enVision Mathematics

Volume 2 Topics 5–8

Authors

Robert Q. Berry, III
Professor of Mathematics
Education, Department of
Curriculum, Instruction and
Special Education, University
of Virginia, Charlottesville,
Virginia

Zachary Champagne
Assistant in Research
Florida Center for Research
in Science, Technology,
Engineering, and
Mathematics (FCR-STEM)
Jacksonville, Florida

Eric Milou
Professor of Mathematics
Rowan University,
Glassboro, New Jersey

Jane F. Schielack
Professor Emerita
Department of Mathematics
Texas A&M University,
College Station, Texas

Jonathan A. Wray
Mathematics Supervisor,
Howard County Public
Schools, Ellicott City,
Maryland

Randall I. Charles
Professor Emeritus
Department of Mathematics
San Jose State University
San Jose, California

Francis (Skip) Fennell
Professor Emeritus of
Education and Graduate
and Professional Studies,
McDaniel College
Westminster, Maryland

SAVVAS
LEARNING COMPANY

Mathematician Reviewers

Gary Lippman, Ph.D.
Professor Emeritus
Mathematics and Computer Science
California State University, East Bay
Hayward, California

Karen Edwards, Ph.D.
Mathematics Lecturer
Arlington, MA

Additional Reviewers

Kristine Peterfeso
Teacher Middle School Math,
Palm Beach County School District

Tamala Ferguson
Math Curriculum Coach,
School District of Osceola County

Melissa Nelson
Math Coach and Assessment
Coordinator, St. Lucie Public Schools

ISBN-13: 978-0-13-498356-1
ISBN-10:   0-13-498356-4
7 2022

CONTENTS

TOPICS

1 Use Positive Rational Numbers

2 Integers and Rational Numbers

3 Numeric and Algebraic Expressions

4 Represent and Solve Equations and Inequalities

5 Understand and Use Ratio and Rate

6 Understand and Use Percent

7 Solve Area, Surface Area, and Volume Problems

8 Display, Describe, and Summarize Data

DIGITAL RESOURCES

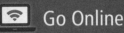 Go Online

 INTERACTIVE STUDENT EDITION
Access online or offline

 VISUAL LEARNING
Interact with visual learning animations

 ACTIVITY
Use with *Solve & Discuss It, Explore It,*
and *Explain It* activities and Examples

VIDEOS
Watch clips to support *3-Act
Mathematical Modeling* Lessons
and *enVision® STEM Projects*

PRACTICE
Practice what you've learned and
get immediate feedback

 TUTORIALS
Get help from *Virtual Nerd*
any time you need it

 MATH TOOLS
Explore math with digital tools

 GAMES
Play math games to help you learn

 KEY CONCEPT
Review important lesson content

 GLOSSARY
Read and listen to English and
Spanish definitions

ASSESSMENT
Show what you've learned

realize™
Everything you need for
math anytime, anywhere.

TOPIC 1

Use Positive Rational Numbers

TOPIC 2

Integers and Rational Numbers

TOPIC 3

Numeric and Algebraic Expressions

TOPIC 4

Represent and Solve Equations and Inequalities

Understand and Use Ratio and Rate

TOPIC 7

Solve Area, Surface Area, and Volume Problems

TOPIC 8

Display, Describe, and Summarize Data

Math Practices and Problem Solving Handbook

The **Math Practices and Problem Solving Handbook** is available online.

1 Make sense of problems and persevere in solving them.

2 Reason abstractly and quantitatively.

3 Construct viable arguments and critique the reasoning of others.

4 Model with mathematics.

5 Use appropriate tools strategically.

6 Attend to precision.

7 Look for and make use of structure.

8 Look for and express regularity in repeated reasoning.

A rancher is building a fence on a 200-foot stretch of field. He has 30 posts and 225 feet of fencing. He plans to place one post every 6 feet. Will he have enough posts to build the fence as planned?

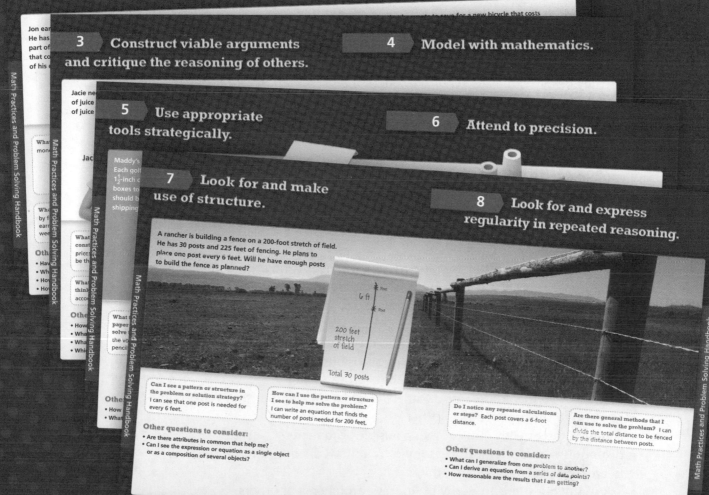

6 ft — Post / Post

200 feet stretch of field

Total 30 posts

Can I see a pattern or structure in the problem or solution strategy? I can see that one post is needed for every 6 feet.

How can I use the pattern or structure I see to help me solve the problem? I can write an equation that finds the number of posts needed for 200 feet.

Do I notice any repeated calculations or steps? Each post covers a 6-foot distance.

Are there general methods that I can use to solve the problem? I can divide the total distance to be fenced by the distance between posts.

Other questions to consider:
- Are there attributes in common that help me?
- Can I see the expression or equation as a single object or as a composition of several objects?

Other questions to consider:
- What can I generalize from one problem to another?
- Can I derive an equation from a series of data points?
- How reasonable are the results that I am getting?

Math Practices and Problem Solving Handbook

Math Practices

1 Make sense of problems and persevere in solving them.

Mathematically proficient students:
- can explain the meaning of a problem
- look for entry points to begin solving a problem
- analyze givens, constraints, relationships, and goals
- make conjectures about the solution
- plan a solution pathway
- think of similar problems, and try simpler forms of the problem
- evaluate their progress toward a solution and change pathways if necessary
- can explain similarities and differences between different representations
- check their solutions to problems.

2 Reason abstractly and quantitatively.

Mathematically proficient students:
- make sense of quantities and their relationships in problem situations:
  - They *decontextualize*—create a coherent representation of a problem situation using numbers, variables, and symbols; and
  - They *contextualize* – attend to the meaning of numbers, variables, and symbols in the problem situation
- know and use different properties of operations to solve problems.

3 Construct viable arguments and critique the reasoning of others.

Mathematically proficient students:
- use definitions and problem solutions when constructing arguments
- make conjectures about the solutions to problems
- build a logical progression of statements to support their conjectures and justify their conclusions
- analyze situations and recognize and use counterexamples
- reason inductively about data, making plausible arguments that take into account the context from which the data arose
- listen or read the arguments of others, and decide whether they make sense
- respond to the arguments of others
- compare the effectiveness of two plausible arguments
- distinguish correct logic or reasoning from flawed, and—if there is a flaw in an argument—explain what it is
- ask useful questions to clarify or improve arguments of others.

4 ▶ Model with mathematics.

Mathematically proficient students:

- can develop a representation—drawing, diagram, table, graph, expression, equation–to model a problem situation
- make assumptions and approximations to simplify a complicated situation
- identify important quantities in a practical situation and map their relationships using a range of tools
- analyze relationships mathematically to draw conclusions
- interpret mathematical results in the context of the situation and propose improvements to the model as needed.

5 ▶ Use appropriate tools strategically.

Mathematically proficient students:

- consider appropriate tools when solving a mathematical problem
- make sound decisions about when each of these tools might be helpful
- identify relevant mathematical resources, and use them to pose or solve problems
- use tools and technology to explore and deepen their understanding of concepts.

6 ▶ Attend to precision.

Mathematically proficient students:

- communicate precisely to others
- use clear definitions in discussions with others and in their own reasoning
- state the meaning of the symbols they use
- specify units of measure, and label axes to clarify their correspondence with quantities in a problem
- calculate accurately and efficiently
- express numerical answers with a degree of precision appropriate for the problem context.

7 ▶ Look for and make use of structure.

Mathematically proficient students:

- look closely at a problem situation to identify a pattern or structure
- can step back from a solution pathway and shift perspective
- can see complex representations, such as some algebraic expressions, as single objects or as being composed of several objects.

8 ▶ Look for and express regularity in repeated reasoning.

Mathematically proficient students:

- notice if calculations are repeated, and look both for general methods and for shortcuts
- maintain oversight of the process as they work to solve a problem, while also attending to the details
- continually evaluate the reasonableness of their intermediate results.

TOPIC 5

UNDERSTAND AND USE RATIO AND RATE

? Topic Essential Question

What are ratios and rates? How can you use ratios and rates to describe quantities and solve problems?

Topic Overview

5-1 Understand Ratios

5-2 Generate Equivalent Ratios

5-3 Compare Ratios

5-4 Represent and Graph Ratios

5-5 Understand Rates and Unit Rates

5-6 Compare Unit Rates

5-7 Solve Unit Rate Problems

3-Act Mathematical Modeling: Get in Line

5-8 Ratio Reasoning: Convert Customary Units

5-9 Ratio Reasoning: Convert Metric Units

5-10 Relate Customary and Metric Units

Topic Vocabulary

- circumference of a circle
- constant speed
- conversion factor
- diameter
- dimensional analysis
- equivalent ratios
- Pi (π)
- rate
- ratio
- term
- unit price
- unit rate

Lesson Digital Resources

INTERACTIVE STUDENT EDITION
Access online or offline.

VISUAL LEARNING ANIMATION
Interact with visual learning animations.

ACTIVITY Use with *Solve & Discuss It, Explore I* and *Explain It* activities, and to explore Example

VIDEOS Watch clips to support *3-Act Mathematical Modeling Lessons* and *STEM Proje*

Go online

Get in Line

 Get in Line

It is hard to call it a freeway when you are stuck in the middle of a traffic jam. To keep vehicles moving on the freeway, some on-ramps have traffic signals. Controlling when cars enter the freeway is not only about reducing delays. It can decrease air pollution and collisions.

These ramp meters typically have alternating green and red lights. The time for one cycle depends on the time of day and the amount of traffic on the freeway. Think about this during the 3-Act Mathematical Modeling lesson.

 PRACTICE Practice what you've learned.

 TUTORIALS Get help from *Virtual Nerd*, right when you need it.

 MATH TOOLS Explore math with digital tools.

 GAMES Play Math Games to help you learn.

 KEY CONCEPT Review important lesson content.

A-Z **GLOSSARY** Read and listen to English/Spanish definitions.

 ASSESSMENT Show what you've learned.

enVision® STEM Project

 VIDEO

Did You Know?

Gears are found in the mechanisms of many common objects, such as cars, bicycles, analog watches, and wind turbines.

Gears have been utilized for centuries. Wooden gears, with wooden teeth, can be found in windmills and watermills.

Gears have equally spaced teeth that enable them to interlock with other gears.

The gears of a bicycle are connected and driven by a chain.

Bicycles often have multiple gears that allow riders to make adjustments to power output and speed.

Riders back in the 19th century were not as lucky—no gears meant a lot of pedaling!

Your Task: Get into Gear ▶

Cyclists strive to achieve efficiency during continuous riding. But, which pairing of gears is the best or most efficient? And does the answer change depending on the terrain? You and your classmates will explore gear ratios and how they can affect pedaling and riding speeds.

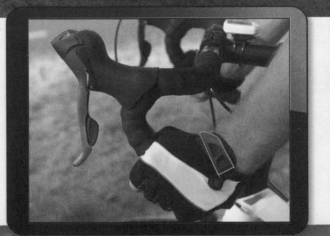

Review What You Know!

Vocabulary

Choose the best term from the box to complete each definition.

> common factor
> common multiple
> equivalent fractions
> fraction

1. Fractions that name the same amount are called _____.

2. The number 3 is a _____ of 9 and 12.

3. A number that can be used to describe a part of a set or a part of a whole

   is a(n) _____.

Equivalent Fractions

Write two fractions equivalent to the given fraction.

4. $\frac{3}{4}$

5. $\frac{7}{8}$

6. $\frac{12}{5}$

7. $\frac{1}{2}$

8. $\frac{8}{9}$

9. $\frac{2}{3}$

Equations

Write an equation that represents the pattern in each table.

10.

x	2	3	4	5	6
y	16	24	32	40	48

11.

x	2	4	6	8	10
y	5	7	9	11	13

Units of Measure

Choose the best unit of measure by writing *inch, foot, yard, ounce, pound, ton, cup, quart,* or *gallon*.

12. serving of trail mix

13. height of a person

14. weight of a newborn kitten

15. gasoline

Measurement Conversions

16. Michael is 4 feet tall. Explain how Michael could find his height in inches. Then explain how he could find his height in yards.

Language Development

A bag contains the following marbles:

3 red　　**2 blue**　　**6 yellow**　　**4 green**

Complete each math statement.

The following **ratio** statement reads, for every 1 red marble, there are [ ] yellow marbles.

A **ratio** that **compares** the yellow marbles to the green marbles is [ ] to [ ].

3 : 4 is the **ratio** of red marbles to [ ] marbles.

The following **ratio** statement reads, for every 1 blue marble, there are 2 [ ] marbles.

$\frac{3}{2}$ represents the [ ] of red marbles to blue marbles.

4 to 15 is the **ratio** of green marbles to the [ ] number of marbles.

In the **ratio** of yellow marbles to blue marbles, **6 : 2**, the **quantities** 6 and 2 are called [ ].

A [ ] **compares** one [ ] to another [ ].

PROJECT 5A

What animal would you most like to have as a pet?

PROJECT: COMPARE COSTS OF PET FOODS

PROJECT 5B

How fast do you think you can throw a baseball?

PROJECT: ANALYZE A SPORT STATISTIC

PROJECT 5C

What color would you want to paint a room?

PROJECT: EXPERIMENT WITH COMBINATIONS OF COLORS

PROJECT 5D

If you could visit any U.S. National Park, which would it be?

PROJECT: PLAN A TOUR

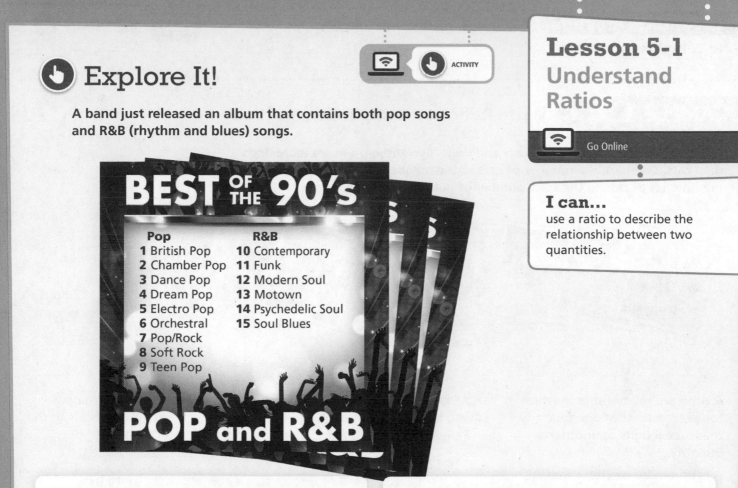

Explore It!

ACTIVITY

A band just released an album that contains both pop songs and R&B (rhythm and blues) songs.

BEST OF THE 90's

Pop
1 British Pop
2 Chamber Pop
3 Dance Pop
4 Dream Pop
5 Electro Pop
6 Orchestral
7 Pop/Rock
8 Soft Rock
9 Teen Pop

R&B
10 Contemporary
11 Funk
12 Modern Soul
13 Motown
14 Psychedelic Soul
15 Soul Blues

POP and R&B

I can...
use a ratio to describe the relationship between two quantities.

A. How can you describe the relationship between the number of pop songs and the number of R&B songs on the album?

B. How does the bar diagram represent the relationship between the number of pop songs and the number of R&B songs?

Pop Songs

R&B Songs

Focus on math practices

Reasoning Another album has 2 pop songs and 10 R&B songs. Draw a bar diagram that you could use to represent the relationship between the number of pop songs and the number of R&B songs.

? Essential Question What is a mathematical way to compare quantities?

VISUAL LEARNING   ASSESS

EXAMPLE 1 👁 **Write Ratios to Compare Quantities**

Scan for Multimedia

Tom's Pet Service takes care of cats and dogs. Currently, there are more dogs than cats. Compare the number of cats to the number of dogs. Then compare the number of cats to the total number of pets at Tom's Pet Service.

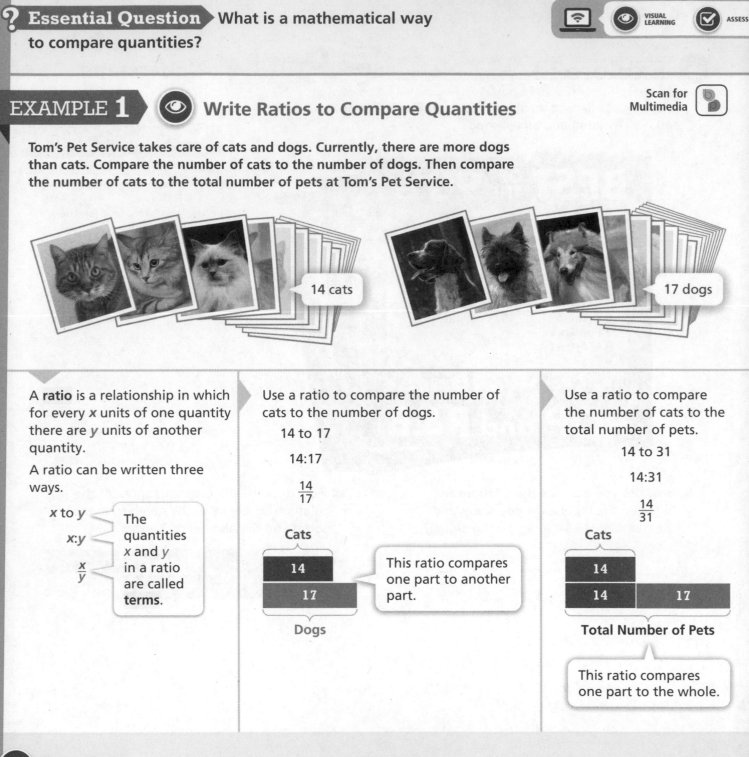

14 cats

17 dogs

A **ratio** is a relationship in which for every *x* units of one quantity there are *y* units of another quantity.

A ratio can be written three ways.

x to *y*
x:*y*
$\frac{x}{y}$

The quantities *x* and *y* in a ratio are called **terms**.

Use a ratio to compare the number of cats to the number of dogs.

14 to 17

14:17

$\frac{14}{17}$

Cats

| 14 |
| 17 |

This ratio compares one part to another part.

Dogs

Use a ratio to compare the number of cats to the total number of pets.

14 to 31

14:31

$\frac{14}{31}$

Cats

| 14 |
| 14 | 17 |

Total Number of Pets

This ratio compares one part to the whole.

☑ **Try It!**

What are three ways to write the ratio of the number of dogs to the total number of pets?

Convince Me! Is the ratio of dogs to cats the same as the ratio of cats to dogs? Explain.

EXAMPLE **2**

Use a Bar Diagram to Solve a Ratio Problem

The ratio of footballs to soccer balls at a sporting goods store is 5 to 3. If the store has 100 footballs in stock, how many soccer balls does it have?

Use a bar diagram to show the ratio 5:3.

Use 5 boxes for footballs.

Footballs

1	1	1	1	1
1	1	1		

Soccer balls

Use 3 boxes for soccer balls.

Use the same diagram to represent 100 footballs.

Because 100 ÷ 5 = 20, write 20 in each red box.

Footballs

20	20	20	20	20

Soccer balls

Each box represents the same value. Write 20 in each green box.

Footballs

20	20	20	20	20
20	20	20		

Soccer balls

There are 3 green boxes, so the total number of soccer balls is 3 × 20, or 60.

The sporting goods store has 60 soccer balls in stock.

EXAMPLE **3**

Use a Double Number Line Diagram to Solve a Ratio Problem

Chen can ride his bike 3 miles in 15 minutes. At this rate, how long will it take Chen to ride his bike 18 miles?

Use a double number line diagram. Show 15 minutes for every 3 miles.

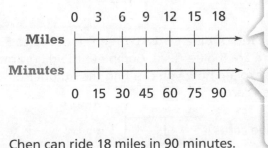

Miles   0 3 6 9 12 15 18

Count by 3s along the top number line until you get to 18 miles.

Minutes   0 15 30 45 60 75 90

Count by 15s for the same number of spaces along the bottom number line.

Chen can ride 18 miles in 90 minutes.

3 miles

Model with Math A double number line diagram can represent a constant relationship between two values with different units.

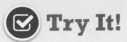 **Try It!**

Chen's friend Alisa can ride her bike 2 miles in 7 minutes. Use a bar diagram or a double number line diagram to find how long it would take Alisa to ride 10 miles if she rides at the same rate.

A ratio compares two quantities. A ratio can be written 3 ways: x to y, x:y, or $\frac{x}{y}$. Ratios can be represented using bar diagrams and double number line diagrams.

Oranges

Apples

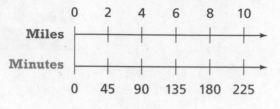

The ratio of oranges to apples is 2:3, 2 to 3, or $\frac{2}{3}$.

The ratio of miles to minutes is 2:45, 2 to 45, or $\frac{2}{45}$.

Do You Understand?

1. **? Essential Question** What is a mathematical way to compare quantities?

2. **Reasoning** What are two different types of comparisons that a ratio can be used to make?

    part to part
    part to whole

3. A science classroom has 5 turtles and 7 frogs. What is the ratio of frogs to total animals?

    7:12

4. Tye is making trail mix with 3 cups of nuts for every 4 cups of granola. If Tye has 6 cups of nuts, how many cups of granola should he use?

Do You Know How?

In 5–7, use three different ways to write a ratio for each comparison.

A sixth-grade basketball team has 3 centers, 5 forwards, and 6 guards.

5. Forwards to guards

    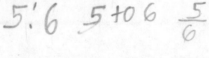
    5:6   5 to 6 $\frac{5}{6}$

6. Centers to total players

    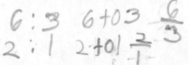
    3:14   3 to 14 $\frac{3}{14}$

7. Guards to centers

    6:3   6 to 3 $\frac{6}{3}$
    2:1   2 to 1 $\frac{2}{1}$

8. The ratio of blue cards to green cards is 2 to 5. There are 8 blue cards. Complete the diagram and explain how you can find the number of green cards.

    Blue cards

    Green cards

    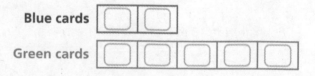

Practice & Problem Solving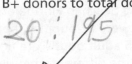

In 9–14, use the data to write a ratio for each comparison in three different ways.

A person's blood type is denoted with the letters A, B, and O, and the symbols + and −. The blood type A+ is read as *A positive*. The blood type B− is read as *B negative*.

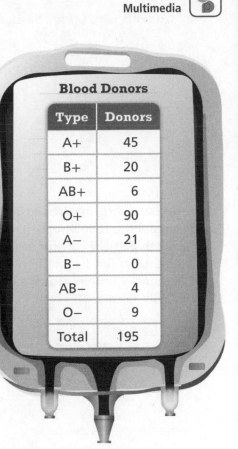

Blood Donors

Type	Donors
A+	45
B+	20
AB+	6
O+	90
A−	21
B−	0
AB−	4
O−	9
Total	195

9. O+ donors to A+ donors

90:45

10. AB− donors to AB+ donors

4:6 AB+

11. B+ donors to total donors

20:195

12. O− donors to A− donors

9:21

13. A+ and B+ donors to AB+ donors

65:6

14. A− and B− donors to AB− donors

21:4

15. Which comparison does the ratio $\frac{90}{9}$ represent?

O+ to O−

16. Which comparison does the ratio 20:21 represent?

B+ to A−

17. Sam is packing gift boxes with fruit. For each apple, he packs 3 plums and 5 oranges. If he puts 3 apples in a box, how many plums and oranges will Sam put in the box? Draw a diagram to solve the problem.

18. Write a ratio that compares the number of teal squares to the total number of squares in the quilt.

19. Reasoning Rita's class has 14 girls and 16 boys. How does the ratio 14:30 describe Rita's class?

20. A math class surveyed students about their musical preferences and recorded the results in the table. Use the data to write a ratio for each comparison in three different ways.

Favorite Music

Music Type	Number of Students
Rock	10
Classical	4
Techno	12
Hip-Hop	15
Country	8
Alternative	4

a. Students who prefer classical to students who prefer techno

4:12

b. Students who prefer hip-hop to total number of students surveyed

15:53

21. Construct Arguments Justin used blocks to model the following situation: A car dealership sells 7 cars for every 4 minivans it sells. How can Justin use his model to find the number of minivans the dealership sells if it sells 35 cars?

22. Make Sense and Persevere The ratio of adult dogs to puppies at a dog beach in Florida on Monday was 3:2. There were 12 puppies there that day. On Tuesday, 15 adult dogs were at the dog beach. What is the difference between the number of adult dogs at the dog beach on Monday and Tuesday?

23. Higher Order Thinking At 9:30 A.M., Sean started filling a swimming pool. At 11:30 A.M., he had filled 1,800 gallons. At what time will the pool be full?

4,500 gallon capacity

☑ Assessment Practice

24. The diagram below represents the relationship between the number of students taking Spanish and the number of students taking French in a foreign language class.

Spanish

French

What is the ratio of the number of students taking Spanish to the number of students taking French?

Ⓐ 8 : 3

Ⓑ 8 : 5

Ⓒ 8 : 8

Ⓓ 8 : 13

Solve & Discuss It!

ACTIVITY

Sally used all of the paint shown below to make a certain tint of orange paint. How many pints of red paint should be mixed with 24 pints of yellow paint to make the same tint of orange?

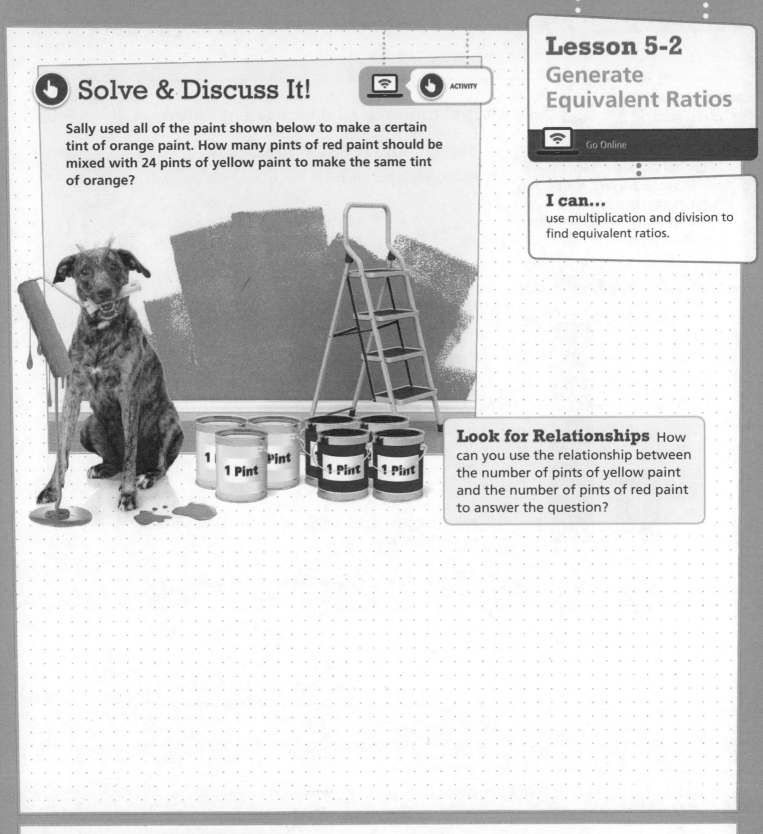

1 Pint
1 Pint
1 Pint
1 Pint
1 Pint

I can...
use multiplication and division to find equivalent ratios.

Look for Relationships How can you use the relationship between the number of pints of yellow paint and the number of pints of red paint to answer the question?

Focus on math practices

Reasoning If Sally uses the same ratio of yellow paint to red paint, how many pints of yellow paint should she mix with 16 pints of red paint?

EXAMPLE 1 Use Multiplication to Find Equivalent Ratios

Scan for Multimedia

For every 16 basketball players in Crystal County schools, there are 48 soccer players. If the ratio remains constant and there are 64 basketball players, how many soccer players are there?

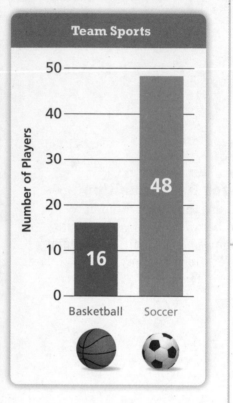

Team Sports

ONE WAY Make a table with equivalent ratios.

Equivalent ratios are ratios that express the same relationship.

Multiply both terms of the original ratio by the same number to find an equivalent ratio.

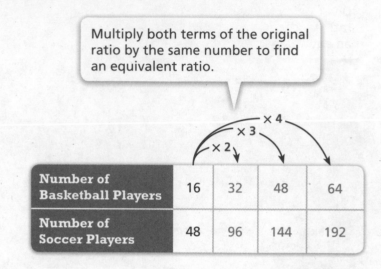

Number of Basketball Players	16	32	48	64
Number of Soccer Players	48	96	144	192

There are 192 soccer players when there are 64 basketball players.

ANOTHER WAY Use multiplication. Multiply both terms by the same nonzero number.

Multiply 16 × 4 for the 64 basketball players.

$$\frac{16 \times 4}{48 \times 4} = \frac{64}{192}$$

Multiply 48 × 4 to find the number of soccer players.

There are 192 soccer players when there are 64 basketball players.

✓ Try It!

If you extend the table above, how would you find the next ratio of basketball players to soccer players?

Convince Me! What is the relationship between the number of basketball players and the number of soccer players in each column in the table?

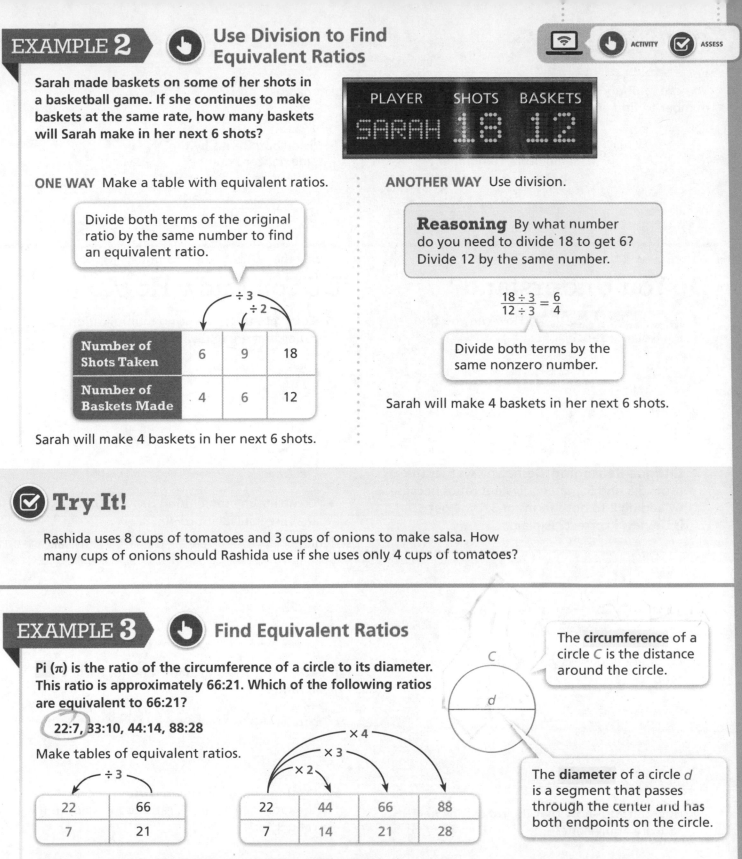

EXAMPLE **2**　Use Division to Find Equivalent Ratios

ACTIVITY　ASSESS

Sarah made baskets on some of her shots in a basketball game. If she continues to make baskets at the same rate, how many baskets will Sarah make in her next 6 shots?

PLAYER　SHOTS　BASKETS
SARAH　18　12

ONE WAY Make a table with equivalent ratios.

Divide both terms of the original ratio by the same number to find an equivalent ratio.

÷ 3
÷ 2

Number of Shots Taken	6	9	18
Number of Baskets Made	4	6	12

Sarah will make 4 baskets in her next 6 shots.

ANOTHER WAY Use division.

Reasoning By what number do you need to divide 18 to get 6? Divide 12 by the same number.

$$\frac{18 \div 3}{12 \div 3} = \frac{6}{4}$$

Divide both terms by the same nonzero number.

Sarah will make 4 baskets in her next 6 shots.

☑ Try It!

Rashida uses 8 cups of tomatoes and 3 cups of onions to make salsa. How many cups of onions should Rashida use if she uses only 4 cups of tomatoes?

EXAMPLE **3**　Find Equivalent Ratios

Pi (π) is the ratio of the circumference of a circle to its diameter. This ratio is approximately 66:21. Which of the following ratios are equivalent to 66:21?

22:7, 33:10, 44:14, 88:28

The **circumference** of a circle C is the distance around the circle.

C

d

Make tables of equivalent ratios.

× 4
× 3
× 2

÷ 3

22	66
7	21

22	44	66	88
7	14	21	28

The **diameter** of a circle d is a segment that passes through the center and has both endpoints on the circle.

The ratios 22:7, 44:14, and 88:28 are equivalent to 66:21.

☑ Try It!

Which of the following ratios are equivalent to 16:20?

2:3, 4:5, 18:22, 20:25

You can multiply or divide both terms of a ratio by the same nonzero number to find equivalent ratios.

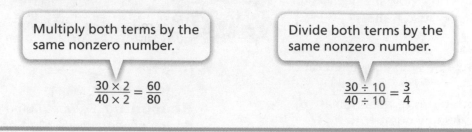

Multiply both terms by the same nonzero number.	Divide both terms by the same nonzero number.

$$\frac{30 \times 2}{40 \times 2} = \frac{60}{80}$$ $$\frac{30 \div 10}{40 \div 10} = \frac{3}{4}$$

Do You Understand?

1. **Essential Question** How can you find equivalent ratios?

2. **Critique Reasoning** Deshawn says that the ratios 3:5 and 5:7 are equivalent ratios because by adding 2 to both terms of 3:5 you get 5:7. Is Deshawn correct? Explain.

3. What are two ways you can find an equivalent ratio for $\frac{12}{16}$?

4. How can you show that the ratios 10:4 and 15:6 are equivalent?

Do You Know How?

5. Complete the table using multiplication to find ratios that are equivalent to 4:5.

4	8	12	16
5	10	15	20

6. Complete the table using division to find ratios that are equivalent to 40:28.

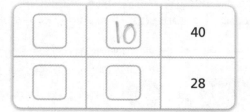

	10	40
		28

In 7–10, write an equivalent ratio for each given ratio.

7. $\frac{12}{21}$ 8. 1:3   9. 6 to 8

10. Pi (π) can be approximated using decimals as the ratio 3.14:1. Find 3 ratios equivalent to the ratio 3.14:1.

Name: _____

Practice & Problem Solving

PRACTICE TUTORIAL

Scan for Multimedia

11. Eva is making French toast. How many ounces of milk should Eva use with 10 eggs?

The recipe calls for 5 ounces of milk for every 2 eggs.

Milk (oz)	5	10	15	20	25
Eggs	2	4	6	8	10

$\frac{8}{2}$ $\frac{4}{2}=2$ $\frac{6}{2}=3$ $\frac{10}{2}=5$

In **12–15**, write three ratios that are equivalent to the given ratio.

12. $\frac{6}{7}$

13. $\frac{9}{5}$

14. 8:14

15. 7:9

---

16. A teacher kept track of what students consumed at a school picnic. For three grades, the ratios of the amount of water consumed to the amount of fruit juice consumed were equivalent. Complete the table.

Grade	Water (gallons)	Juice (gallons)
5th	6	7
6th	24	28
7th	18	21

17. The attendant at a parking lot compared the number of hybrid vehicles to the total number of vehicles in the lot during a weekend. The ratios for the three days were equivalent. Complete the table.

Day	Hybrids	Total
Fri.	4	9
Sat.	28	63
Sun.	32	72

---

18. Shiloh is sharing jellybeans. The jar of jellybeans has the ratio shown. If Shiloh keeps the ratio the same and gives his friend 7 pink jellybeans, how many green jellybeans should he also share?

32 green jellybeans
56 pink jellybeans

Green Jellybeans	4	12	16	32
Pink Jellybeans	7	21	28	56

19. Use Appropriate Tools Equivalent ratios can be found by extending pairs of rows or columns in a multiplication table. Write three ratios equivalent to $\frac{2}{5}$ using the multiplication table.

X	0	1	2	3	4	5	6
0	0	0	0	0	0	0	0
1	0	1	2	3	4	5	6
2	0	2	4	6	8	10	12
3	0	3	6	9	12	15	18
4	0	4	8	12	16	20	24
5	0	5	10	15	20	25	30
6	0	6	12	18	24	30	36

20. If 5 mi ≈ 8 km, about how many miles would be equal to 50 km? Explain.

21. Vocabulary How is the word *term* defined when used to describe a ratio relationship? How is the word *term* defined in the context of an expression?

22. Higher Order Thinking Three sisters are saving for a special vacation in Orlando, Florida. The ratio of Ada's savings to Ellie's savings is 7:3, and the ratio of Ellie's savings to Jasmine's savings is 3:4. Together all three girls have saved $56. How much has each girl saved? Complete the table. Explain how the table can be used to solve the problem.

Ada's savings	$7		$21	
Ellie's savings		$6		
Jasmine's savings	$4			$16

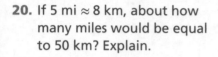
Assessment Practice

23. Corey is making key lime pies for the school fair. For every 3 egg yolks, he uses 2 tablespoons of key lime zest.

PART A

Complete the table to find equivalent ratios.

Egg Yolks	3			
Lime Zest (tbsp)	2	4	6	8

PART B

How can you use the table to find how many egg yolks are needed for 8 tablespoons of lime zest?

24. Which ratios can be represented by Pi (π)? Select all that apply.

- ☐ Diameter : Circumference
- ☐ Circumference : Diameter
- ☐ Circumference : Radius
- ☐ Radius : Circumference
- ☐ Circumference : Twice the radius

Solve & Discuss It!

ACTIVITY

Scott is making a snack mix using almonds and raisins. For every 2 cups of almonds in the snack mix, there are 3 cups of raisins. Ariel is making a snack mix that has 3 cups of almonds for every 5 cups of sunflower seeds. If Scott and Ariel each use 6 cups of almonds to make a batch of snack mix, who will make a larger batch?

I can...
compare ratios to solve problems.

Scott's almonds

Ariel's almonds

Scott's raisins

Ariel's sunflower seeds

Model with Math How can you use ratio tables to represent Scott's and Ariel's snack mixes?

Focus on math practices

Look for Relationships Scott and Ariel want to make as much snack mix as possible, but no more than 25 cups of mix. If they can use only full cups of ingredients, who can make more mix without going over?

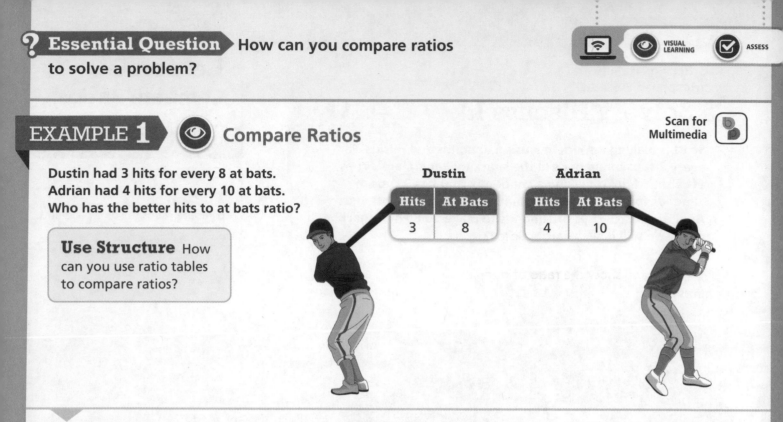

? **Essential Question** How can you compare ratios to solve a problem?

VISUAL LEARNING   ASSESS

EXAMPLE 1 👁 Compare Ratios

Scan for Multimedia

Dustin had 3 hits for every 8 at bats.
Adrian had 4 hits for every 10 at bats.
Who has the better hits to at bats ratio?

Use Structure How can you use ratio tables to compare ratios?

Dustin

Hits	At Bats
3	8

Adrian

Hits	At Bats
4	10

Extend and complete the ratio tables for Dustin and Adrian until the number of at bats is the same in each table. Compare the number of hits that Dustin and Adrian each get with 40 at bats.

Dustin

Hits	At Bats
3	8
6	16
9	24
12	32
15	40

Adrian

Hits	At Bats
4	10
8	20
12	30
16	40

Dustin gets 15 hits for every 40 at bats.

Adrian gets 16 hits for every 40 at bats.

Because Adrian gets more hits in 40 at bats, he has the better hits to at bats ratio.

☑ **Try It!**

Marlon had 6 hits in 15 at bats. How does Marlon's hits to at bats ratio compare to Adrian's?

Convince Me! Based on their hits to at bats ratios, who would you expect to have more hits in a game, Marlon or Dustin? Explain.

Due to compatibility and size restrictions, only certain types of fish can live together in an aquarium. If there are 15 mollies in each tank with the ratios shown at the right, which tank has more fish?

Tank 1

Tank 2

4 Guppies : 5 Mollies

2 Angelfish : 3 Mollies

STEP 1

Make a table to show the ratio of guppies to mollies in Tank 1.

Guppies	Mollies
4	5
8	10
12	15
16	20
20	25

There are 12 guppies for every 15 mollies.

STEP 2

Make a table to show the ratio of angelfish to mollies in Tank 2.

Angelfish	Mollies
2	3
4	6
6	9
8	12
10	15

There are 10 angelfish for every 15 mollies.

STEP 3

Add to find the total number of fish in each aquarium.

Tank 1: 12 guppies + 15 mollies = 27 fish

Tank 2: 10 angelfish + 15 mollies = 25 fish

27 > 25

Tank 1 has more fish.

✅ **Try It!**

Tank 3 has a ratio of 3 guppies for every 4 angelfish. Complete the ratio table to find the number of angelfish in Tank 3 with 12 guppies.

Using the information in Example 2 and the table at the right, which tank with guppies has more fish?

Guppies	3			
Angelfish	4			

You can use ratio tables to compare ratios when one of the corresponding terms is the same.

Theresa's Purple Paint Mixture

Cups of Blue Paint	2	4	6
Cups of Red Paint	5	10	15

Hala's Purple Paint Mixture

Cups of Blue Paint	3	6	9
Cups of Red Paint	7	14	21

Theresa used more cups of red paint than Hala.

Do You Understand?

1. **? Essential Question** How can you compare ratios to solve a problem?

2. In Example 1, how many hits would Adrian have in 50 at bats? Explain.

3. **Reasoning** During the first week of a summer camp, 2 out of 3 campers were boys. During the second week, 3 out of 5 campers were boys. There were 15 total campers each week. During which week were there more boy campers? Explain.

Do You Know How?

4. To make plaster, Kevin mixes 3 cups of water with 4 pounds of plaster powder. Complete the ratio table. How much water will Kevin mix with 20 pounds of powder?

Cups of Water	3			
Pounds of Powder	4	8	12	

5. Jenny makes plaster using a ratio of 4 cups of water to 5 pounds of plaster powder. Whose plaster recipe uses more water? Use the ratio table here and in Exercise 4 to compare.

Cups of Water	4	8		
Pounds of Powder	5			

6. Kevin and Jenny each use 12 cups of water to make plaster. Who will make more plaster? Explain.

Practice & Problem Solving

Scan for
Multimedia

In 7–10, use the ratio table at the right.

7. Local radio station *WMTH* schedules 2 minutes of news for every 20 minutes of music. Complete the ratios shown in the table at the right.

Minutes of Music	20	?	40	?	60
Minutes of News	2	3	?	5	?

8. What is the ratio of minutes of music to minutes of news?

9. Radio station *WILM* broadcasts 4 minutes of news for every 25 minutes of music. Which radio station broadcasts more news each hour?

10. Which station will have to be on the air longer to broadcast 4 minutes of news? Explain.

11. **Reasoning** The ratio tables at the right show the comparison of books to games for sale at Bert's Store and at Gloria's Store. Complete the ratio tables. Which store has the greater ratio of books to games? Explain.

Bert's Store

Books	4				
Games	6				

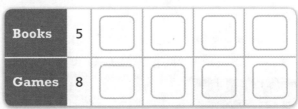

Gloria's Store

Books	5				
Games	8				

12. The ratio of soy sauce to lime juice in a homemade salad dressing is 7:6. The ratio of soy sauce to lime juice in a store-bought dressing is 11:9. Which dressing has the greater ratio of soy sauce to lime juice?

Homemade Salad Dressing

Soy Sauce	7				
Lime Juice	6				

Store-Bought Salad Dressing

Soy Sauce	11				
Lime Juice	9				

13. One bouquet of flowers has 3 milkweeds for every 5 tickseeds. Another bouquet has 4 tickseeds for every 5 canna lilies. If both bouquets have 20 tickseeds, which bouquet has more flowers?

Milkweeds and Tickseeds

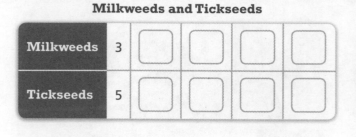

Tickseeds and Canna lilies

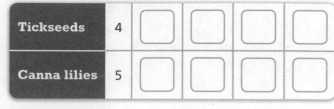

14. Higher Order Thinking Lauren can drive her car 320 miles on 10 gallons of gasoline. Melissa can drive her car 280 miles on 8 gallons of gasoline. Who can drive farther on 40 gallons of gasoline? Complete the ratio tables to justify your solution.

Lauren's Car

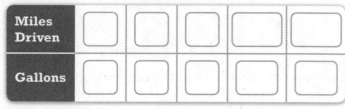

Melissa's Car

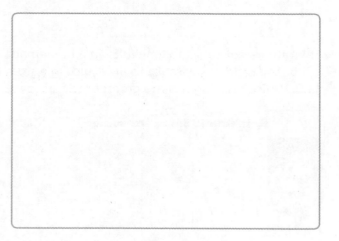

✅ Assessment Practice

15. Fran buys Florida cone seashells in packages that contain 9 purple-dyed Florida cone seashells for every 3 pink-dyed Florida cone seashells. Mia buys Florida cone seashells in packages with a ratio of 2 pink-dyed Florida cone seashells to 4 purple-dyed Florida cone seashells.

PART A

Complete the tables using the ratios given.

Fran's Shell Packages

Purple cone shells	9		27	
Pink cone shells	3	6		12

Mia's Shell Packages

Purple cone shells	4	8		16
Pink cone shells	2		6	

PART B

If the girls each buy packages that contain 6 pink-dyed Florida cone seashells, how many purple-dyed Florida cone seashells would each have? Explain.

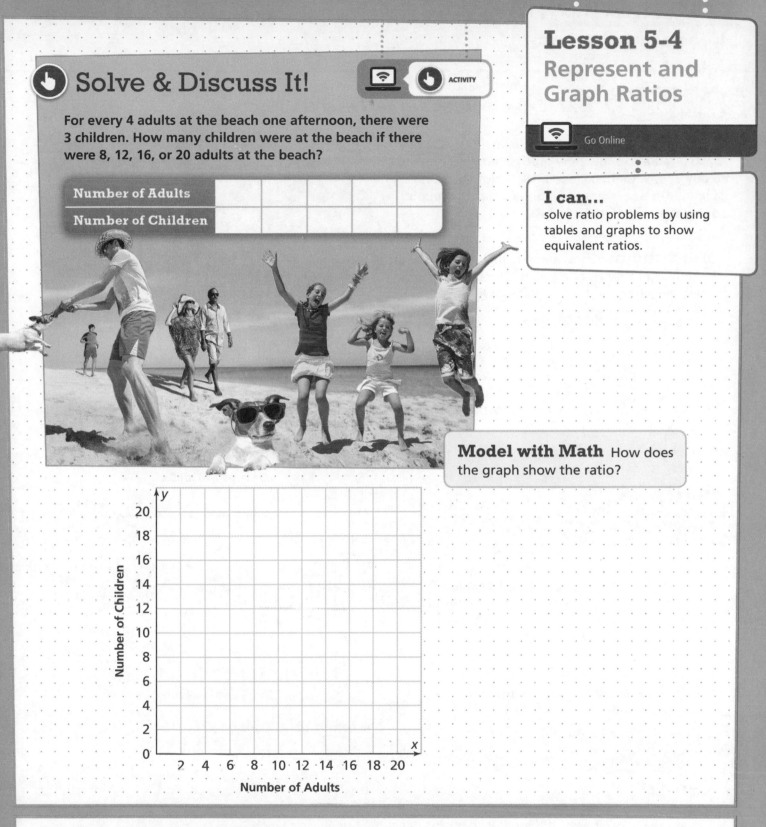
Solve & Discuss It!

ACTIVITY

For every 4 adults at the beach one afternoon, there were 3 children. How many children were at the beach if there were 8, 12, 16, or 20 adults at the beach?

Number of Adults					
Number of Children					

I can...
solve ratio problems by using tables and graphs to show equivalent ratios.

Model with Math How does the graph show the ratio?

Focus on math practices

Critique Reasoning There were 25 children and 15 adults at the beach. Emery said that there were 5 children for every 3 adults. Is he correct? Explain.

VISUAL LEARNING

ASSESS

EXAMPLE 1 ◉ Explore Ratios in Tables and Graphs

Scan for Multimedia

Ellen is shopping for supplies at Jake's Party Store. Make a table to show how much Ellen would spend to buy 3, 6, 9, or 12 balloons. Then plot the pairs of values in a coordinate graph and use the graph to find the cost of 18 balloons.

Use Structure How can you make a table of equivalent ratios or a graph to find the costs for other numbers of balloons?

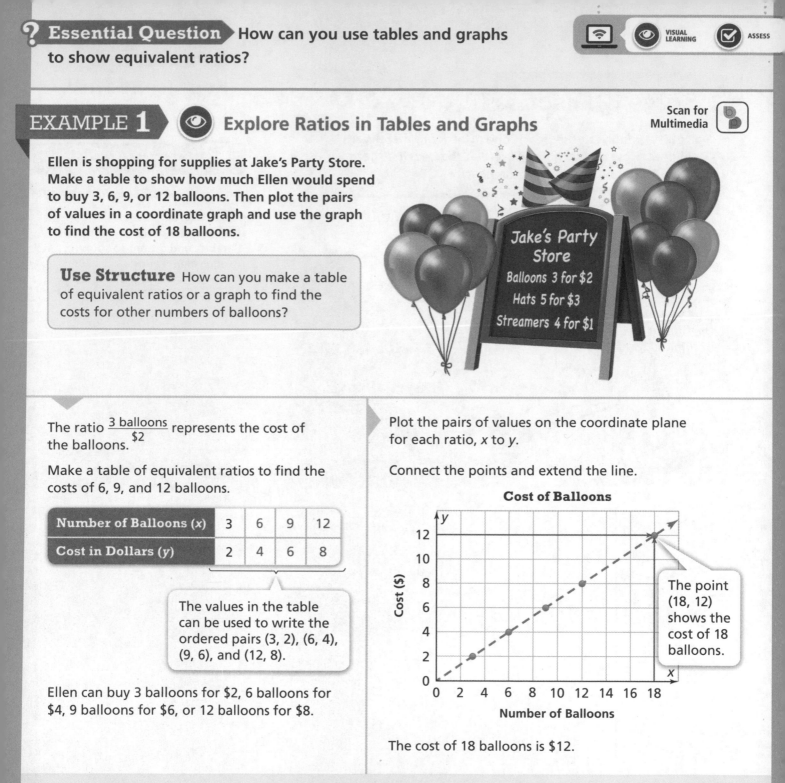

Jake's Party Store
Balloons 3 for $2
Hats 5 for $3
Streamers 4 for $1

The ratio $\frac{3 \text{ balloons}}{\$2}$ represents the cost of the balloons.

Make a table of equivalent ratios to find the costs of 6, 9, and 12 balloons.

Number of Balloons (x)	3	6	9	12
Cost in Dollars (y)	2	4	6	8

The values in the table can be used to write the ordered pairs (3, 2), (6, 4), (9, 6), and (12, 8).

Ellen can buy 3 balloons for $2, 6 balloons for $4, 9 balloons for $6, or 12 balloons for $8.

Plot the pairs of values on the coordinate plane for each ratio, x to y.

Connect the points and extend the line.

Cost of Balloons

The point (18, 12) shows the cost of 18 balloons.

The cost of 18 balloons is $12.

☑ Try It!

What are the coordinates of the point that represents the number of balloons you can buy for $6?

Convince Me! How can you use the graph to find the cost of 15 balloons?

EXAMPLE **2** 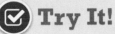 Graph Ratios Using Repeated Addition

ACTIVITY   ASSESS

Jack is making juice. He has 25 celery sticks. If Jack uses all 25 celery sticks, how many apples will he need to make the juice?

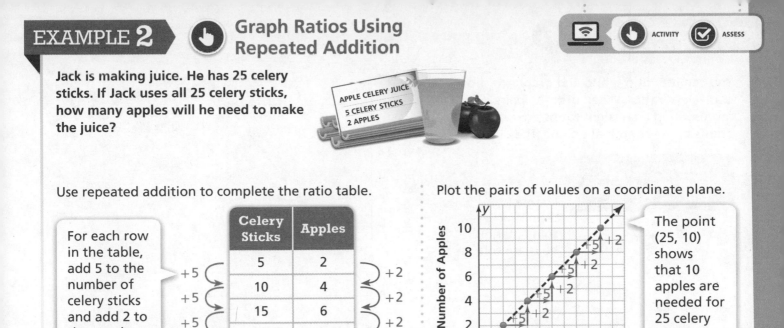

APPLE CELERY JUICE
5 CELERY STICKS
2 APPLES

Use repeated addition to complete the ratio table.

For each row in the table, add 5 to the number of celery sticks and add 2 to the number of apples.

Celery Sticks	Apples
5	2
10	4
15	6
20	8
25	10

+5
+5
+5
+5

+2
+2
+2
+2

Plot the pairs of values on a coordinate plane.

The point (25, 10) shows that 10 apples are needed for 25 celery sticks.

Jack needs 10 apples to make the juice.

EXAMPLE **3** Graph Ratios Related to Pi (π)

The measurements of different circular objects are given in a ratio table. What do you notice about the graph of the pairs of values given in the ratio table?

Object	Diameter, d	Circumference, C
Fruit Plate	7 in.	22 in.
Clock Face	14 in.	44 in.
Hula Hoop	35 in.	110 in.

Plot the pairs of values on a coordinate plane.

(35, 110)
(14, 44)
(7, 22)

The graph of the values in the ratio table are on the same line.

✓ Try It!

Can you draw an object with a diameter of 10 inches and a circumference of 50 inches? Explain.

You can use ratio tables and graphs to show equivalent ratios. When ordered pairs representing equivalent ratios are graphed as points in the coordinate plane, they form a line.

Tennis Rackets Sold	Tennis Balls Sold
3	4
6	8
9	12
12	16

For every 3 tennis rackets sold, 4 tennis balls are sold.

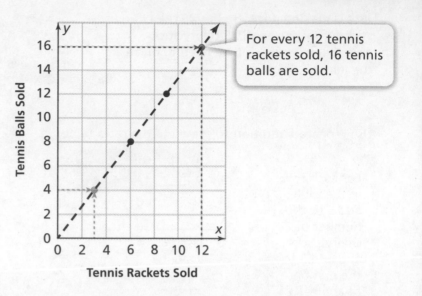

For every 12 tennis rackets sold, 16 tennis balls are sold.

Do You Understand?

1. **Essential Question** How can you use tables and graphs to show equivalent ratios?

2. **Look for Relationships** In Example 2, how could you use the graph to find the number of apples needed for 30 celery sticks?

3. How could you use repeated addition to show ratios equivalent to 1:3 on a graph?

Do You Know How?

4. Complete the table to show equivalent ratios representing a cost of $8 for every 3 boxes. Then write the pairs of values as points to be plotted on a coordinate plane.

Number of Boxes	Cost of Boxes ($)
3	8
6	16
9	24
☐	☐
☐	☐

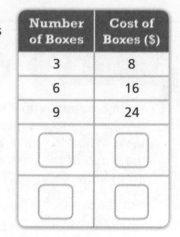

5. **Model with Math** Plot the equivalent ratios (3, 4), (6, 8), and (9, 12) on the graph. Use the graph to find the number of nonfiction books purchased if 10 fiction books are purchased.

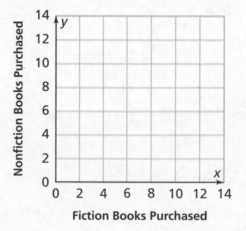

Practice & Problem Solving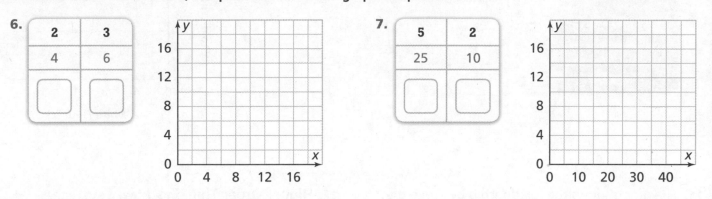

Scan for
MultImedia

Leveled Practice In **6** and **7**, complete the table and graph the pairs of values.

6.

2	3
4	6
☐	☐

7.

5	2
25	10
☐	☐

8. A student runs 2 minutes for every 10 minutes she walks.

a. Complete the table. Graph the pairs of values.

Running (min)	Walking (min)
2	10
4	20
☐	☐

Exercise Times

b. For how long would the student walk if she runs for 7 minutes?

9. A car magazine reports the number of miles driven for different amounts of gas for three cars. Which car travels the farthest on 1 gallon of gas? Explain.

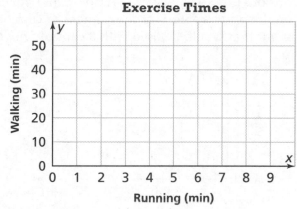

Car A

Miles Driven	☐	☐	200	300	☐
Gallons of Gas	1	4	8	☐	16

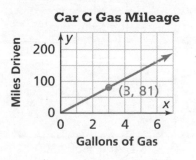

Car C Gas Mileage

(3, 81)

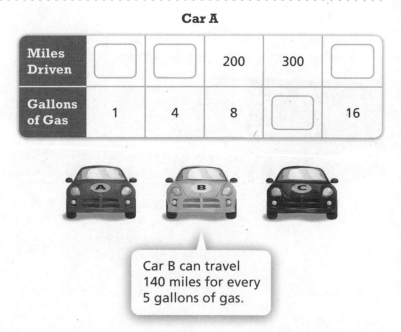

Car B can travel 140 miles for every 5 gallons of gas.

10. **Model with Math** A bread recipe calls for 4 cups of white flour for every 5 cups of whole-wheat flour. Complete the table to show how many cups of whole-wheat flour are needed to mix with 16 cups of white flour. Then graph the pairs of values.

White Flour (c)	4	8	12	16
Whole-Wheat Flour (c)	☐	☐	☐	☐

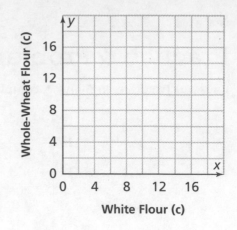

11. The graph shows the relationship between the number of cups of sugar and the number of cups of flour in a key-lime bread recipe. What point on the graph represents the number of cups of sugar that would be used with 8 cups of flour?

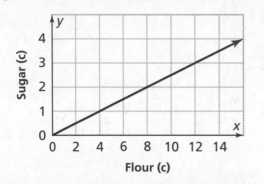

12. **Higher Order Thinking** Ishwar can read 5 pages in 15 minutes. Anne can read 15 pages in 1 hour. Explain how you could use a table or graph to find how much longer it would take Anne to read a 300-page book than Ishwar.

☑ Assessment Practice

13. The measurements of a circular object are given in the ratio table.

    PART A

    Find the missing dimensions of other circular objects by completing the ratio table.

Diameter, d	42 mm	☐	301 mm
Circumference, C	132 mm	198 mm	☐

    PART B

    Graph the pairs of values.

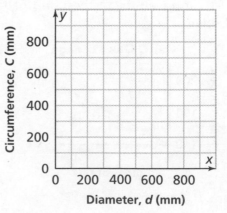

1. **Vocabulary** How can a *ratio* be used to compare quantities? *Lesson 5-1*

2. The circumference of the outside of a ring is 66 mm, and it has an outer diameter of 21 mm. If the circumference of the inside of the ring is 50 mm, what is the inner diameter of the ring? *Lesson 5-4*

3. During the breakfast service, the D-Town Diner sells 12 cups of coffee for every 10 glasses of orange juice. How many cups of coffee would the diner have sold if 40 glasses of orange juice had been sold? Complete the table with equivalent ratios. *Lesson 5-2*

Cups of Coffee	12			
Glasses of Orange Juice	10			40

4. The ratio of cows to chickens at Old McDonald's Farm is 2:7. Select all the farms that have a greater ratio of cows to chickens than Old McDonald's Farm. *Lessons 5-3*

☐ Red's Farm: 3 cows for every 5 chickens

☐ Cluck & Moo Farm: 1 cow for every 5 chickens

☐ T Family Farm: 1 cow for every 3 chickens

☐ Pasture Farm: 2 cows for every 9 chickens

☐ C & C Farm: 3 cows for every 8 chickens

5. A package of 3 notebooks costs $5. Complete the ratio table and graph the pairs of values. How much will 18 notebooks cost? *Lesson 5-4*

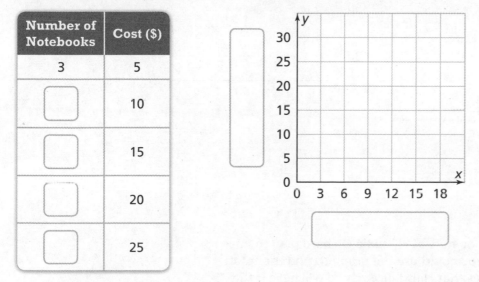

Number of Notebooks	Cost ($)
3	5
	10
	15
	20
	25

How well did you do on the mid-topic checkpoint? Fill in the stars.

MID-TOPIC PERFORMANCE TASK

Hillsdale Orchard grows Fuji apples and Gala apples. There are 160 Fuji apple trees and 120 Gala apple trees in the orchard.

PART A

Hillsdale Orchard's owners decide to plant 30 new Gala apple trees. Complete the ratio table to find the number of new Fuji apple trees the owners should plant if they want to maintain the same ratio of Fuji apple trees to Gala apple trees.

Fuji Apple Trees			160
Gala Apple Trees	30		120

PART B

Use the ratio table to complete a graph that shows the relationship between the number of Fuji apple trees and Gala apple trees at Hillsdale Orchard.

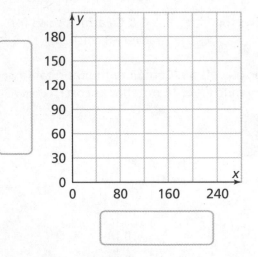

PART C

By the end of the next season, the owners of Hillsdale Orchard plan to have 240 Fuji apple trees. Explain how you could use the graph to find the total number of Fuji and Gala apple trees that Hillsdale Orchard will have if the owners achieve their goal.

Solve & Discuss It!

ACTIVITY

What is the cost of 10 bottles of fruit juice?

Fruit Juice
Buy **4** for **$10**

I can...
solve problems involving rates.

Make Sense and Persevere
How can you use tables or diagrams to make sense of the quantities in the problem?

Focus on math practices

Critique Reasoning Monica says, "If 4 bottles cost $10, then 2 bottles cost $5, and 8 bottles cost $20. So 10 bottles cost $5 + $20." Is Monica correct? Explain.

VISUAL LEARNING   ASSESS

EXAMPLE 1 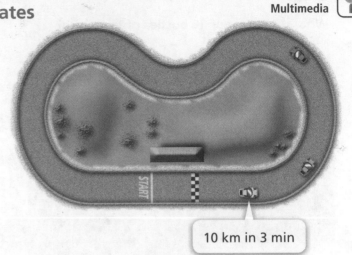 Find Equivalent Rates

A rate is a special type of ratio that compares quantities with unlike units of measure.

If the race car continues to travel at the same rate, how long will it take it to travel 25 kilometers?

> **Generalize** You can find equivalent rates the same ways that you find equivalent ratios.

Scan for Multimedia

10 km in 3 min

START

ONE WAY Use a ratio table to find rates that are equivalent to $\frac{10 \text{ km}}{3 \text{ min}}$.

Distance (km)	Time (min)
5	$1\frac{1}{2}$
10	3
15	$4\frac{1}{2}$
20	6
25	$7\frac{1}{2}$

It will take the race car $7\frac{1}{2}$ minutes to travel 25 kilometers.

ANOTHER WAY Write the rate as a fraction. Multiply both terms of the rate by the same number to find an equivalent rate.

> Think, $10 \times ? = 25$.

$$\frac{10 \text{ km}}{3 \text{ min}} = \frac{25 \text{ km}}{x \text{ min}}$$

$$\frac{10 \text{ km} \times 2.5}{3 \text{ min} \times 2.5} = \frac{25 \text{ km}}{7.5 \text{ min}}$$

> Multiply both terms by 2.5.

It will take the race car 7.5 minutes to travel 25 kilometers.

✓ Try It!

At the same rate, how long would it take the car to travel 60 kilometers?

It will take the car [ ] minutes to travel [ ] kilometers.

Convince Me! Sal draws the double number line diagram at the right. He says it shows that at this rate the race car will travel 35 kilometers in 10.5 minutes. Critique Sal's reasoning. Is he correct? Explain.

$$\frac{10 \text{ km} \times \boxed{}}{3 \text{ min} \times \boxed{}} = \frac{60 \text{ km}}{\boxed{} \text{ min}}$$

km
0 ——— 10 ——— 20 ——— 30 35 40

0 ——— 3 ——— 6 ——— 9 10.5 12
min

EXAMPLE 2 ▶ 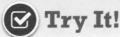 Compare Quantities in Two Ways

ACTIVITY ✓ ASSESS

Harvest Market sells a crate of Fuji apples for $12.00. What are
two different unit rates that could represent the situation?

Find the unit rate in
pounds per dollar.

$$\frac{15 \text{ pounds}}{\$12.00}$$

$$\frac{15 \text{ pounds} \div 12}{\$12.00 \div 12} = \frac{1.25 \text{ pounds}}{\$1.00}$$

The unit rate in pounds per dollar is $\frac{1.25 \text{ pounds}}{\$1.00}$.

Find the unit rate in
dollars per pound.

$$\frac{\$12.00}{15 \text{ pounds}}$$

$$\frac{\$12.00 \div 15}{15 \text{ pounds} \div 15} = \frac{\$0.80}{1 \text{ pound}}$$

The unit rate in dollars per pound is $\frac{\$0.80}{1 \text{ pound}}$.

✓ Try It!

A recipe for scrambled eggs uses 2 tablespoons of milk for every
3 eggs. What are two unit rates that could represent the recipe?

EXAMPLE 3 ▶ 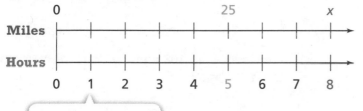 Use Unit Rates to Solve Problems

A unit rate is a rate in which the comparison is to 1 unit.

How far could the family travel in 8 hours if they maintain
the same rate of speed?

A family bicycles
25 miles in 5 hours.

1 hour is the unit.

STEP 1

Find the unit rate in miles per hour.

$$\frac{25 \text{ miles}}{5 \text{ hours}} \text{ or } \frac{25}{5}$$

$$\frac{25 \div 5}{5 \div 5} = \frac{5}{1}$$

Write an equivalent rate
with a denominator of 1.

The unit rate is $\frac{5}{1}$, or 5 miles per hour.

Generalize The unit rate is an equivalent
rate with a denominator of 1.

STEP 2

Use the unit rate to find how far the family
could travel in 8 hours.

$$\frac{5 \times 8}{1 \times 8} = \frac{40}{8} \text{ or } \frac{40 \text{ miles}}{8 \text{ hours}}$$

The family could travel 40 miles in 8 hours.

✓ Try It!

A canoeing club travels 78 miles in 3 days. How far could they travel in 5 days
if they maintain the same speed?

A rate compares quantities with unlike units of measure.

$$\frac{\$3.50}{7 \text{ oranges}}$$

A unit rate compares a quantity to 1 unit of another quantity.

$$\frac{\$3.50}{7 \text{ oranges}} = \frac{\$0.50}{1 \text{ orange}}$$

Do You Understand?

1. **Essential Question** What are rates and unit rates?

2. **Be Precise** Use what you know about ratios to describe a rate.

3. **Reasoning** A bathroom shower streams 5 gallons of water in 2 minutes.

   a. Find the unit rate for gallons per minute and describe it in words.

   b. Find the unit rate for minutes per gallon and describe it in words.

5 gallons in two minutes

Do You Know How?

In **4** and **5**, find the value of *n*.

4.

Miles	45	135
Hours	4	n

5.

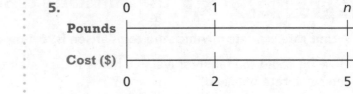

6. Jenny packaged 108 eggs in 9 cartons. Write this statement as a rate.

7. Anna Maria read 40 pages in 60 minutes. What is her unit rate in pages per minute?

In **8** and **9**, use the unit rates that you found in Exercise 3.

8. How many gallons of water does the shower stream in 6 minutes?

9. How long can someone shower to use only 10 gallons of water?

Practice & Problem Solving

In **10** and **11**, write each statement as a rate.

10. Jan saw 9 full moons in 252 days.

11. It took Hannah 38 minutes to run 8 laps.

In **12** and **13**, find the value of *x*.

12.

Fish	16	48
Bowls	2	*x*

13.

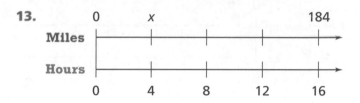

Leveled Practice In **14** and **15**, find the unit rate.

14. $\dfrac{320 \text{ mi}}{16 \text{ gal}}$

$$\frac{320 \div 16}{16 \div 16} = \frac{\boxed{}}{1}$$

$$\frac{\boxed{} \text{ mi}}{1 \text{ gal}}$$

15. $\dfrac{75 \text{ cm}}{5 \text{ h}}$

$$\frac{75 \div \boxed{}}{5 \div 5} = \frac{\boxed{}}{1}$$

$$\frac{\boxed{} \text{ cm}}{1 \text{ h}}$$

In **16–19**, complete each table.

16.

Pages	9			
Minutes	18	1	10	15

17.

Beans	186			
Bags	3	1	7	11

18.

Ounces		24.6		123
Bags	1	2	5	

19.

Miles	25		125	
Gallons		3	5	12

20. Which runner set the fastest pace? Explain.

Runner	Laps	Time
Martha	20	32 min
Allison	16	25 min
Rachel	17	27.2 min

21. Model with Math Over the summer, Alexis read 15 books in 12 weeks. The diagram below can be used to track her progress. If Alexis read at the same rate each week, how many books had she read in 4 weeks? In 8 weeks? Complete the diagram.

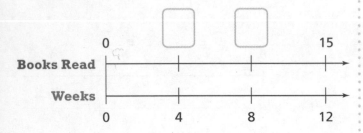

22. An elephant charges an object that is 0.35 kilometer away. How long will it take the elephant to reach the object?

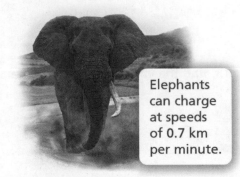

Elephants can charge at speeds of 0.7 km per minute.

23. A machine takes 1 minute to fill 6 cartons of eggs. At this rate, how many minutes will it take to fill 420 cartons?

24. Higher Order Thinking How are the ratios $\frac{24 \text{ laps}}{1 \text{ hour}}$ and $\frac{192 \text{ laps}}{8 \text{ hours}}$ alike? How are they different?

Assessment Practice

25. A bakery sells 12 gourmet orange-zest cupcakes for $36.00. Select all the statements that are true.

☐ $\frac{\$3.00}{1 \text{ cupcake}}$ is a unit rate for the cost per cupcake.

☐ $\frac{36}{12}$ represents the ratio of $36.00 for 12 cupcakes.

☐ Using the same rate, the bakery can sell 6 cupcakes for $20.00.

☐ Using the same rate, the bakery can sell 2 dozen cupcakes for $72.00.

☐ Using the same rate, it would cost $24.50 for 8 cupcakes.

Solve & Discuss It!

ACTIVITY

Rick and Nikki own remote-control cars. They use a stopwatch to record the speed of each car. Whose car is faster?

Speed of Rick's Car		Speed of Nikki's Car	
Distance (feet)	Time (seconds)	Distance (feet)	Time (seconds)
150	30	80	20

Rick's Car

Nikki's Car

I can...
compare unit rates to solve problems.

Be Precise Use precise numbers and units to describe and compare rates.

Focus on math practices

Make Sense and Persevere If each car maintains its rate of speed, how long will it take Rick's car to travel 300 feet? How long will it take Nikki's car to travel the same distance? Explain.

? Essential Question How can you use unit rates to make comparisons?

VISUAL LEARNING   ASSESS

EXAMPLE 1 ◉ **Compare to Find the Greater Unit Rate**

Scan for Multimedia

Ethan swam 11 laps in the pool in 8 minutes. Austin swam 7 laps in the same pool in 5 minutes. Which boy swam at a faster rate?

Make Sense and Persevere
Is the faster rate a fewer number of laps per minute or a greater number of laps per minute?

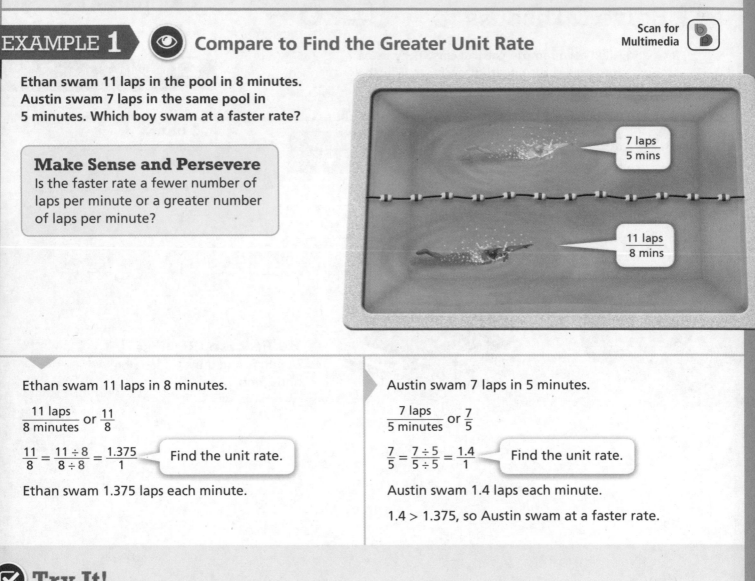

7 laps / 5 mins

11 laps / 8 mins

Ethan swam 11 laps in 8 minutes.

$\frac{11 \text{ laps}}{8 \text{ minutes}}$ or $\frac{11}{8}$

$\frac{11}{8} = \frac{11 \div 8}{8 \div 8} = \frac{1.375}{1}$ ← Find the unit rate.

Ethan swam 1.375 laps each minute.

Austin swam 7 laps in 5 minutes.

$\frac{7 \text{ laps}}{5 \text{ minutes}}$ or $\frac{7}{5}$

$\frac{7}{5} = \frac{7 \div 5}{5 \div 5} = \frac{1.4}{1}$ ← Find the unit rate.

Austin swam 1.4 laps each minute.

1.4 > 1.375, so Austin swam at a faster rate.

☑ **Try It!**

Ashley is Austin's older sister. She trains in the same pool and can swim 9 laps in 6 minutes. Is Ashley a faster swimmer than Austin?

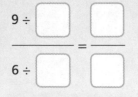

$\dfrac{9 \div \boxed{}}{6 \div \boxed{}} = \dfrac{\boxed{}}{\boxed{}}$

Ashley swims 1.5 laps per minute. Because $\boxed{}$ $\boxed{}$ 1.4, Ashley is a $\boxed{}$ swimmer than Austin.

Convince Me! How can you use the unit rate in minutes per lap to compare Ashley's speed to Austin's speed?

EXAMPLE 2

Compare to Find the Lesser Unit Rate

Is the lunch special or the weekend special a better value? Find the unit price of each special.

A unit price is a unit rate that gives the price of one item.

> **Make Sense and Persevere**
> Is the lesser unit price or the greater unit price a better value?

Find the unit price of the lunch special.

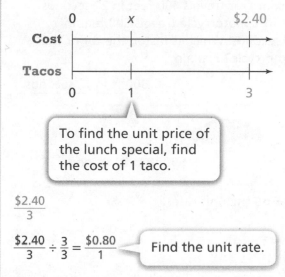

> To find the unit price of the lunch special, find the cost of 1 taco.

$$\frac{\$2.40}{3}$$

$$\frac{\$2.40}{3} \div \frac{3}{3} = \frac{\$0.80}{1}$$ — Find the unit rate.

The unit price for the lunch special is $0.80 per taco.

Find the unit price of the weekend special.

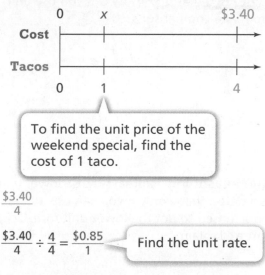

> To find the unit price of the weekend special, find the cost of 1 taco.

$$\frac{\$3.40}{4}$$

$$\frac{\$3.40}{4} \div \frac{4}{4} = \frac{\$0.85}{1}$$ — Find the unit rate.

The unit price for the weekend special is $0.85 per taco.

$0.80 per taco < $0.85 per taco, so the lunch special is a better value.

✓ Try It!

Explain how to decide which is the better value, 4 greeting cards for $10 or 6 greeting cards for $14.

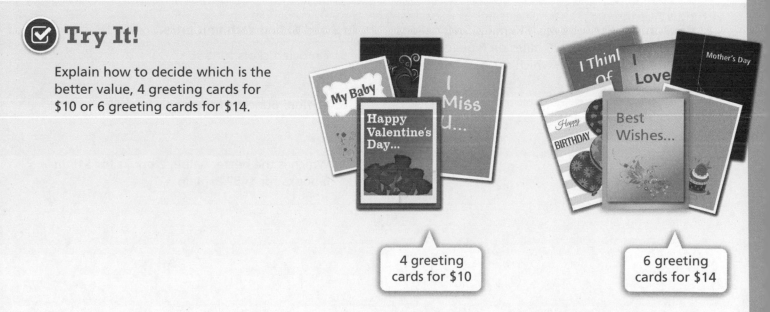

> 4 greeting cards for $10

> 6 greeting cards for $14

You can use unit rates to make comparisons.

$8.50 per hour > $8.00 per hour

$$\frac{7 \text{ laps}}{1 \text{ min}} < \frac{9 \text{ laps}}{1 \text{ min}}$$

$$\frac{32 \text{ cm}}{1 \text{ sec}} < \frac{45 \text{ cm}}{1 \text{ sec}}$$

175 words per minute > 95 words per minute

Do You Understand?

1. Essential Question How can you use unit rates to make comparisons?

2. Critique Reasoning Paul says that a lower unit rate is a better value only if you can use all the items purchased to get the lower unit rate. Do you agree? Explain.

3. Reasoning Car A travels 115 miles on 5 gallons of gas. Car B travels 126 miles on 6 gallons of gas. How can you find which car gets better gas mileage?

Do You Know How?

4. Hakim's car travels 600 feet in 20 seconds. Andre's motorcycle travels 300 feet in 12 seconds. Which is faster, the car or the motorcycle? Explain.

300 ft in 12 seconds

600 ft in 20 seconds

a. Find the unit rates.

b. Compare the unit rates.

In 5 and 6, find each unit price.

5. 7 movie tickets for $56

6. 12 fluid ounces of shampoo for $2.76

7. Which is the better value, 2 books for $15 or 6 books for $45? Explain.

Name: _____

Practice & Problem Solving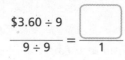

 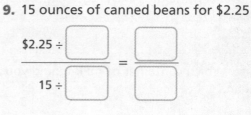

Leveled Practice In **8** and **9**, find each unit price.

8. 9 pens for $3.60

$$\frac{\$3.60 \div 9}{9 \div 9} = \frac{\boxed{}}{1}$$

9. 15 ounces of canned beans for $2.25

$$\frac{\$2.25 \div \boxed{}}{15 \div \boxed{}} = \frac{\boxed{}}{\boxed{}}$$

- -

In **10** and **11**, determine which is the better value.

10. 3 kilograms of charcoal for $7.95 or
5 kilograms of charcoal for $12.50

11. 50 envelopes for $2.49 or
90 envelopes for $5.50

- -

In **12–15**, compare the rates to find which is greater.

12. 35 points in 20 minutes or 49 points in
35 minutes

13. 12 laps in 8 minutes or 16 laps in 10 minutes

14. 45 strikeouts in 36 innings or 96 strikeouts in
80 innings

15. 480 stickers on 6 sheets or 120 stickers on
2 sheets

- -

In **16–18**, compare the rates to find which is the better value.

16. $27 for 4 large pizzas or $32 for 5 large pizzas

17. $30 for 100 flyers or $65 for 250 flyers

18. 36 pictures for $8 or 24 pictures for $5

19. **Model with Math** Katrina and Becca exchanged 270 text messages in 45 minutes. An equal number of texts was sent each minute. The girls can send 90 more text messages before they are charged additional fees. Complete the double number line diagram. At this rate, for how many more minutes can the girls exchange texts before they are charged extra?

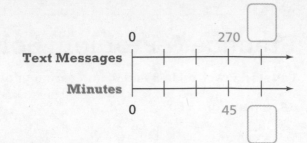

20. **Reasoning** Which container of milk would you buy? Explain.

½ gallon for $2.29

1 gallon for $3.99

21. **Higher Order Thinking** Amil and Abe rode in a bike-a-thon. Abe rode for 77 minutes at a faster rate per mile than Amil. Find Amil's unit rate. Then explain how you could use it to find a possible unit rate for Abe.

Amil rode 15 miles in 55 minutes.

✅ Assessment Practice

22. A food warehouse sells cans of soup in boxes. Bargain shoppers have four options.

PART A

Complete the table to find the unit price for each option.

Boxes of Soup	Unit Price
12 cans for $10.56	
16 cans for $13.60	
20 cans for $17.20	
24 cans for $21.36	

PART B

Compare the unit rates found in Part A and identify the best value.

👆 Solve & Discuss It!

📶 👆 ACTIVITY

Suppose you are traveling by train to visit a friend who lives 275 miles away. How long will the trip take? Moving at a constant speed, how long would it take the train to travel 385 miles?

> The train travels at a constant speed of 55 miles per hour.

I can...
use unit rates to solve problems.

> **Model with Math** How can you use what you know about unit rates to model and solve this problem?

Focus on math practices

Reasoning Suppose the train was traveling at a constant speed that is twice as fast as 55 miles per hour. How long would it take the train to go 275 miles? Explain.

VISUAL LEARNING   ASSESS

EXAMPLE 1   👁 Solve Constant Speed Problems

Scan for Multimedia

The jet flies at a constant speed.

Constant speed means that the speed stays the same over time.

If the jet continues to fly at the same rate, how far could it fly in 85 minutes?

The jet flies 175 miles in 7 minutes.

ONE WAY Use a table to record equivalent rates to find how far the jet could fly in 85 minutes.

Time (min)	Distance (mi)
1	25
7	175
25	625
50	1,250
85	2,125

×85   ×85

The jet could fly 2,125 miles in 85 minutes.

ANOTHER WAY Use the unit rate to find how far the jet could fly in 85 minutes.

$$\frac{175 \text{ miles} \div 7}{7 \text{ minutes} \div 7} = \frac{25 \text{ miles}}{1 \text{ minute}}$$

$$\frac{25 \text{ miles} \times 85}{1 \text{ minute} \times 85} = \frac{2,125 \text{ miles}}{85 \text{ minutes}}$$

Find an equivalent rate.

Look for Relationships The table and the equation represent the same relationship.

The jet could fly 2,125 miles in 85 minutes.

☑ Try It!

At the same rate, how far would the jet fly in 75 minutes?

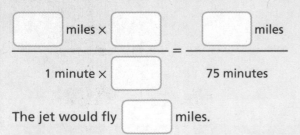

$$\frac{\boxed{} \text{ miles} \times \boxed{}}{1 \text{ minute} \times \boxed{}} = \frac{\boxed{} \text{ miles}}{75 \text{ minutes}}$$

The jet would fly ☐ miles.

Convince Me! How could you use the table from Example 1 to find how far the jet would fly in 75 minutes? Explain.

EXAMPLE 2 ▶ 👆 **Solve Unit Price Problems**

Grocery Giant is having a sale on Swiss cheese. How much would it cost to buy 5 slices of cheese at the same rate?

24 slices for $7.20

> **Reasoning** How can you use the unit price to solve the problem?

ONE WAY Use a ratio table to solve.

Slices	Price
1	$0.30
5	$1.50
24	$7.20

×5   ÷24   ×5   ÷24

ANOTHER WAY Use the unit price to solve.

$$\frac{\$7.20 \div 24}{24 \text{ slices} \div 24} = \frac{\$0.30}{1 \text{ slice}}$$

$$\frac{\$0.30 \times 5}{1 \text{ slice} \times 5} = \frac{\$1.50}{5 \text{ slices}}$$

At this rate, it would cost $1.50 for 5 slices of cheese.

✅ **Try It!**

Jarod paid $13.80 for 5 tickets to the game. At the same rate, how much would 3 tickets cost?

EXAMPLE 3 ▶ 👆 **Use an Equation to Represent Unit Rate Problems**

A ferryboat travels at a constant speed of 57.5 miles in 2.5 hours. How long would it take the ferryboat to travel 92 miles at that rate?

STEP 1 Find the unit rate.

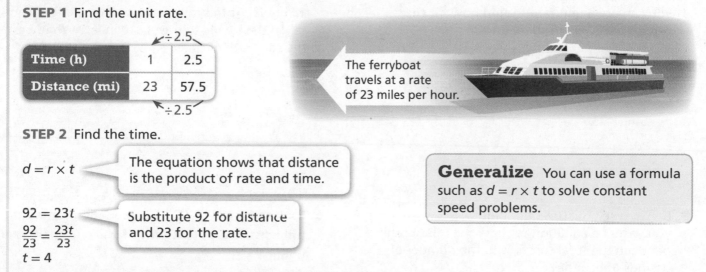

		÷2.5
Time (h)	1	2.5
Distance (mi)	23	57.5

÷2.5

The ferryboat travels at a rate of 23 miles per hour.

STEP 2 Find the time.

$d = r \times t$ — The equation shows that distance is the product of rate and time.

$92 = 23t$ — Substitute 92 for distance and 23 for the rate.
$$\frac{92}{23} = \frac{23t}{23}$$
$t = 4$

> **Generalize** You can use a formula such as $d = r \times t$ to solve constant speed problems.

It would take 4 hours for the ferryboat to travel 92 miles.

✅ **Try It!**

A submarine travels 19 miles in $\frac{1}{2}$ hour. Write an equation to find out how long it would take the submarine to travel 57 miles at the same rate. Then find the time.

You can use ratio tables or unit rates to solve rate problems, including constant speed problems.

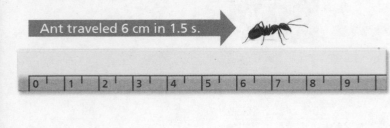

Ant traveled 6 cm in 1.5 s.

Time (s)	Distance (cm)
1	4
1.5	6
3	12
4.5	18
6	24

×6 ... ×6

Do You Understand?

1. **? Essential Question** How can you use unit rates to solve problems?

2. **Construct Arguments** An ostrich runs 6 miles in 12 minutes at a constant speed. Explain how you can use a unit rate to find how far the ostrich could run in 40 minutes.

3. Bananas sell for $0.58 per pound. How could you write an equation to show the relationship between the total cost, c, and the number of pounds of bananas, p?

Do You Know How?

In 4 and 5, use unit rates to solve.

4. A football player runs 80 yards in 25 seconds. If he maintains the same rate of speed, how far could he run in 60 seconds?

5. On a family vacation, Amy's dad drove the car at a constant speed and traveled 585 miles in 13 hours. At this rate, how long would it have taken the family to travel 810 miles? What was the car's rate of speed?

6. Look at Exercise 5. Write an equation to find the total distance, d, that Amy's family traveled after t hours.

Name: _____

Practice & Problem Solving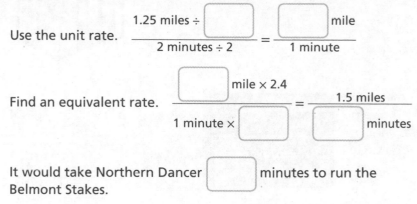

Scan for Multimedia

Leveled Practice In 7–9, solve the rate problems.

7. A horse named Northern Dancer won the Kentucky Derby with a time of exactly 2 minutes. At this constant rate, how long would it take Northern Dancer to run the Belmont Stakes?

Use the unit rate. $\dfrac{1.25 \text{ miles} \div \boxed{}}{2 \text{ minutes} \div 2} = \dfrac{\boxed{} \text{ mile}}{1 \text{ minute}}$

Find an equivalent rate. $\dfrac{\boxed{} \text{ mile} \times 2.4}{1 \text{ minute} \times \boxed{}} = \dfrac{1.5 \text{ miles}}{\boxed{} \text{ minutes}}$

It would take Northern Dancer $\boxed{}$ minutes to run the Belmont Stakes.

Kentucky Derby $1\frac{1}{4}$ miles

Belmont Stakes $1\frac{1}{2}$ miles

8. If a cyclist rides at a constant rate of 24 miles per hour, how long would it take the cyclist to ride 156 miles?

9. The price of an 8-minute phone call is $1.20. What is the price of a 17-minute phone call?

In 10 and 11, use the map at the right.

The Garcia family is driving from Sacramento, California, to Key West, Florida. In 5 days, they have traveled 2,045 miles. At this rate, how long will it take them to travel from Sacramento to Key West?

10. How can you use rate reasoning to solve this problem? Explain.

Sacramento, California

3,272 miles

Key West, Florida

11. **Be Precise** Show how to use numbers, units, and symbols precisely to solve the problem.

12. Vik wrote the equation $470 \cdot h = 3{,}008$, where h is the number of hours it took a plane flying at a constant speed of 470 miles per hour to travel 3,008 miles. Solve for h.

13. A nursery owner buys 7 panes of glass to fix some damage to his greenhouse. The 7 panes cost $15.05. Unfortunately, he breaks 2 more panes while repairing the damage. What is the cost of another 2 panes of glass?

14. Cheyenne drew a circle with diameter 1 meter. She measured the circumference to estimate the value of Pi. Complete the table, and then write an equation to find the circumference, C, for a circle with diameter d.

Diameter, d (meters)	1	2	3	4
Circumference, C (meters)	3.14			

15. Jayden bought 70 feet of speaker wire for $18.20. He needs 30 more feet. If the unit price is the same, how much will Jayden pay for the extra 30 feet of wire? Explain.

16. Higher Order Thinking Sasha runs at a constant speed of 3.8 meters per second for $\frac{1}{2}$ hour. Then she walks at a constant rate of 1.5 meters per second for $\frac{1}{2}$ hour. How far did Sasha run and walk in 60 minutes?

☑ Assessment Practice

17. Suppose that a leatherback turtle swam 7.5 kilometers in 3 hours at a constant speed.

PART A

How many kilometers per hour did the turtle swim?

PART B

At this rate, how long would it take the turtle to swim 10 kilometers?

3-ACT MATH ▷ ▷ ▷

Get in Line

ACT 1

1. After watching the video, what is the first question that comes to mind?

2. Write the Main Question you will answer.

3. Construct Arguments Predict an answer to this Main Question. Explain your prediction.

4. On the number line below, write a number that is too small to be the answer. Write a number that is too large.

Too small   Too large

←——|————————————————————|——→

5. Plot your prediction on the same number line.

6. What information in this situation would be helpful to know? How would you use that information?

7. Use Appropriate Tools What tools can you use to solve the problem? Explain how you would use them strategically.

8. Model with Math Represent the situation using mathematics. Use your representation to answer the Main Question.

9. What is your answer to the Main Question? Is it higher or lower than your prediction? Explain why.

FREEWAY
ENTRANCE
500 feet

10. Write the answer you saw in the video.

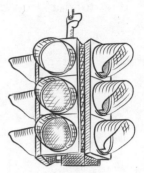

11. Reasoning Does your answer match the answer in the video? If not, what are some reasons that would explain the difference?

12. Make Sense and Persevere Would you change your model now that you know the answer? Explain.

Reflect

13. Model with Math Explain how you used a mathematical model to represent the situation. How did the model help you answer the Main Question?

14. Generalize Will your model work on other lights? Explain your reasoning.

15. Use Structure Later that week, it took between 20 and 21 minutes to get through the same light. How many cars were in line?

Solve & Discuss It!

ACTIVITY

If 6.5 feet of snow were to fall in a 24-hour period, would the 1921 record be broken? There are 12 inches in 1 foot.

THE NEWS

April 15, 1921   Silver Lake, Colorado

RECORD BREAKING SNOWFALL

75.8 INCHES IN 24 HOURS

BREAKING NEWS

Man digging his pickup truck out from snow.

I can...
use ratio reasoning to convert customary measurements.

Reasoning Use the relationship between inches and feet to solve the problem.

Focus on math practices

Make Sense and Persevere How many feet of snow would need to fall in Silver Lake, Colorado, to break the 1921 24-hour snowfall record from 1921?

VISUAL LEARNING   ASSESS

EXAMPLE **1** 👁 **Convert Customary Units of Length**

Scan for Multimedia

The sidewalk in front of a store is 4.5 feet wide. The city regulations establish a maximum width for sidewalks of 66 inches. Does the sidewalk meet the city regulations?

Customary Units

Length
1 ft = 12 in.
1 yd = 36 in.
1 yd = 3 ft
1 mi = 5,280 ft
1 mi = 1,760 yd

Model with Math The conversions in the table can be written as rates that compare equivalent measurements.

4.5 ft

ONE WAY

Write the width of the sidewalk in inches.

> Identify the conversion rate that relates feet to inches.

12 in. = 1 ft

Find an equivalent rate.

$$\frac{12 \text{ in.} \times 4.5}{1 \text{ ft} \times 4.5} = \frac{54 \text{ in.}}{4.5 \text{ ft}}$$

> Multiply both terms of the rate by 4.5.

The sidewalk is 54 inches wide. It meets the city regulations.

ANOTHER WAY

Use **dimensional analysis** to convert measures by including measurement units when you multiply by a conversion factor. A **conversion factor** is a rate that compares equivalent measures.

$$4.5 \cancel{ft} \times \frac{12 \text{ in.}}{1 \cancel{ft}}$$
$$= 4.5 \times 12 \text{ in.}$$
$$= 54 \text{ in.}$$

> Multiply by the conversion factor that relates the measures and leaves you with the units needed to solve the problem. Divide out the common units.

The sidewalk is 54 inches wide. It meets the city regulations.

☑ **Try It!**

According to city regulations, how many feet wide is the maximum sidewalk width? Explain.

Convince Me! What conversion factor would you use when converting 66 inches to feet? Explain.

EXAMPLE **2** ▶ 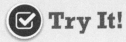 **Convert Customary Units of Capacity**

Jonah has 15 gallons of water for a camping trip. How many quarts of water does he have?

ONE WAY Use an equivalent rate.

4 qt = 1 gal ◁ Identify the conversion rate.

$\frac{4 \text{ qt} \times 15}{1 \text{ gal} \times 15} = \frac{60 \text{ qt}}{15 \text{ gal}}$ ◁ Multiply both terms of the rate by 15.

Jonah has 60 quarts of water.

ANOTHER WAY Use dimensional analysis.

15 g̶a̶l̶ $\times \frac{4 \text{ qt}}{1 \text{ g̶a̶l̶}}$ ◁ Multiply by the conversion factor. Divide out the common units.

$= 15 \times 4 \text{ qt}$

$= 60 \text{ qt}$

Jonah has 60 quarts of water.

Customary Units

Capacity	
1 tbsp = 3 tsp	1 pt = 2 c
1 fl oz = 2 tbsp	1 qt = 2 pt
1 c = 8 fl oz	1 gal = 4 qt

Make Sense and Persevere
How can you use the conversion table to identify an appropriate conversion rate?

 Try It!

Brandon is making bread. His recipe says to use $2\frac{1}{2}$ tablespoons of sugar. How many teaspoons of sugar should he use?

EXAMPLE **3** ▶ 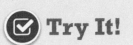 **Convert Customary Units of Weight**

The alpine pika is a small mammal in the rabbit family. How much does the alpine pika weigh in pounds?

The number of ounces in the conversion rate is greater than the number of ounces that the pika weighs. Use division to find the equivalent rate.

Customary Units

Weight
1 lb = 16 oz
1 T = 2,000 lb

ONE WAY Use an equivalent rate.

16 oz = 1 lb ◁ Identify the conversion rate.

$\frac{16 \text{ oz} \div 1.6}{1 \text{ lb} \div 1.6} = \frac{10 \text{ oz}}{0.625 \text{ lb}}$ ◁ Divide both terms of the rate by 1.6.

The alpine pika weighs 0.625 pound.

ANOTHER WAY Use dimensional analysis.

10 o̶z̶ $\times \frac{1 \text{ lb}}{16 \text{ o̶z̶}}$ ◁ Multiply by the conversion factor. Divide out the common units.

$= \frac{10}{16} \text{ lb}$

$= 0.625 \text{ lb}$

The alpine pika weighs 0.625 pound.

 Try It!

How many pounds does the elephant weigh?

Stella weighs approximately 3.3 tons.

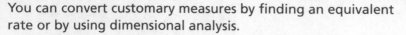
You can convert customary measures by finding an equivalent rate or by using dimensional analysis.

Use an equivalent rate.	Use dimensional analysis.
1 mi = 5,280 ft	$4.25 \ \cancel{mi} \times \dfrac{5,280 \ ft}{1 \ \cancel{mi}}$
$\dfrac{5,280 \ ft \times 4.25}{1 \ mi \times 4.25} = \dfrac{22,440 \ ft}{4.25 \ mi}$	$= 4.25 \times 5,280 \ ft$
	$= 22,440 \ ft$

Customary Units

Length
1 ft = 12 in.
1 yd = 36 in.
1 yd = 3 ft
1 mi = 5,280 ft
1 mi = 1,760 yd

Do You Understand?

1. **? Essential Question** How can you use ratios to convert customary units of measure?

2. What is a conversion factor that relates miles to yards?

3. **Construct Arguments** Jenna used the conversion factor $\dfrac{1 \ T}{2,000 \ lb}$ to convert 50 tons to pounds. Did she use the correct conversion factor? Explain.

4. How can you use the conversion rates of fluid ounces to cups, and cups to pints, to find the number of fluid ounces in a pint?

Do You Know How?

5. Convert 27 inches to yards by finding an equivalent rate.

6. Use dimensional analysis to convert 1.8 pounds to ounces.

7. **Critique Reasoning** Sam is tripling a recipe for an organic cleaning solution. The new recipe calls for 15 tsp of orange oil. To find how many tbsp this is, Sam converted this way:

Conversion factor: $\dfrac{3 \ tsp}{1 \ tbsp}$

$15 \ \cancel{tsp} \times \dfrac{3 \ \cancel{tsp}}{1 \ tbsp} = \dfrac{45}{1} \ tbsp = 45 \ tbsp$

What error did Sam make?

Practice & Problem Solving

In **8–13**, complete each conversion.

8. 5 pt = [   ] c

9. $2\frac{1}{2}$ gal = [   ] qt

10. 2,640 yd = [   ] mi

11. Convert 16 yards to feet.
Use the conversion rate
3 feet = 1 yard.

12. Convert 10 pints to quarts.
Use the conversion rate
1 quart = 2 pints.

13. Convert 12 ounces to pounds.
Use the conversion rate
16 ounces = 1 pound.

14. Two neighbors in a rural area want to know the distance between their homes in miles. What should the neighbors use as a conversion factor to convert this distance to miles?

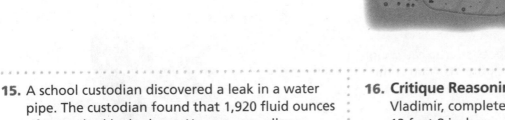

4,224 feet

15. A school custodian discovered a leak in a water pipe. The custodian found that 1,920 fluid ounces of water had leaked out. How many gallons of water is this? Use the conversion factor $\frac{1 \text{ gallon}}{128 \text{ fluid ounces}}$.

16. Critique Reasoning Two students, Stella and Vladimir, complete the conversion statement 12 feet 8 inches = _____ inches.

Stella stated that 12 feet 8 inches = 152 inches. Vladimir stated that 12 feet 8 inches = 9 inches.

Which student is incorrect? Explain.

17. The hole for a support post needs to be 6 feet deep. It is currently 1 foot 8 inches deep. How much deeper must the hole be?
Use the conversion factor $\frac{12 \text{ inches}}{1 \text{ foot}}$.

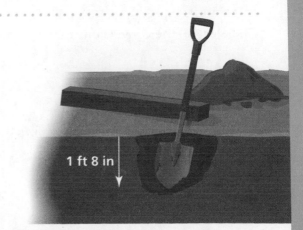

1 ft 8 in

In **18** and **19**, use the recipe card.

18. **Look for Relationships** Cheryl has measured 3 cups of water. Is this enough water for Cheryl to make a double recipe of green slime for a class project? Explain.

Green Slime Recipe

• 1 pint water
• $\frac{1}{2}$ cup cornstarch
• Green food coloring

Add hot water to cornstarch and stir constantly. Then add green food coloring, and stir. Allow the slime to cool to room temperature. This makes a messy slime that goes from liquid to solid. Make sure to play with it on a plastic covered surface. Always have adult supervision when using hot water.

19. There are 16 tablespoons in 1 cup. How many tablespoons of cornstarch would Cheryl need to make the green slime recipe 15 times?

20. **Make Sense and Persevere** Len plans to run at least 3 miles each day to get ready for a cross-country race. One lap of the school track is 440 yards. If Len runs 10 laps each day, will he cover at least 3 miles? Explain.

21. **Higher Order Thinking** Hunter is splitting a quart of ice cream with 7 members of his family. If the quart is split evenly, how many cups will each family member get? Explain.

22. A fully loaded and fueled space shuttle can weigh close to 4.5 million pounds at liftoff. What is this weight expressed in tons?

Weighs almost 4.5 million pounds

✓ Assessment Practice

23. Select all the conversions that are true.

- ☐ 18 ft = 6 yd
- ☐ 18 yd = 6 ft
- ☐ 0.5 mi = 10,560 ft
- ☐ 0.5 mi = 2,640 ft
- ☐ $\frac{1}{2}$ mi = 880 yd

Customary Units

Length
1 ft = 12 in.
1 yd = 36 in.
1 yd = 3 ft
1 mi = 5,280 ft
1 mi = 1,760 yd

Solve & Discuss It!

ACTIVITY

Sam needs to fill a 5-liter water jug for his team. If Sam uses the water bottle to fill the jug, how many times does he need to fill the water bottle to fill the jug?

250 ml

I can...
use unit rates to convert metric measurements.

Reasoning How many milliliters are in 5 liters?

Metric Units of Capacity

1,000 milliliters (mL) = 1 liter (L)
100 centiliters (cL) = 1 liter
10 deciliters (dL) = 1 liter
1 dekaliter (daL) = 10 liters
1 hectoliter (hL) = 100 liters
1 kiloliter (kL) = 1,000 liters

Focus on math practices

Be Precise How many liters of water does Sam's water bottle hold when full?

EXAMPLE 1 👁 Convert Metric Units of Length

Scan for Multimedia

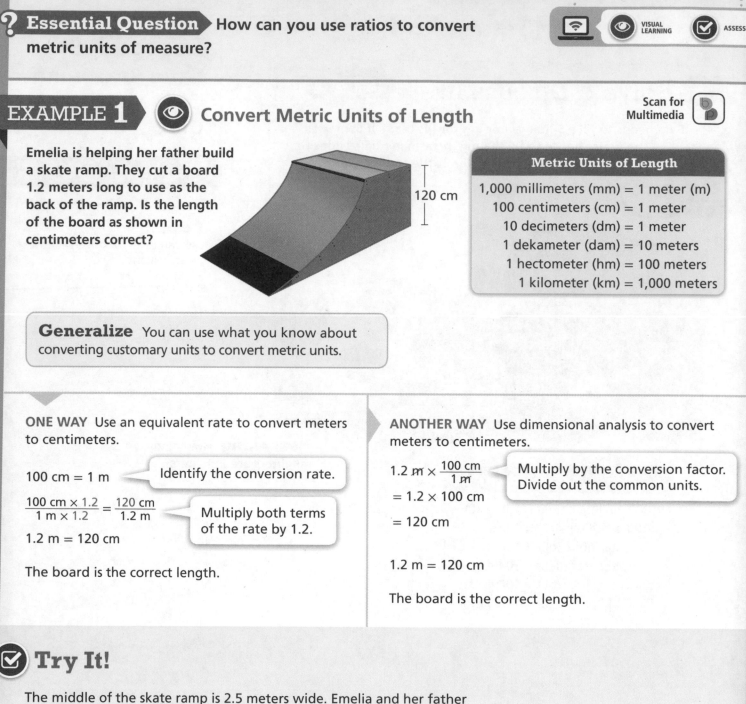

Emelia is helping her father build a skate ramp. They cut a board 1.2 meters long to use as the back of the ramp. Is the length of the board as shown in centimeters correct?

120 cm

Metric Units of Length

1,000 millimeters (mm) = 1 meter (m)
100 centimeters (cm) = 1 meter
10 decimeters (dm) = 1 meter
1 dekameter (dam) = 10 meters
1 hectometer (hm) = 100 meters
1 kilometer (km) = 1,000 meters

Generalize You can use what you know about converting customary units to convert metric units.

ONE WAY Use an equivalent rate to convert meters to centimeters.

100 cm = 1 m ← Identify the conversion rate.

$\frac{100 \text{ cm} \times 1.2}{1 \text{ m} \times 1.2} = \frac{120 \text{ cm}}{1.2 \text{ m}}$ ← Multiply both terms of the rate by 1.2.

1.2 m = 120 cm

The board is the correct length.

ANOTHER WAY Use dimensional analysis to convert meters to centimeters.

$1.2 \text{ m} \times \frac{100 \text{ cm}}{1 \text{ m}}$ ← Multiply by the conversion factor. Divide out the common units.

= 1.2 × 100 cm

= 120 cm

1.2 m = 120 cm

The board is the correct length.

☑ Try It!

The middle of the skate ramp is 2.5 meters wide. Emelia and her father want to use a board that is 23.5 decimeters long. Is this board wide enough for them to use? Convert the decimeters to meters to explain.

Convince Me! How can you convert 2.5 meters to decimeters to determine whether the board is wide enough?

EXAMPLE **2** 👆 **Convert Metric Units of Capacity**

📶 👆 ACTIVITY ☑ ASSESS

Raji poured 150 liters of water into an aquarium. How much more water does Raji need to fill the aquarium?

2.2 hectoliters total capacity

Metric Units of Capacity
1,000 milliliters (mL) = 1 liter (L)
100 centiliters (cL) = 1 liter
10 deciliters (dL) = 1 liter
1 dekaliter (daL) = 10 liters
1 hectoliter (hL) = 100 liters
1 kiloliter (kL) = 1,000 liters

ONE WAY Use an equivalent rate.

1 hectoliter = 100 liters

$$\frac{1 \text{ hL} \times 2.2}{100 \text{ L} \times 2.2} = \frac{2.2 \text{ hL}}{220 \text{ L}}$$

220 L − 150 L = 70 L

Subtract 150 L from the capacity of the aquarium.

Raji needs 70 more liters of water.

ANOTHER WAY Use dimensional analysis.

$$2.2 \text{ hL} \times \frac{100 \text{ L}}{1 \text{ hL}}$$

= 2.2 × 100 L

= 220 L

220 L − 150 L = 70 L

Subtract 150 L from the capacity of the aquarium.

Raji needs 70 more liters of water.

EXAMPLE **3** 👆 **Convert Metric Units of Mass**

Lyle has a bowl that contains 0.8 kilogram of salt. He uses a spoon to remove 850 centigrams of salt. How much salt, in centigrams, remains?

Calculate the conversion rate of kilograms to centigrams.

$$1 \text{ kg} = 1,000 \text{ g} \times \frac{100 \text{ cg}}{1 \text{ g}}$$

1 kg = 1,000 × 100 cg

1 kg = 100,000 cg

Convert 0.8 kilogram to centigrams.

$$\frac{1 \text{ kg} \times 0.8}{100,000 \text{ cg} \times 0.8} = \frac{0.8 \text{ kg}}{80,000 \text{ cg}}$$

80,000 cg − 850 cg = 79,150 cg

Subtract 850 cg from the original mass.

79,150 cg of salt remains in the bowl.

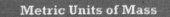

Metric Units of Mass
1,000 milligrams (mg) = 1 gram (g)
100 centigrams (cg) = 1 gram
10 decigrams (dg) = 1 gram
1 dekagram (dag) = 10 grams
1 hectogram (hg) = 100 grams
1 kilogram (kg) = 1,000 grams

Look for Relationships
You could also convert kilograms to centigrams using dimensional analysis.

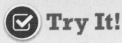 **Try It!**

To make violet paint, Iris mixes 0.25 liter of red paint, 0.25 liter of blue paint, and 4.5 centiliters of white paint. How many centiliters of paint are in the mixture?

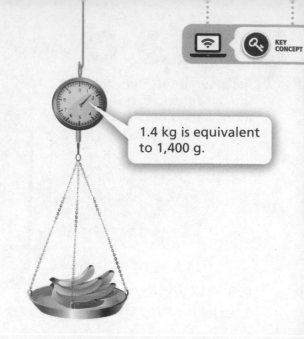

1.4 kg is equivalent to 1,400 g.

You can convert metric measures by finding an equivalent rate or by using dimensional analysis.

Use an equivalent rate.

1 kg = 1,000 g

$$\frac{1 \text{ kg} \times 1.4}{1,000 \text{ g} \times 1.4} = \frac{1.4 \text{ kg}}{1,400 \text{ g}}$$

Use dimensional analysis.

$$1.4 \text{ kg} \times \frac{1,000 \text{ g}}{1 \text{ kg}}$$

$$= 1.4 \times 1,000 \text{ g}$$

$$= 1,400 \text{ g}$$

Do You Understand?

1. **? Essential Question** How can you use ratios to convert metric units of measure?

2. **Be Precise** How are the metric units kilometer and kilogram the same? How are they different?

3. **Reasoning** Which is greater, 250 m or 0.25 km? Justify your reasoning.

4. How can you find the conversion rate for milliliters to kiloliters?

Do You Know How?

5. What is the conversion factor when converting from liters to milliliters?

6. Use an equivalent rate to convert 35 centimeters to meters.

7. **Critique Reasoning** Maddy wants to know how many centigrams are in 0.75 gram. She converted 0.75 gram to its equivalent in centigrams as shown. Is her work correct? Explain.

$$\frac{10 \text{ cg} \times 0.75}{1 \text{ g} \times 0.75} = \frac{7.5 \text{ cg}}{0.75 \text{ g}}$$

8. Look at Exercise 7. Use dimensional analysis to convert 0.75 gram to centigrams.

Name: _____

Practice & Problem Solving

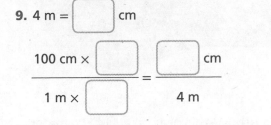

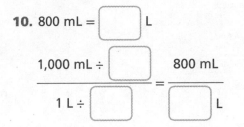

Leveled Practice In **9** and **10**, complete each conversion using an equivalent rate.

9. 4 m = [ ] cm

$$\frac{100 \text{ cm} \times \boxed{}}{1 \text{ m} \times \boxed{}} = \frac{\boxed{} \text{ cm}}{4 \text{ m}}$$

10. 800 mL = [ ] L

$$\frac{1,000 \text{ mL} \div \boxed{}}{1 \text{ L} \div \boxed{}} = \frac{800 \text{ mL}}{\boxed{} \text{ L}}$$

Leveled Practice In **11** and **12**, complete each conversion using dimensional analysis.

11. 200 cL = [ ] L

$$200 \text{ cL} \times \frac{\boxed{} \text{ L}}{\boxed{} \text{ cL}} = \frac{\boxed{}}{\boxed{}} \text{ L} = \boxed{} \text{ L}$$

12. 2.5 kg = [ ] g

$$2.5 \text{ kg} \times \frac{\boxed{} \text{ g}}{\boxed{} \text{ kg}} = \frac{\boxed{}}{\boxed{}} \text{ g} = \boxed{} \text{ g}$$

In **13** and **14**, complete each conversion.

13. 80 cm = [ ] m

14. 2.1 g = [ ] mg

In **15–17**, use the table showing the amount of liquid that Whitney drinks each day.

15. How many liters of water does Whitney drink each day?

Drink	Amount
Juice	250 mL
Milk	400 mL
Water	1,500 mL

16. What is the total amount of liquid, in liters, that Whitney drinks each day?

17. Troy drinks 1.8 L of water each day. How many more milliliters of water does Troy drink each day than Whitney?

18. There are 10 millimeters in 1 centimeter, so about how many millimeters long is this dinosaur bone? Explain.

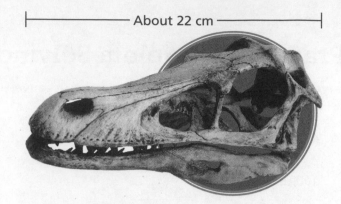

About 22 cm

19. Critique Reasoning Savannah says that 1 kilogram is equivalent to 1,000,000 milligrams. Is Savannah correct? Explain.

20. Model with Math Lucas hiked 14,300 meters through the Everglades in the morning. After lunch, he continued hiking. When he finished the hike, he had covered 31.5 kilometers in all. Write an equation that can be used to find how far Lucas hiked after lunch.

21. Tariq has a collection of 35 quarters that he wants to send to his cousin. What is the total weight of the quarters in kilograms?

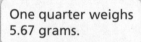

One quarter weighs 5.67 grams.

5.67 g

22. Higher Order Thinking Louis has a bag of 25 pen shells. Each pen shell is 18 centimeters long. What is the combined length of the pen shells in meters?

Assessment Practice

23. Select all the conversions that are equivalent to the capacity of a 5.5-liter pitcher of lemonade.

☐ 0.0055 kL

☐ 55 mL

☐ 0.055 kL

☐ 550 mL

☐ 5,500 mL

24. Select all the conversions that are equivalent to the mass of a 425-gram football.

☐ 42,000 mg

☐ 42,500 cg

☐ 450 dg

☐ 4.25 hg

☐ 0.425 kg

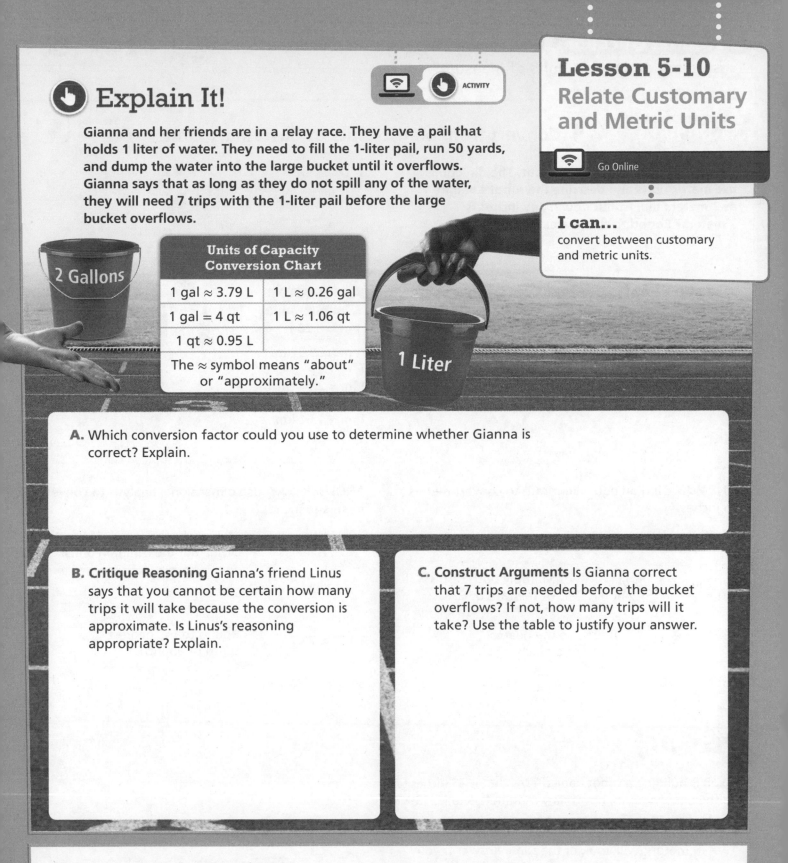

Explain It!

ACTIVITY

Gianna and her friends are in a relay race. They have a pail that holds 1 liter of water. They need to fill the 1-liter pail, run 50 yards, and dump the water into the large bucket until it overflows. Gianna says that as long as they do not spill any of the water, they will need 7 trips with the 1-liter pail before the large bucket overflows.

2 Gallons

1 Liter

Units of Capacity Conversion Chart

1 gal ≈ 3.79 L	1 L ≈ 0.26 gal
1 gal = 4 qt	1 L ≈ 1.06 qt
1 qt ≈ 0.95 L	

The ≈ symbol means "about" or "approximately."

Lesson 5-10
Relate Customary and Metric Units

Go Online

I can...
convert between customary and metric units.

A. Which conversion factor could you use to determine whether Gianna is correct? Explain.

B. Critique Reasoning Gianna's friend Linus says that you cannot be certain how many trips it will take because the conversion is approximate. Is Linus's reasoning appropriate? Explain.

C. Construct Arguments Is Gianna correct that 7 trips are needed before the bucket overflows? If not, how many trips will it take? Use the table to justify your answer.

Focus on math practices

Construct Arguments Morgan says that 4 liters is less than 1 gallon. Construct an argument to show that Morgan is incorrect.

327

? **Essential Question** How can you use ratios to convert customary and metric units of measure?

VISUAL LEARNING   ASSESS

EXAMPLE 1 👁 **Convert from Metric Units to Customary Units**

Scan for Multimedia

Tyrel is using a kit to build a robot. The directions use metric units and describe the robot's height as 2 meters tall. About how many inches is 2 meters? Round to the nearest tenth.

Make Sense and Persevere When relating customary and metric units, exact whole-number conversions are rare. The table shows approximate equivalents.

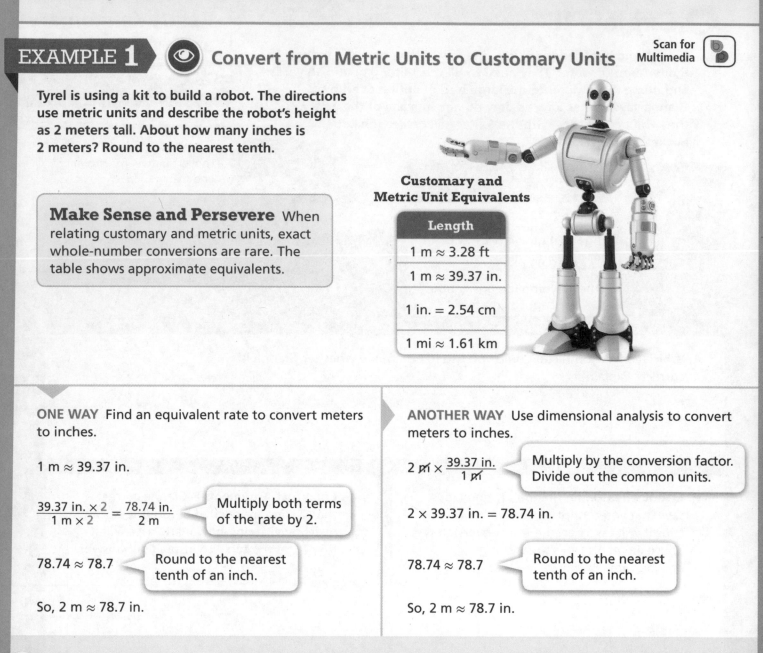

Customary and Metric Unit Equivalents

Length
1 m ≈ 3.28 ft
1 m ≈ 39.37 in.
1 in. = 2.54 cm
1 mi ≈ 1.61 km

ONE WAY Find an equivalent rate to convert meters to inches.

1 m ≈ 39.37 in.

$$\frac{39.37 \text{ in.} \times 2}{1 \text{ m} \times 2} = \frac{78.74 \text{ in.}}{2 \text{ m}}$$

Multiply both terms of the rate by 2.

78.74 ≈ 78.7

Round to the nearest tenth of an inch.

So, 2 m ≈ 78.7 in.

ANOTHER WAY Use dimensional analysis to convert meters to inches.

$$2 \text{ m} \times \frac{39.37 \text{ in.}}{1 \text{ m}}$$

Multiply by the conversion factor. Divide out the common units.

2 × 39.37 in. = 78.74 in.

78.74 ≈ 78.7

Round to the nearest tenth of an inch.

So, 2 m ≈ 78.7 in.

☑ **Try It!**

Jacob is building a robot named T3-X that is 75 inches tall. To the nearest tenth, how many centimeters tall is T3-X?

Convince Me! If you want to find the height of T3-X in meters, will you get the same answer if you convert inches to centimeters, and then centimeters to meters, as you would if you convert inches to feet, and then feet to meters? Explain.

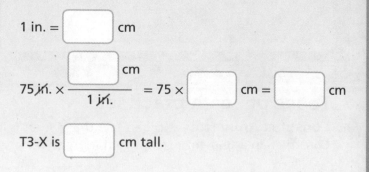

1 in. = [   ] cm

$$75 \text{ in.} \times \frac{[\quad] \text{ cm}}{1 \text{ in.}} = 75 \times [\quad] \text{ cm} = [\quad] \text{ cm}$$

T3-X is [   ] cm tall.

EXAMPLE 2 — Convert from Customary Units to Metric Units

Jenna's Alaskan husky weighs 21 pounds. What is her husky's approximate weight in kilograms? Round to the nearest tenth.

Generalize When relating customary and metric units, use what you know about converting within one measurement system.

Use dimensional analysis.

$$21 \text{ lb} \times \frac{1 \text{ kg}}{2.20 \text{ lb}}$$

$$\frac{21 \text{ kg}}{2.20} \approx 9.5 \text{ kg}$$

Divide to simplify. Round to the nearest tenth.

Jenna's Alaskan husky weighs about 9.5 kilograms.

Customary and Metric Unit Equivalents

Weight/Mass
1 oz ≈ 28.35 g
1 kg ≈ 2.20 lb
1 metric ton (t) ≈ 1.102 T

EXAMPLE 3 — Convert Using Two Steps

If Deva drank all the water in her bottle, how many cups of water did she drink? Round to the nearest tenth.

Convert liters to quarts, and then quarts to cups.

H2O Ultra 0.75 liter

Customary and Metric Equivalents	Customary Units
Capacity	**Capacity**
1 gal ≈ 3.79 L	1 tbsp = 3 tsp
1 qt ≈ 0.95 L	1 fl oz = 2 tbsp
1 L ≈ 0.26 gal	1 c = 8 fl oz
1 L ≈ 1.06 qt	1 pt = 2 c
	1 qt = 2 pt
	1 gal = 4 qt

STEP 1

1 L ≈ 1.06 qt

$$0.75 \text{ L} \times \frac{1.06 \text{ qt}}{1 \text{ L}}$$

Multiply by the conversion factor. Divide out the common units.

$$0.75 \times 1.06 = 0.795$$

$$0.75 \text{ L} \approx 0.795 \text{ qt}$$

STEP 2

1 qt = 4 c

Identify the conversion factors: 1 qt = 2 pt and 2 pt = 4 c.

$$0.795 \text{ qt} \times \frac{4 \text{ c}}{1 \text{ qt}}$$

Multiply by the conversion factor. Divide out the common units.

$$0.795 \times 4 = 3.18 \text{ c}$$

Multiply the remaining factors.

To the nearest tenth, Deva drank about 3.2 cups of water.

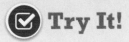 Try It!

Find the length of a 100-yard football field in meters. Use 1 yard = 3 feet and 1 meter ≈ 3.28 feet. Round to the nearest tenth.

You can use what you know about converting within one measurement system to relate customary and metric units. You can convert measures with customary and metric units by finding an equivalent rate or using dimensional analysis.

Use an equivalent rate.

1 kg ≈ 2.20 lb

$$\frac{1\ kg \times 5}{2.20\ lb \times 5} = \frac{5\ kg}{11\ lb}$$

5 kg ≈ 11 lb

Use dimensional analysis.

$5\ \cancel{kg} \times \dfrac{2.20\ lb}{1\ \cancel{kg}}$

5 × 2.20 = 11 lb

5 kg ≈ 11 lb

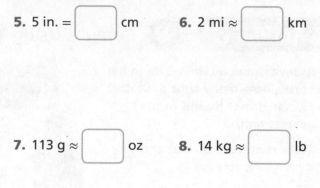

Do You Understand?

1. ❓**Essential Question** How can you use ratios to convert customary and metric units of measure?

2. **Reasoning** When converting centimeters to inches, do you multiply or divide by 2.54? Explain.

3. **Use Structure** How can you find the approximate number of liters in 1 pint?

   Remember: 1 quart = 2 pints

4. How is the conversion from inches to centimeters different from other conversions between customary and metric units?

Do You Know How?

In 5–8, find the equivalent measure. Round to the nearest tenth.

5. 5 in. = ☐ cm

6. 2 mi ≈ ☐ km

7. 113 g ≈ ☐ oz

8. 14 kg ≈ ☐ lb

9. Convert 30 gallons to liters by finding an equivalent rate.

10. Approximately how many ounces are equivalent to 1 kilogram?

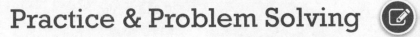

Practice & Problem Solving

Scan for
Multimedia

In 11–18, find the equivalent measure. Round to the nearest tenth.

11. 9 qt ≈ [　　] L

12. 2 gal ≈ [　　] L

13. 2 in. ≈ [　　] cm

14. 5 km ≈ [　　] mi

15. 10 L ≈ [　　] qt

16. 5.5 t ≈ [　　] T

17. 50 lb ≈ [　　] kg

18. 10 oz ≈ [　　] g

19. A chef at a restaurant uses 12 pounds of butter each day. About how many grams of butter does the chef use each day? Use the conversion factors $\frac{16 \text{ ounces}}{1 \text{ pound}}$ and $\frac{28.35 \text{ grams}}{1 \text{ ounce}}$.

20. Reasoning Simone wants to know whether a new chest of drawers will fit next to her bed. The chest she would like to buy is 73 centimeters wide. She knows that her room is 86 inches wide. The bed is 76 inches wide. Will the chest fit next to her bed? Explain.

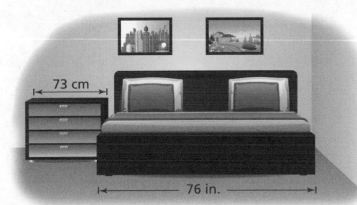

73 cm

76 in.

21. **Be Precise** Denali is the highest mountain in the United States. What is its height in meters? Round to the nearest whole number.

Denali is approximately 20,320 ft high.

22. **Construct Arguments** Francesca wants to convert 1 foot to centimeters. Use what you know about customary units to explain how she can do this.

23. **Higher Order Thinking** At the state fair, a person must be at least 138 centimeters tall to ride the roller coaster. Billy wants to ride the coaster. He is 4 feet 7 inches tall. Is Billy tall enough to ride the coaster? Explain.

24. Paul's car holds a maximum of 19 gallons of gas. About how many liters of gas does Paul need to fill his gas tank?

gallons remaining

☑ Assessment Practice

25. The posted speed limit is 65 miles per hour. Select all the metric measures that are faster than 65 miles per hour.

☐ 65 km per hour

☐ 97.5 km per hour

☐ 104 km per hour

☐ 105.7 km per hour

☐ 120.3 km per hour

26. Boys competing in the long jump event must jump at least 15 feet to qualify for the state track and field meet. Select all the metric measures that are less than 15 feet.

☐ 6.5 m

☐ 5.0 m

☐ 4.5 m

☐ 3.92 m

☐ 3.5 m

? Topic Essential Question

What are ratios and rates? How can you use ratios and rates to describe quantities and solve problems?

Vocabulary Review

Complete each definition and then provide an example of each vocabulary word.

Vocabulary   constant speed   conversion factor   rate
                 ratio   term   unit price

Definition	Example
1. A relationship in which there are y units of a quantity for every x units of a quantity is a _____.	
2. The price of a single item is called a _____.	
3. A ratio that compares quantities with unlike units of measure is a _____.	

Use Vocabulary in Writing

Explain how you can convert 52 ounces to pounds. Use vocabulary words in your explanation.

Concepts and Skills Review

LESSON **5-1** **Understand Ratios**

Quick Review

A **ratio** is a relationship in which for every *x* units of one quantity there are *y* units of another quantity. A ratio can be written using the word "to," a colon, or a fraction bar to separate the two terms.

Example

The ratio of men to women at a small wedding is 6:4. If there are 16 women at the wedding, how many men are at the wedding?

Draw a diagram to represent the ratio. Because 4 boxes represent 16 women, each box represents 4 women.

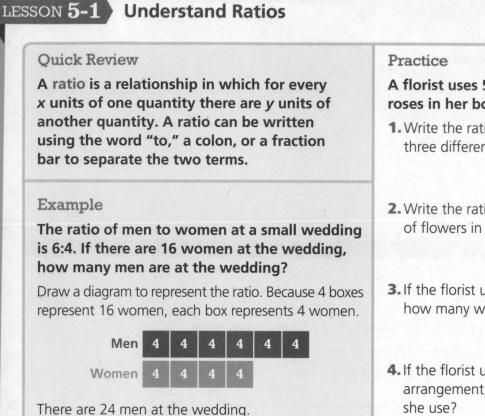

There are 24 men at the wedding.

Practice

A florist uses 5 red roses for every 2 white roses in her bouquets.

1. Write the ratio of white roses to red roses in three different ways.

2. Write the ratio of red roses to the total number of flowers in three different ways.

3. If the florist uses 10 red roses in a bouquet, how many white roses does she use?

4. If the florist uses 10 white roses in an arrangement, how many red roses does she use?

LESSON **5-2** **Generate Equivalent Ratios**

Quick Review

You can multiply or divide both terms of a ratio by the same nonzero number to find equivalent ratios.

Example

Find two ratios that are equivalent to $\frac{21}{126}$.

One Way

Multiply.

$$\frac{21 \times 2}{126 \times 2} = \frac{42}{252}$$

Another Way

Divide.

$$\frac{21 \div 3}{126 \div 3} = \frac{7}{42}$$

Practice

In **1–4**, find two ratios equivalent to the given ratio.

1. $\frac{5}{12}$

2. 14:32

3. 3 to 4

4. $\frac{7}{8}$

5. For every 4 bagels sold at a bakery, 7 muffins are sold. How many muffins are sold when the bakery sells 24 bagels? Complete the table.

Bagels	4	8	12	16	20	24
Muffins	7					

LESSON 5-3 Compare Ratios

Quick Review

To compare ratios, make a table to show each ratio and then find a value in which one of the terms is the same in both tables.

Example

Erica

Math Facts	Seconds
25	30
50	60
75	90
100	120
125	150

Klayton

Math Facts	Seconds
38	50
76	100
114	150
152	200
190	250

Erica can complete more facts than Klayton.

Practice

1. The school soccer team buys 3 soccer balls for every 2 players. The school volleyball team buys 7 volleyballs for every 5 players. Which team buys more balls per player?

2. Jenna walks 12 miles in 5 days. Alex walks 7 miles in 3 days. Who walks more miles per day?

LESSON 5-4 Represent and Graph Ratios

Quick Review

You can solve some ratio problems by making a table of equivalent ratios and then graphing the pairs of values on a coordinate plane.

Example

Days of Rain	1	2	3	n
Days of Sun	2	4	6	8

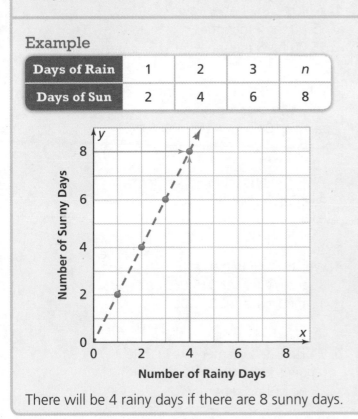

There will be 4 rainy days if there are 8 sunny days.

Practice

1. In gym class, the sixth graders walk 2 laps for every 3 laps they run. If the students run 12 laps, how many laps will they walk? Complete the table. Then plot the pairs of values on the coordinate plane.

Run (laps)	3	6	9	12
Walk (laps)	2			

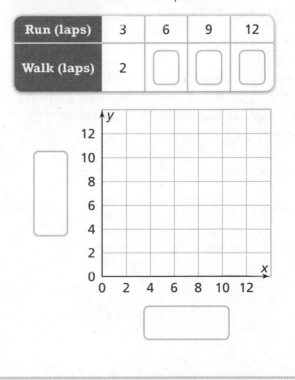

LESSON 5-5 ▸ Understand Rates and Unit Rates

Quick Review

A **rate** is a ratio that relates two quantities with different units. A **unit rate** relates a quantity to 1 unit of another quantity. You can use what you know about dividing fractions to write a ratio of fractions as a unit rate.

Example

Write 20 meters in 4 minutes as a rate and as a unit rate.

Rate:

$$\frac{20 \text{ meters}}{4 \text{ minutes}}$$

Unit Rate:

$$\frac{20 \text{ meters} \div 4}{4 \text{ minutes} \div 4} = \frac{5 \text{ meters}}{1 \text{ minute}}$$

> The unit rate is an equivalent rate with a denominator of 1 unit.

Practice

Write each statement as a unit rate.

1. 78 miles on 3 gallons

2. 18 laps in 6 minutes

3. 48 sandwiches for 16 people

4. 49 houses in 7 blocks

5. 6 desks in 2 rows

LESSON 5-6 ▸ Compare Unit Rates

Quick Review

A unit rate compares a quantity to 1 unit of another quantity. To compare unit rates, compare the first terms.

Example

On Pet Day, Meg's turtle crawled 30 feet in 6 minutes, and Pat's turtle crawled 25 feet in 5 minutes. Whose turtle crawled at a faster rate?

Write each rate.

Meg's turtle $\frac{30 \text{ ft}}{6 \text{ min}}$ $\frac{25 \text{ ft}}{5 \text{ min}}$ Pat's turtle

Find each unit rate.

$\frac{5 \text{ ft}}{1 \text{ min}}$ $\frac{5 \text{ ft}}{1 \text{ min}}$

Both turtles crawled at the same rate.

Practice

1. Which is the better value? Circle it.
   $5.00 for 4 mangoes
   $6.00 for 5 mangoes

2. Who earned more each month? Circle it.
   Atif: $84 over 3 months
   Jafar: $100 over 4 months

3. Which is a faster rate? Circle it.
   3 laps in 5 minutes
   4 laps in 7 minutes

4. Which is the better value? Circle it.
   3 sandwiches for $15.00
   4 sandwiches for $21.00

5. Which is the greater rate? Circle it.
   6 points in 3 attempts
   15 points in 5 attempts

LESSON 5-7 ▶ Solve Unit Rate Problems

Quick Review

You can use a ratio table or a unit rate to solve problems involving ratios or rates.

Example

A plane travels at a rate of 780 miles in 2 hours. At this rate, how far will it travel in 3.5 hours?

Find the unit rate.

$$\frac{780 \text{ miles} \div 2}{2 \text{ hours} \div 2} = \frac{390 \text{ miles}}{1 \text{ hour}}$$

Find an equivalent rate.

$$\frac{390 \text{ miles} \times 3.5}{1 \text{ hour} \times 3.5} = \frac{1,365 \text{ miles}}{3.5 \text{ hours}}$$

The plane will travel 1,365 miles in 3.5 hours.

Practice

1. Doug has 5 hours to make an on-time delivery 273 miles away. Doug drives at a constant speed of 55 miles per hour. Will Doug make the delivery by the deadline? Explain.

2. Marie has 8 hours to write a 45-page chapter for her book. Marie writes at a constant speed of 4 pages per hour. Will Marie complete the chapter in time? Explain.

LESSON 5-8 ▶ Ratio Reasoning: Convert Customary Units

Quick Review

You can convert customary measures by finding equivalent rates or by using dimensional analysis.

Example

How many pints are equivalent to 4 quarts?

Find an equivalent rate:

2 pints = 1 quart ········ Identify the conversion rate.

$$\frac{2 \text{ pints} \times 4}{1 \text{ quart} \times 4} = \frac{8 \text{ pints}}{4 \text{ quarts}}$$

Use dimensional analysis:

4 quarts $\times \dfrac{2 \text{ pints}}{1 \text{ quart}} =$ 8 pints ········ Multiply by the conversion factor.

So, 8 pints are equivalent to 4 quarts.

Practice

In 1–4, complete each conversion.

1. 2 mi = [ ] ft

2. 144 in. = [ ] yd

3. 4 oz = [ ] lb

4. 3 gal = [ ] qt

5. The hippo at the zoo weighs 1.5 tons. How many pounds does the hippo weigh?

Ratio Reasoning: Convert Metric Units

Quick Review

To convert metric units, use the same methods used for converting customary units. Either use the conversion rate to find an equivalent rate or use dimensional analysis.

Example

Tariq rode his bike 15,100 meters. How many kilometers did he ride his bike?

Find an equivalent rate:

$$1,000 \text{ meters} = 1 \text{ kilometer}$$

$$\frac{1,000 \text{ m} \times 15.1}{1 \text{ km} \times 15.1} = \frac{15,100 \text{ m}}{15.1 \text{ km}}$$

Use dimensional analysis:

$$15,100 \text{ m} \times \frac{1 \text{ km}}{1,000 \text{ m}} = \frac{15,100}{1,000} \text{ km} = 15.1 \text{ km}$$

Tariq rode 15.1 kilometers.

Practice

In 1–4, complete each conversion.

1. 3 m = ☐ mm

2. 3,520 mm = ☐ cm

3. 4.2 kg = ☐ g

4. 300 mL = ☐ L

5. Li needs to buy 2 kilograms of apples. If she buys 9 apples that each weigh approximately 150 grams, will she have enough? Explain.

Relate Customary and Metric Units

Quick Review

To convert between metric and customary units, use the conversion rate and find an equivalent rate, or use dimensional analysis. Most conversions will be approximate because, except in the case of inches to centimeters, the conversion rates are approximate.

Example

Gwen has a cooler that holds 3 quarts. About how many liters does the cooler hold?

$$1 \text{ qt} \approx 0.95 \text{ L}$$

$$3 \text{ qt} \times \frac{0.95 \text{ L}}{1 \text{ qt}} = (3 \times 0.95) \text{ L} = 2.85 \text{ L}$$

Gwen's cooler holds approximately 2.85 liters.

Practice

In 1–4, find the equivalent measure. Round to the nearest tenth.

1. 100 g ≈ ☐ oz

2. 6 ft ≈ ☐ m

3. 57 gal ≈ ☐ L

4. 27 km ≈ ☐ mi

5. The science class is raising monarch caterpillars. One of the caterpillars weighs 2.3 ounces. About how many grams does the caterpillar weigh? Round to the nearest tenth.

Pathfinder

Shade a path from START to FINISH. Follow the sums and differences in which the digit in the ones place is greater than the digit in the tenths place. You can only move up, down, right, or left.

I can...
add and subtract multidigit decimals.

START ↓

31.2 − 5.73	1.84 + 19.26	25 − 8.53	2 − 0.95	12.3 − 4.81
14.27 + 4.9	7.29 − 0.8	12.95 + 9.06	1.07 + 0.27	4.22 + 2.8
18 + 4.301	3.007 − 1.71	8.38 − 6.42	10 − 8.94	21 − 3.303
43.397 + 17.81	15.75 − 8.8	4.02 − 3.83	17.54 + 6.82	3.8 + 1.89
2.35 + 1.08	1.035 − 0.641	29.06 + 2.87	28.12 − 5.016	0.62 + 5.38

↓
FINISH

? Topic Essential Question

What is the meaning of percent? How can percent be estimated and found?

Topic Overview

6-1 Understand Percent

6-2 Relate Fractions, Decimals, and Percents

6-3 Represent Percents Greater Than 100 or Less Than 1

6-4 Estimate to Find Percent

6-5 Find the Percent of a Number

6-6 Find the Whole Given a Part and the Percent

3-Act Mathematical Modeling: Ace the Test

Topic Vocabulary

• percent

Lesson Digital Resources

INTERACTIVE STUDENT EDITION
Access online or offline.

VISUAL LEARNING ANIMATION
Interact with visual learning animations.

ACTIVITY Use with *Solve & Discuss It, Explore I* and *Explain It* activities, and to explore Example

VIDEOS Watch clips to support *3-Act Mathematical Modeling Lessons* and *STEM Proje*

📶 Go online

Ace the Test

 Ace the Test

Numbers, percents, letters—teachers use grades as a language to help explain how you are doing in class. When you know how your grade is determined, it is easier to understand your teacher's expectations. Think about this during the 3-Act Mathematical Modeling lesson.

 PRACTICE Practice what you've learned.

 TUTORIALS Get help from *Virtual Nerd*, right when you need it.

 MATH TOOLS Explore math with digital tools.

 GAMES Play Math Games to help you learn.

 KEY CONCEPT Review important lesson content.

A-Z **GLOSSARY** Read and listen to English/Spanish definitions.

 ASSESSMENT Show what you've learned.

:enVision® STEM Project

Did You Know?

Extinction normally occurs at a rate of about one to five species per year. The earth is now **losing species** at 1,000 to 10,000 times that rate, with dozens going extinct every day.

There are 1,373 species of birds identified as **threatened**.

13%
of all bird species
threatened

Polar Bears need ice floes to rest when they travel long distances to find food or migrate. Due to **melting ice**, the population will likely decrease by more than **30%** in the next three generations.

50%
decline

Scientists estimate that the **population** of nearly 17,000 eastern lowland gorillas has **declined** by more than **50%**.

Conservation efforts helped the total number of **black rhinos** to grow from 2,410 to 4,880 in 15 years.

According to the Chinese government, the population of wild giant pandas has reached 1,864, up from 1,596 at last count.

In **100 years**, the number of the world's tigers **declined** from 100,000 to 3,200.

Your Task: Engineering to Prevent Extinction

Engineers help to to prevent extinction with both direct and indirect solutions. Materials engineers develop wood alternatives. Mechanical and chemical engineers produce clean energy. You and your classmates will research threatened species and identify ways that engineers can help to prevent the extinction of these species.

Review What You Know!

Vocabulary

Choose the best term from the box to complete each definition.

| decimal |
| fraction |
| ratio |
| term |

1. A _____ can be written as x to y, x:y, or $\frac{x}{y}$.

2. The number 2.25 is a _____.

3. A number that can be used to describe a part of a whole is a _____.

Rates

Write an equivalent rate.

4. $\dfrac{60 \text{ mi}}{1 \text{ hr}} = \dfrac{\boxed{} \text{ mi}}{5 \text{ hr}}$

5. $\dfrac{8 \text{ hr}}{2 \text{ days}} = \dfrac{28 \text{ hr}}{\boxed{} \text{ days}}$

6. $\dfrac{16 \text{ limes}}{\boxed{} \text{ bags}} = \dfrac{40 \text{ limes}}{5 \text{ bags}}$

7. $\dfrac{\boxed{} \text{ cups}}{9 \text{ boxes}} = \dfrac{24 \text{ cups}}{4 \text{ boxes}}$

8. $\dfrac{\boxed{} \text{ m}}{3 \text{ s}} = \dfrac{135 \text{ m}}{15 \text{ s}}$

9. $\dfrac{36 \text{ lb}}{\$\boxed{}} = \dfrac{9 \text{ lb}}{\$6}$

Decimal Computation

Find each product or quotient.

10. $21 \div 0.05$

11. 18×1.25

12. $10.2 \div 1.2$

13. 150×0.625

14. $4 \div 100$

15. 0.25×0.1

Equivalent Ratios

Write three equivalent ratios for each ratio.

16. $\frac{8}{12}$

17. $\frac{15}{35}$

18. $\frac{30}{48}$

19. What are two ways to find an equivalent ratio for $\frac{10}{25}$?

Language Development

Fill in the cluster diagram using key phrases, sentences, illustrations, or examples related to percents.

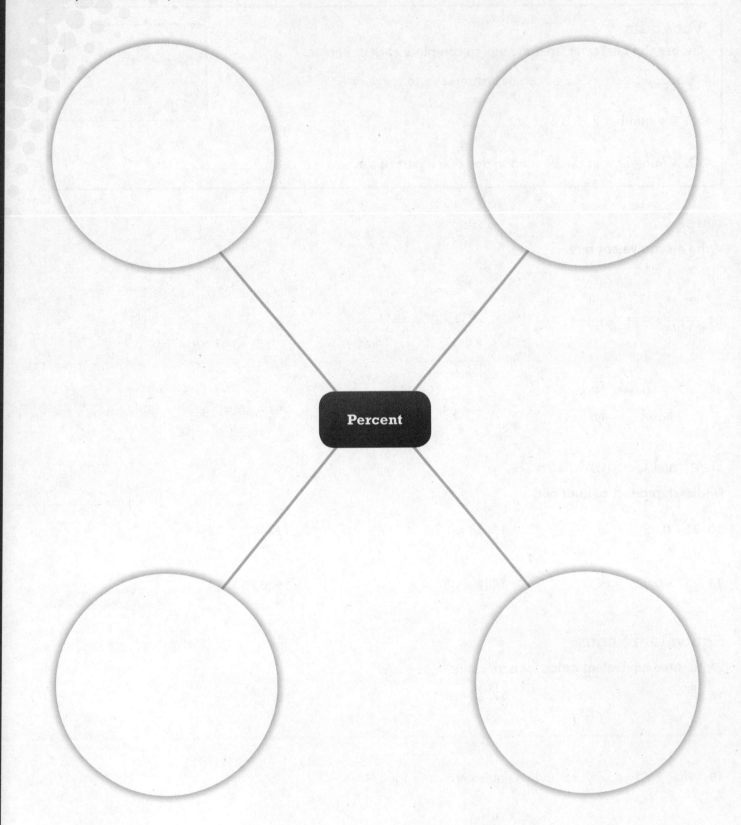

Percent

PROJECT
6A

How would you describe
your favorite work of art?

PROJECT: BUILD A MOSAIC

PROJECT
6B

If you had a jar of coins,
what could you buy?

PROJECT: ESTIMATE PERCENTS

PROJECT 6C

How does advertising make you want to buy something?

PROJECT: DESIGN FLYERS

PROJECT 6D

Which do you think grows faster—a koala or a panda bear?

PROJECT: MAKE A GROWTH CHART

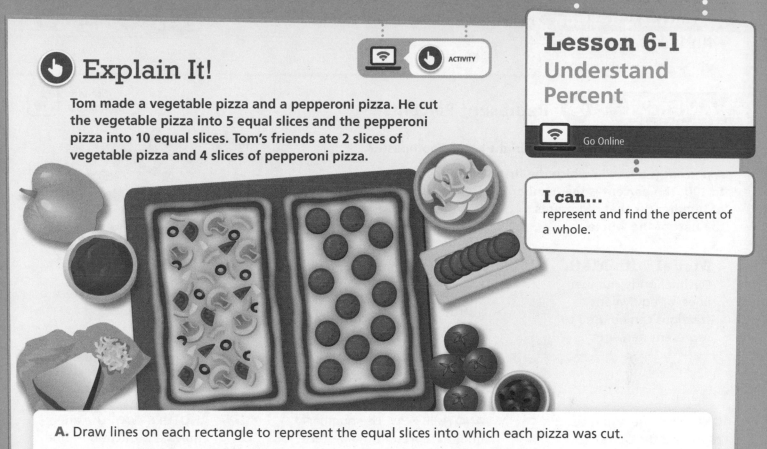

👆 Explain It!

ACTIVITY

Tom made a vegetable pizza and a pepperoni pizza. He cut the vegetable pizza into 5 equal slices and the pepperoni pizza into 10 equal slices. Tom's friends ate 2 slices of vegetable pizza and 4 slices of pepperoni pizza.

I can...
represent and find the percent of a whole.

A. Draw lines on each rectangle to represent the equal slices into which each pizza was cut.

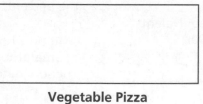

Vegetable Pizza

Pepperoni Pizza

B. Construct Arguments Tom says his friends ate the same amount of vegetable pizza as pepperoni pizza. How could that be true?

Focus on math practices

Model with Math What if Tom's friends ate $\frac{6}{10}$ of the pepperoni pizza? How could you use the rectangles above to find an equal amount of vegetable pizza?

347

? **Essential Question** How can you represent a rate with 100 as the whole?

VISUAL LEARNING   ASSESS

EXAMPLE 1 👁 Represent Percents

Scan for Multimedia

What percent of people prefer Bright White Toothpaste?

A percent is a rate in which the first term is compared to 100. The percent is the number of hundredths that represents the part of the whole.

Model with Math
Decimal grids, number lines, or equivalent fractions can be used to represent percents.

Seven out of ten people prefer Bright White Toothpaste.

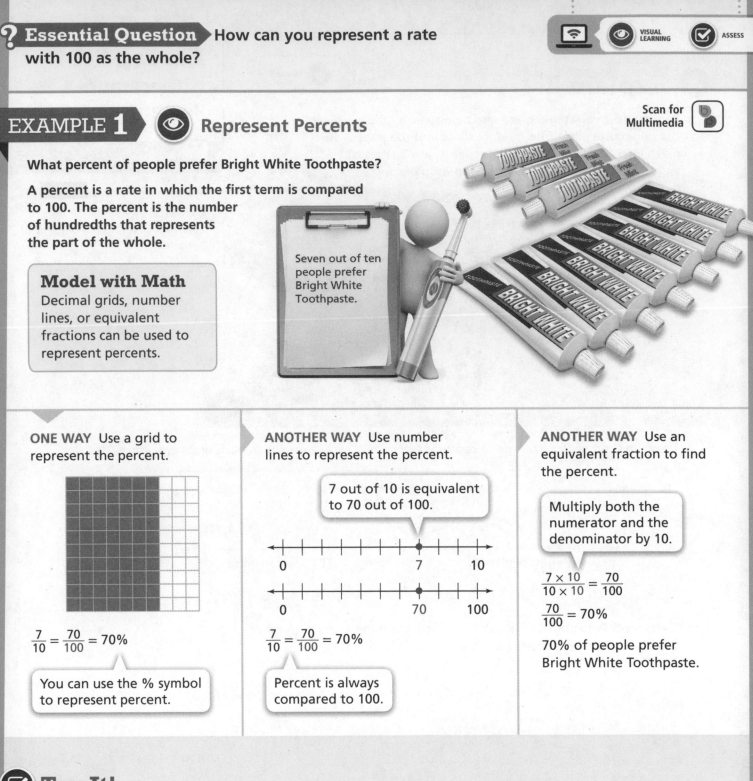

ONE WAY Use a grid to represent the percent.

$\frac{7}{10} = \frac{70}{100} = 70\%$

You can use the % symbol to represent percent.

ANOTHER WAY Use number lines to represent the percent.

7 out of 10 is equivalent to 70 out of 100.

$\frac{7}{10} = \frac{70}{100} = 70\%$

Percent is always compared to 100.

ANOTHER WAY Use an equivalent fraction to find the percent.

Multiply both the numerator and the denominator by 10.

$\frac{7 \times 10}{10 \times 10} = \frac{70}{100}$

$\frac{70}{100} = 70\%$

70% of people prefer Bright White Toothpaste.

☑ Try It!

Jane won 9 out of the 10 video games she played. What percent of the video games did Jane win?

Convince Me! When using an equivalent fraction to find a percent, why do you write 100 as the denominator?

EXAMPLE **2** ▶ 👆 **Examine Percents and Wholes**

🖥 👆 **ACTIVITY** ☑ **ASSESS**

Each line segment represents 100%, but the segments are not the same length. Use equivalent rates to find the percent, or part, of each line segment that points *A* and *B* represent.

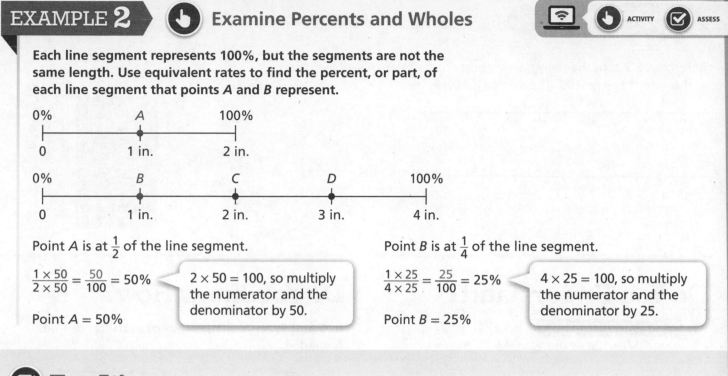

Point *A* is at $\frac{1}{2}$ of the line segment.

$\frac{1 \times 50}{2 \times 50} = \frac{50}{100} = 50\%$

> 2 × 50 = 100, so multiply the numerator and the denominator by 50.

Point *A* = 50%

Point *B* is at $\frac{1}{4}$ of the line segment.

$\frac{1 \times 25}{4 \times 25} = \frac{25}{100} = 25\%$

> 4 × 25 = 100, so multiply the numerator and the denominator by 25.

Point *B* = 25%

☑ Try It!

Which point represents 50% on the second line segment? Explain.

EXAMPLE **3** ▶ 👆 **Use Percents**

You can use percent and mental math to find the length of a line segment.

A. If $\overline{CD}$ represents 10%, what is the length of a line segment that is 100%?

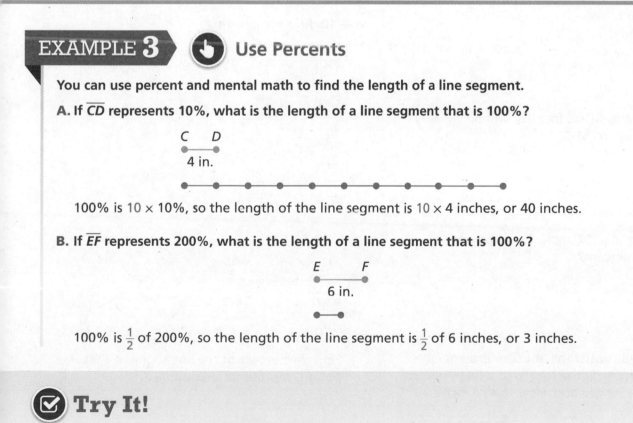

100% is 10 × 10%, so the length of the line segment is 10 × 4 inches, or 40 inches.

B. If $\overline{EF}$ represents 200%, what is the length of a line segment that is 100%?

100% is $\frac{1}{2}$ of 200%, so the length of the line segment is $\frac{1}{2}$ of 6 inches, or 3 inches.

☑ Try It!

If $\overline{CD}$ represents 100%, what is the length of a line segment that is 25%? Explain.

KEY CONCEPT

A percent is a rate that compares a part to a whole. The second term in the rate is always 100. The whole is 100%.

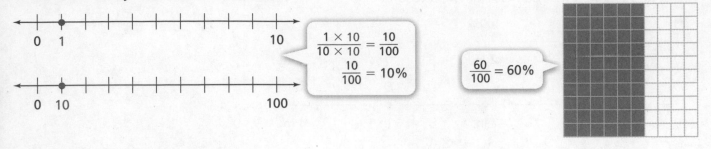

$$\frac{1 \times 10}{10 \times 10} = \frac{10}{100}$$

$$\frac{10}{100} = 10\%$$

$$\frac{60}{100} = 60\%$$

Do You Understand?

1. **Essential Question** How can you represent a rate with 100 as the whole?

2. When writing a percent as a fraction, what number do you write as the whole, or denominator?

3. Why are tenths, fifths, fourths, and halves easy to express as percents?

4. Why is the grid in Example 1 a good way to represent a percent?

5. **Look for Relationships** If $\overline{CD}$ in Example 3 represents 100%, is the length of a line segment that is 300% longer or shorter than 4 inches? Explain.

Do You Know How?

In **6 and 7**, write the percent of each figure that is shaded.

6.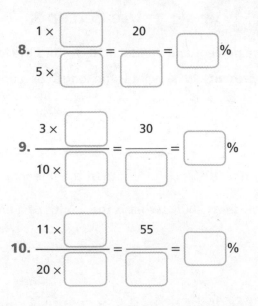

7.

In **8–10**, find the percent.

8. $\dfrac{1 \times \boxed{}}{5 \times \boxed{}} = \dfrac{20}{\boxed{}} = \boxed{}\%$

9. $\dfrac{3 \times \boxed{}}{10 \times \boxed{}} = \dfrac{30}{\boxed{}} = \boxed{}\%$

10. $\dfrac{11 \times \boxed{}}{20 \times \boxed{}} = \dfrac{55}{\boxed{}} = \boxed{}\%$

11. Find the percent of the line segment that point D represents in Example 2.

Practice & Problem Solving

In 12 and 13, shade each model to represent the percent.

12. 14%

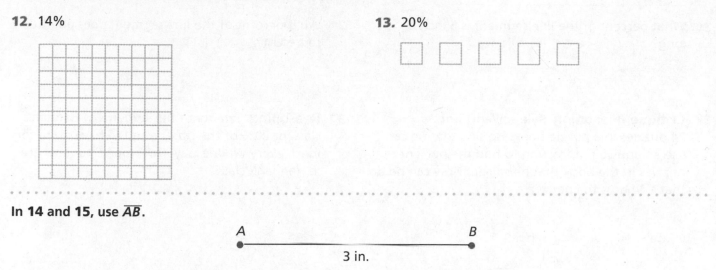

13. 20%

☐ ☐ ☐ ☐ ☐

In 14 and 15, use $\overline{AB}$.

A •————————————————• B

3 in.

14. If $\overline{AB}$ represents 50%, what is the length of a line segment that is 100%?

15. If $\overline{AB}$ is 300%, what is the length of a line segment that is 100%?

16. Your friend shows you a coin collection. In it, $\frac{45}{50}$ of the coins are quarters. What percent of the coins are quarters?

17. Use Structure In a race, 19 out of 50 runners finished in fewer than 30 minutes. What percent of the runners finished in fewer than 30 minutes? Write an equivalent fraction to find the percent.

18. A basketball player made 63 out of 100 attempted free throws. What percent of free throws did the player make?

19. Harry kept a weather journal for September. The sun was shining on 4 out of every 5 days. On what percent of the days was the sun not shining?

In 20 and 21, use the line segment.

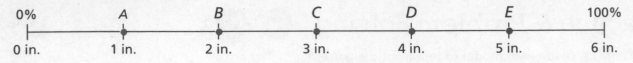

0%   A   B   C   D   E   100%

0 in.   1 in.   2 in.   3 in.   4 in.   5 in.   6 in.

20. What percent of the line segment is 6 inches long?

21. What percent of the line segment does point C represent?

22. Critique Reasoning Kyle solved 18 of 24 puzzles in a puzzle book. He says that he can use an equivalent fraction to find the percent of puzzles in the book that he solved. How can he do that? What is the percent?

23. Reasoning Twenty of the students in Hannah's class, or 80% of the class, voted to have pizza for lunch every Wednesday. How many students are in Hannah's class?

24. According to a survey of workers, $\frac{2}{20}$ of the workers walk to work, $\frac{1}{20}$ bike, $\frac{4}{20}$ carpool, and $\frac{13}{20}$ drive alone. What percent of the workers walk or bike to work?

25. Higher Order Thinking From Monday through Friday, James works in the library on 2 days and in the cafeteria on another day. On Saturday and Sunday, James washes cars 50% of the days. How many days does James work in a week? What percent of the days from Monday through Friday does he work?

☑ Assessment Practice

26. Select all the figures that are shaded to represent 20% of the whole.

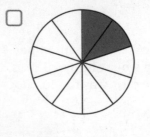

☐   ☐

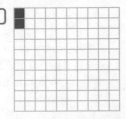

☐ ■ ☐ ☐ ☐ ☐   ☐

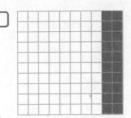

Solve & Discuss It!

ACTIVITY

The grid is shaded with blue, orange, and yellow. What part of the grid is shaded blue? What part is shaded orange? What part of the grid is shaded?

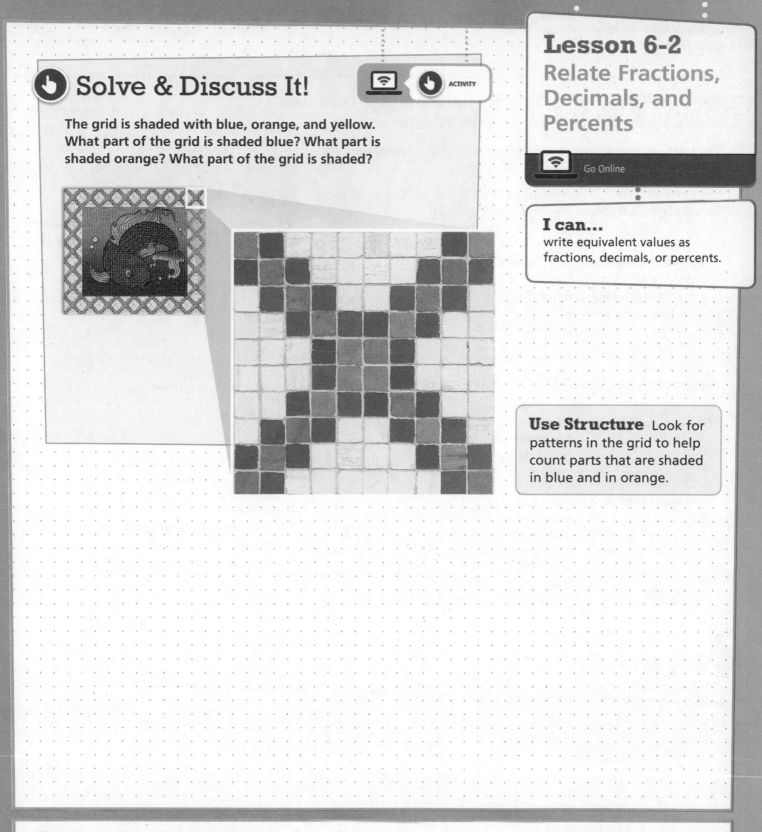

I can...
write equivalent values as fractions, decimals, or percents.

Use Structure Look for patterns in the grid to help count parts that are shaded in blue and in orange.

Focus on math practices

Reasoning Write the part of the grid that is shaded yellow as a decimal and a percent. How are the decimal and the percent alike and how are they different?

🛜 👁 VISUAL LEARNING   ☑ ASSESS

EXAMPLE 1 👁 **Express Percents and Decimals as Parts of a Whole**

Scan for Multimedia 📘

The portion of the time that Teddy spends doing homework for each subject is shown in the bar diagram.

How can you write the amount of time Teddy spends on reading or science as a fraction, decimal, and percent?

> **Reasoning** Fractions, decimals, and percents are three ways to show parts of a whole. How can you use reasoning to write quantities as a fraction, a decimal, or a percent?

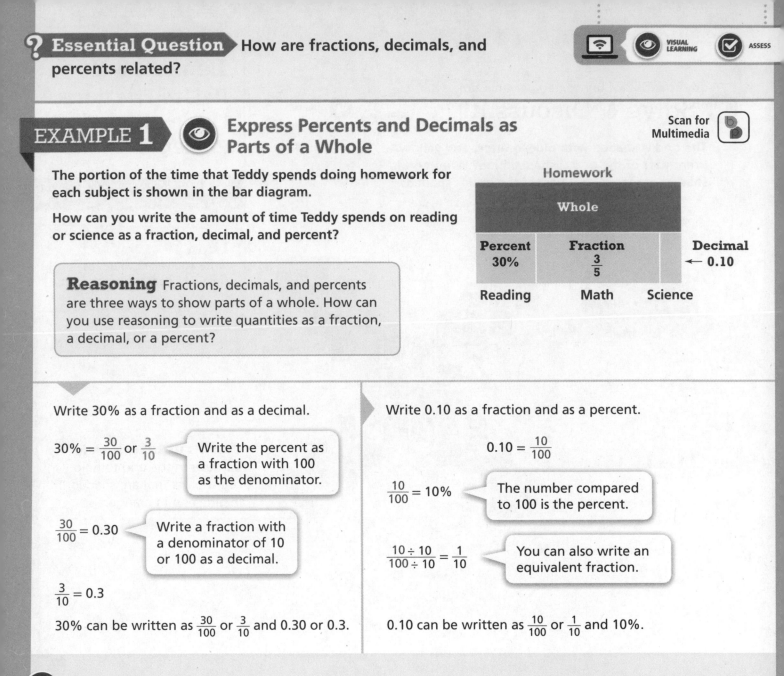

Homework

Whole		
Percent 30%	Fraction $\frac{3}{5}$	Decimal ← 0.10
Reading	Math	Science

Write 30% as a fraction and as a decimal.

$30\% = \frac{30}{100}$ or $\frac{3}{10}$ ⟨ Write the percent as a fraction with 100 as the denominator.

$\frac{30}{100} = 0.30$ ⟨ Write a fraction with a denominator of 10 or 100 as a decimal.

$\frac{3}{10} = 0.3$

30% can be written as $\frac{30}{100}$ or $\frac{3}{10}$ and 0.30 or 0.3.

Write 0.10 as a fraction and as a percent.

$0.10 = \frac{10}{100}$

$\frac{10}{100} = 10\%$ ⟨ The number compared to 100 is the percent.

$\frac{10 \div 10}{100 \div 10} = \frac{1}{10}$ ⟨ You can also write an equivalent fraction.

0.10 can be written as $\frac{10}{100}$ or $\frac{1}{10}$ and 10%.

☑ **Try It!**

Ana spends 0.45 of her homework time reading. What is 0.45 as a percent? Explain.

Convince Me! What relationship do you see when comparing the equivalent fraction and percent?

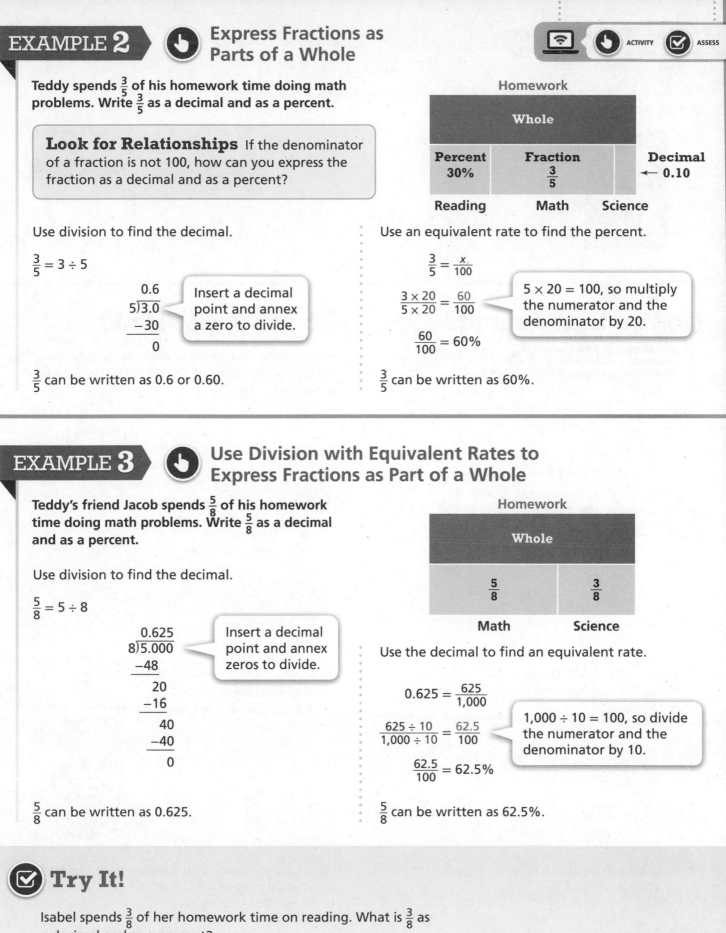

EXAMPLE 2 Express Fractions as Parts of a Whole

ACTIVITY   ASSESS

Teddy spends $\frac{3}{5}$ of his homework time doing math problems. Write $\frac{3}{5}$ as a decimal and as a percent.

Look for Relationships If the denominator of a fraction is not 100, how can you express the fraction as a decimal and as a percent?

Homework

Whole		
Percent 30%	Fraction $\frac{3}{5}$	Decimal ← 0.10
Reading	Math	Science

Use division to find the decimal.

$\frac{3}{5} = 3 \div 5$

$$\begin{array}{r} 0.6 \\ 5\overline{)3.0} \\ -30 \\ \hline 0 \end{array}$$

Insert a decimal point and annex a zero to divide.

$\frac{3}{5}$ can be written as 0.6 or 0.60.

Use an equivalent rate to find the percent.

$\frac{3}{5} = \frac{x}{100}$

$\frac{3 \times 20}{5 \times 20} = \frac{60}{100}$

$5 \times 20 = 100$, so multiply the numerator and the denominator by 20.

$\frac{60}{100} = 60\%$

$\frac{3}{5}$ can be written as 60%.

EXAMPLE 3 Use Division with Equivalent Rates to Express Fractions as Part of a Whole

Teddy's friend Jacob spends $\frac{5}{8}$ of his homework time doing math problems. Write $\frac{5}{8}$ as a decimal and as a percent.

Homework

Whole	
$\frac{5}{8}$	$\frac{3}{8}$
Math	Science

Use division to find the decimal.

$\frac{5}{8} = 5 \div 8$

$$\begin{array}{r} 0.625 \\ 8\overline{)5.000} \\ -48 \\ \hline 20 \\ -16 \\ \hline 40 \\ -40 \\ \hline 0 \end{array}$$

Insert a decimal point and annex zeros to divide.

Use the decimal to find an equivalent rate.

$0.625 = \frac{625}{1,000}$

$\frac{625 \div 10}{1,000 \div 10} = \frac{62.5}{100}$

$1,000 \div 10 = 100$, so divide the numerator and the denominator by 10.

$\frac{62.5}{100} = 62.5\%$

$\frac{5}{8}$ can be written as 0.625.

$\frac{5}{8}$ can be written as 62.5%.

✓ Try It!

Isabel spends $\frac{3}{8}$ of her homework time on reading. What is $\frac{3}{8}$ as a decimal and as a percent?

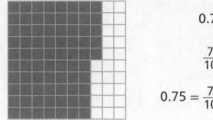
You can use division and equivalent ratios to express fractions, decimals, and percents in equivalent forms.

$$0.75 = \frac{75}{100}$$

$$\frac{75}{100} = 75\%$$

$$0.75 = \frac{75}{100} = 75\%$$

Whole
0.75

Do You Understand?

1. **? Essential Question** How are fractions, decimals, and percents related?

2. Why do you use a denominator of 100 when you write a percent as a fraction?

3. **Look for Relationships** How do you use the digits in a hundredths decimal to write a percent?

4. How do you write a fraction with a denominator of 20 as a decimal?

Do You Know How?

In 5–7, write each number in equivalent forms using the two other forms of notation: fraction, decimal, or percent.

5. 27%

6. 0.91

7. $\frac{6}{100}$

8. Greek yogurt has 25% of the calcium that most people need in a day. What is 25% as a decimal?

9. Linda received $\frac{4}{5}$ of the votes in the election for student council president. What percent of the votes did Linda receive?

Practice & Problem Solving

Leveled Practice In **10–15**, write each number in equivalent forms using the two other forms of notation: fraction, decimal, or percent.

10. 0.25

$0.25 = \dfrac{\boxed{}}{100} = \boxed{}$ %

$0.25 = \dfrac{\boxed{} \div 25}{100 \div \boxed{}} = \dfrac{\boxed{}}{4}$

11. $\dfrac{2}{2}$

$\dfrac{2}{2} = \dfrac{2 \times \boxed{}}{2 \times \boxed{}} = \dfrac{100}{100} = \boxed{}$ %

$\dfrac{2}{2} = 2 \div \boxed{} = \boxed{}.0$

12. 7%

$7\% = \dfrac{\boxed{}}{100}$

$7\% = \dfrac{\boxed{}}{100} = 0.\boxed{}$

13. 38%

14. $\dfrac{7}{8}$

15. 0.04

16. Devon answered 23 out of 25 problems on a math test correctly. What percent of the problems did Devon answer correctly?

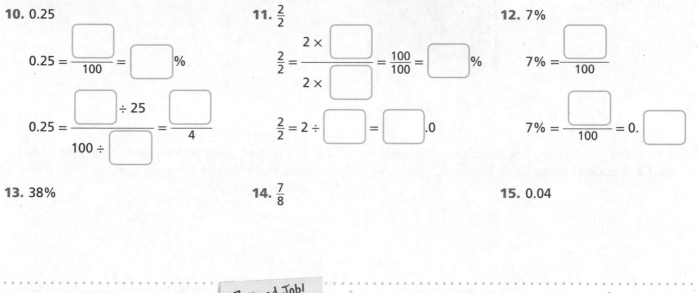

17. Reasoning How could you write $\dfrac{4}{8}$ as a percent without dividing?

In **18–21**, use the circle graph.

18. Many chemical elements can be found in Earth's atmosphere. What fraction of Earth's atmosphere is made up of nitrogen?

Gases in Earth's Atmosphere

1%

21%

78%

Nitrogen

Oxygen

Other gases

19. How much of Earth's atmosphere is made up of oxygen? Write the part as a decimal.

20. What percent of gases in Earth's atmosphere does the whole circle graph represent?

21. What fraction of the gases in Earth's atmosphere are gases other than nitrogen and oxygen?

22. Look for Relationships All T-shirts in a store are on sale as shown. Is this markdown greater than or less than a markdown of $\frac{1}{5}$ off the original price? Explain.

25% OFF

23. Critique Reasoning Enrollment at Jacksonville Middle School increased by 3% this year. Sofia says that the increase, written as a decimal, is 0.3. Is Sofia correct? Explain.

24. Generalize What are the attributes of fractions that are equivalent to 100%?

25. The cost of building a new library is 0.85 of the cost of remodeling the old library. What is the cost as a percent?

26. Nine out of every 20 people walking out of a movie theater say that they would recommend the movie to a friend. What percent of the people would recommend the movie to a friend?

27. Higher Order Thinking Ms. Rose bought a package of sea life stickers. Out of every 10 stickers, 4 are starfish. If there are 60 stickers in the package, what fraction of the stickers are starfish? What percent of the stickers in the package are starfish?

☑ Assessment Practice

28. $\frac{3}{4}$ can be represented as a percent. Select all the fractions and decimals that are also equivalent to this percent.

- ☐ $\frac{51}{68}$
- ☐ 0.34
- ☐ $\frac{36}{50}$
- ☐ 0.75
- ☐ $\frac{39}{52}$

29. There are 110 sixth-grade students in a Florida middle school. 40% of the students enjoy playing video games on the weekends. Using the percent as a rate per 100, how many students enjoy playing video games?

☐

Lesson 6-3
Represent Percents Greater Than 100 or Less Than 1

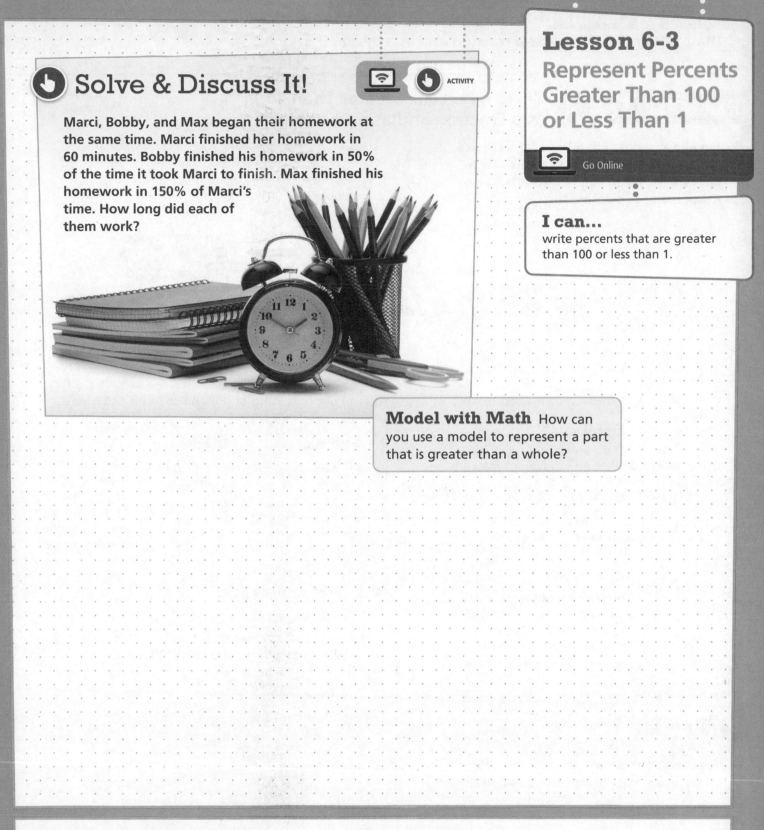

Go Online

I can...
write percents that are greater than 100 or less than 1.

Solve & Discuss It!

ACTIVITY

Marci, Bobby, and Max began their homework at the same time. Marci finished her homework in 60 minutes. Bobby finished his homework in 50% of the time it took Marci to finish. Max finished his homework in 150% of Marci's time. How long did each of them work?

Model with Math How can you use a model to represent a part that is greater than a whole?

Focus on math practices

Reasoning Did Max spend more time or less time on his homework than Marci? Explain.

? **Essential Question** How can you write a percent greater than 100 or less than 1 as a fraction and as a decimal?

VISUAL LEARNING   ASSESS

EXAMPLE 1   👁 Write a Percent Greater Than 100 as a Fraction and as a Decimal

Scan for Multimedia

Jan and Kim built model cars for a science project. Kim's car traveled 140% as far as Jan's car. How can you write 140% as a fraction and as a decimal?

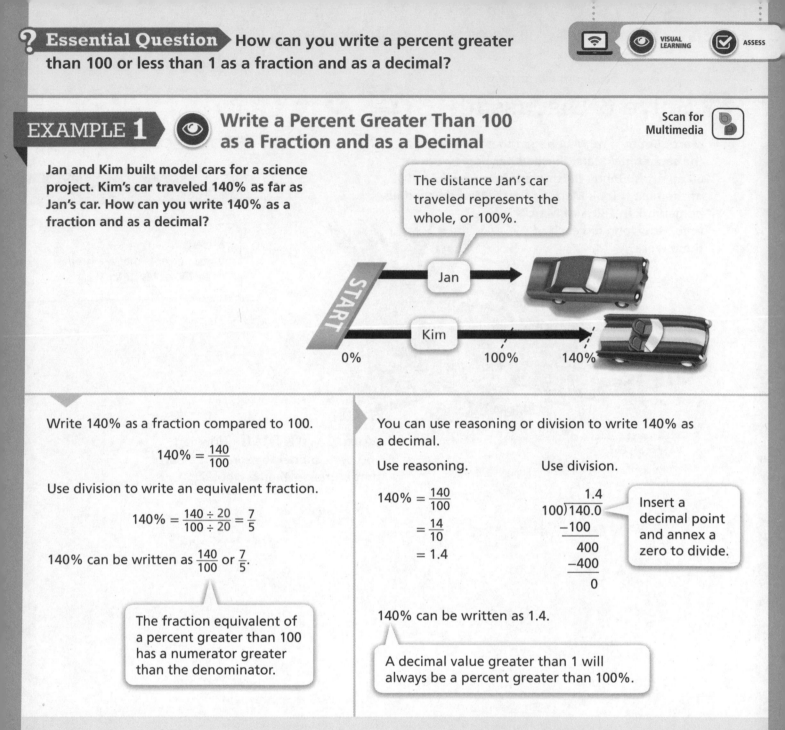

The distance Jan's car traveled represents the whole, or 100%.

START
Jan
Kim
0%   100%   140%

Write 140% as a fraction compared to 100.

$$140\% = \frac{140}{100}$$

Use division to write an equivalent fraction.

$$140\% = \frac{140 \div 20}{100 \div 20} = \frac{7}{5}$$

140% can be written as $\frac{140}{100}$ or $\frac{7}{5}$.

The fraction equivalent of a percent greater than 100 has a numerator greater than the denominator.

You can use reasoning or division to write 140% as a decimal.

Use reasoning.

$$140\% = \frac{140}{100}$$
$$= \frac{14}{10}$$
$$= 1.4$$

Use division.

$$\begin{array}{r} 1.4 \\ 100\overline{)140.0} \\ -100 \\ \hline 400 \\ -400 \\ \hline 0 \end{array}$$

Insert a decimal point and annex a zero to divide.

140% can be written as 1.4.

A decimal value greater than 1 will always be a percent greater than 100%.

☑ Try It!

The area of a new movie theater is 225% of the area of the old theater. What is 225% as a fraction and as a decimal?

Convince Me! How would you write 1.75 as a percent? Give an example in which you would use a percent that is greater than 100.

Write $\frac{1}{2}$% as a fraction and as a decimal.

A percent less than 1 is less than $\frac{1}{100}$ of the whole.

Write $\frac{1}{2}$% as a fraction.

$\frac{1}{2}\% = \frac{\frac{1}{2}}{100}$

Percent means out of 100. Divide $\frac{1}{2}$ by 100.

$= \frac{1}{2} \div 100$

$= \frac{1}{2} \times \frac{1}{100}$

$= \frac{1}{200}$

$\frac{1}{2}$% can be written as $\frac{1}{200}$.

Write $\frac{1}{2}$% as a decimal.

$\frac{1}{2}\% = 0.5\%$

$= \frac{0.5}{100}$

$= \frac{5}{1,000} = 0.005$

$\frac{1}{2}$% can be written as 0.005.

EXAMPLE 3   **Write a Decimal Percent Less Than 1 as a Fraction and as a Decimal**

Write the percent of the solution that is water as a fraction and as a decimal.

0.9% of this solution is water.

0.9% is less than 1%.

Write 0.9% as a fraction.

$0.9\% = 0.9 \div 100$

$= \frac{0.9}{100}$

$= \frac{9}{1,000}$

0.9% can be written as $\frac{9}{1,000}$.

Write 0.9% as a decimal.

$0.9\% = 0.9 \div 100$

$\frac{0.9}{100} = \frac{9}{1,000}$

$= 0.009$

0.9% can be written as 0.009.

✅ Try It!

Write each percent as a fraction and as a decimal.

a. $\frac{2}{5}$%   **b.** 0.3%

You can express percents greater than 100 or less than 1 in equivalent forms.

$$275\% = \frac{275}{100}$$

$$\frac{275 \div 25}{100 \div 25} = \frac{11}{4}$$

$$275\% = \frac{11}{4} = 2.75$$

$$\frac{1}{5}\% = 0.2\%$$

$$\frac{0.2}{100} = \frac{2}{1,000} \text{ or } \frac{1}{500} = 0.002$$

$$\frac{1}{5}\% = \frac{1}{500} = 0.002$$

Do You Understand?

1. **? Essential Question** How can you write a percent greater than 100 or less than 1 as a fraction and as a decimal?

2. **Reasoning** Explain why $\frac{3}{4}$ is less than 100%.

3. **Reasoning** Why is the numerator greater than the denominator in a fraction that is equivalent to a percent greater than 100?

4. Explain the difference between $\frac{1}{2}$ and $\frac{1}{2}\%$.

Do You Know How?

In 5–7, write each percent as a fraction and as a decimal.

5. 150%

6. $\frac{3}{10}\%$

7. 0.24%

8. Kelly saved $\frac{4}{5}\%$ of her allowance. What is this percent expressed as a fraction and as a decimal?

9. Mrs. Sanchez sold her house for 250% of the amount she paid for it. What is this percent expressed as a fraction and as a decimal?

Name: _____

Practice & Problem Solving

Scan for
Multimedia

Leveled Practice In **10–15**, write each percent as a fraction and as a decimal.

10. $\frac{3}{5}\% = \frac{3}{5} \div \boxed{}$

$= \frac{3}{5} \times \dfrac{1}{\boxed{}}$

$= \dfrac{3}{\boxed{}} = \boxed{}$

11. $\frac{3}{4}\% = 0.\boxed{}\ \%$

$= \dfrac{\boxed{}}{100}$

$= \dfrac{\boxed{}}{10,000} = \boxed{}$

12. $0.1\% = 0.1 \div 100$

$= \dfrac{0.1}{\boxed{}} = \dfrac{1}{\boxed{}}$

$= \boxed{}$

13. $0.4\% = 0.4 \div 100$

$= \dfrac{0.4}{\boxed{}} = \dfrac{4}{\boxed{}}$

$= \boxed{}$

14. 322%

15. 210%

---

16. Reasoning Use the art at the right. How do you express the length of the *Queen Mary 2* as it compares to the height of the Washington Monument as a fraction and as a decimal?

17. About $\frac{7}{10}\%$ of the passengers on a cruise ship swam in the ship's pool on the first day of the cruise. How would you express this number as a decimal and as a percent?

The *Queen Mary 2* is more than 200% longer than the Washington Monument is high.

Washington Monument

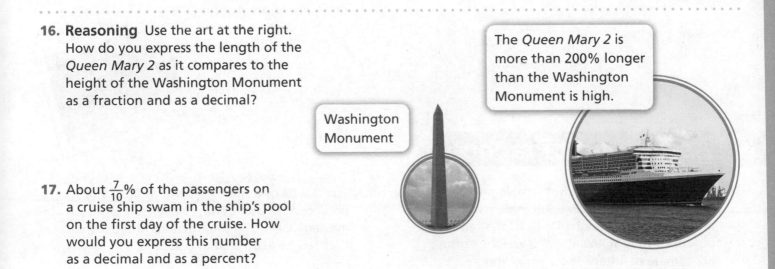

18. The fastest boat can reach speeds more than 710% as fast as the *Queen Mary 2*. How would you express this number as a fraction and as a decimal?

19. The weight of the Washington Monument is about 105% as much as the *Queen Mary 2*. Write this percent as a fraction and as a decimal.

20. Students set a goal for the number of cans to collect for the canned food drive. They reached 120% of their goal. What is 120% expressed as a fraction and as a decimal?

120%
Our goal
Canned Food Drive

21. Use Structure Popcorn sales at a Saturday afternoon matinee were 108% of the sales at the 8:00 showing of the movie. Calvin expressed 108% as 10.8. Is Calvin correct? Explain.

22. Construct Arguments There are 350% more students enrolled in Spanish class than Latin class. How does expressing 350% as a decimal prove that more than 3 times as many students are enrolled in Spanish class as are enrolled in Latin class?

23. Critique Reasoning Free round-trip tickets to Orlando, Florida were given to 0.4% of the people staying at a hotel. Larry says that tickets were given to $\frac{4}{10}$ of the people at the hotel. What did Larry do wrong when he calculated 0.4% as a fraction? What is the correct fraction?

24. The unemployment rate decreased by $\frac{1}{10}$% in one month. Write $\frac{1}{10}$% as a fraction and as a decimal.

25. Higher Order Thinking A photo of a mosquito in a science book is magnified to 635% of the mosquito's actual size. If the mosquito is 16 millimeters long, what is the length of the mosquito in the picture?

? mm

✓ Assessment Practice

26. At a Florida zoo, one adult female panther weighs 100 pounds. An adult male panther at the same zoo weighs 159% of the female panther's weight. What is the weight of the adult male panther? Show your work.

27. The results of a survey show that 0.32% of the people in the survey have never sent a text message. Select all the fractions and decimals that can be expressed as 0.32%.

- ☐ $\frac{32}{100}$
- ☐ $\frac{2}{625}$
- ☐ 0.0032
- ☐ $\frac{8}{2,500}$
- ☐ 0.032

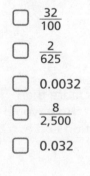

1. Vocabulary Explain how fractions, decimals, and percents are related. *Lesson 6-2*

2. Sarai is mixing a solution. She pours all the liquid from a full small beaker into a large beaker. The liquid fills the large beaker to 15% of its capacity. If the small beaker holds 300 mL, how much does the large beaker hold? *Lessons 6-1 and 6-3*

3. The Murphy family is on a road trip. On the first day, they traveled 30% of their total distance. On the second day, they traveled another $\frac{1}{4}$ of the total distance. What fraction of the total distance do they have left after the second day? What percent? *Lesson 6-2*

4. Complete the table. *Lessons 6-2 and 6-3*

Percent	Fraction	Decimal
70%		
		1.25
	$\frac{11}{20}$	
0.2%		

5. A basketball player made 17 out of 20 free throws at practice. What percent of the free throws did the player miss? *Lesson 6-1*

6. A section of rope 5 inches long represents 20% of the length of the entire rope. How long is the rope? *Lesson 6-1*

How well did you do on the mid-topic checkpoint? Fill in the stars. ☆ ☆ ☆

MID-TOPIC PERFORMANCE TASK

The students in Mr. Anderson's class conducted a survey of 1,000 people. They asked each person to name his or her favorite color. The results are shown in the table.

Color	Number
Blue	450
Red	300
Orange	50
Yellow	10
White	5

PART A

Complete the table to write each result as a fraction, a decimal, and a percent.

Color	Number	Fraction	Decimal	Percent
Blue	450			
Red	300			
Orange	50			
Yellow	10			
White	5			

PART B

Green was chosen by 18% of the people. Which number is equivalent to 18%? Select all that apply.

- [ ] $\frac{18}{1,000}$
- [ ] 0.18
- [ ] $\frac{9}{5}$
- [ ] $\frac{18}{100}$
- [ ] 0.018

PART C

Cecilia noticed that not all of the survey responses were recorded in the table. What percent of the responses were not recorded in the table? Explain.

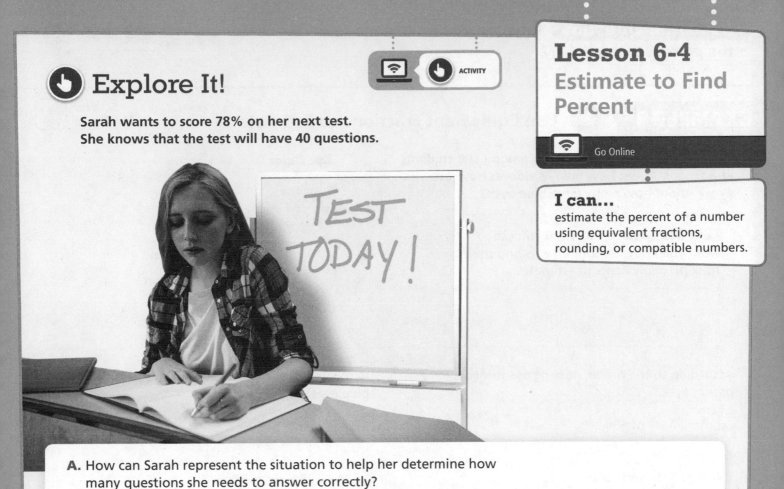

Explore It!

ACTIVITY

Sarah wants to score 78% on her next test.
She knows that the test will have 40 questions.

TEST TODAY!

I can...
estimate the percent of a number using equivalent fractions, rounding, or compatible numbers.

A. How can Sarah represent the situation to help her determine how many questions she needs to answer correctly?

1	2	3	4	5	6	7	8	9	10
11	12	13	14	15	16	17	18	19	20
21	22	23	24	25	26	27	28	29	30
31	32	33	34	35	36	37	38	39	40

B. How could you use the model to help solve the problem?

Focus on math practices

Use Structure On her last test, Sarah answered 82% of 60 questions correctly. About how many questions did Sarah answer correctly? Use estimation.

VISUAL LEARNING   ASSESS

EXAMPLE 1   👁 Use Equivalent Fractions to Estimate

Scan for Multimedia

This graph shows the eye colors among 500 students at a school. About how many students have brown eyes? About how many have blue eyes?

Use Structure How can you use what you know about percents and their fraction equivalents to estimate?

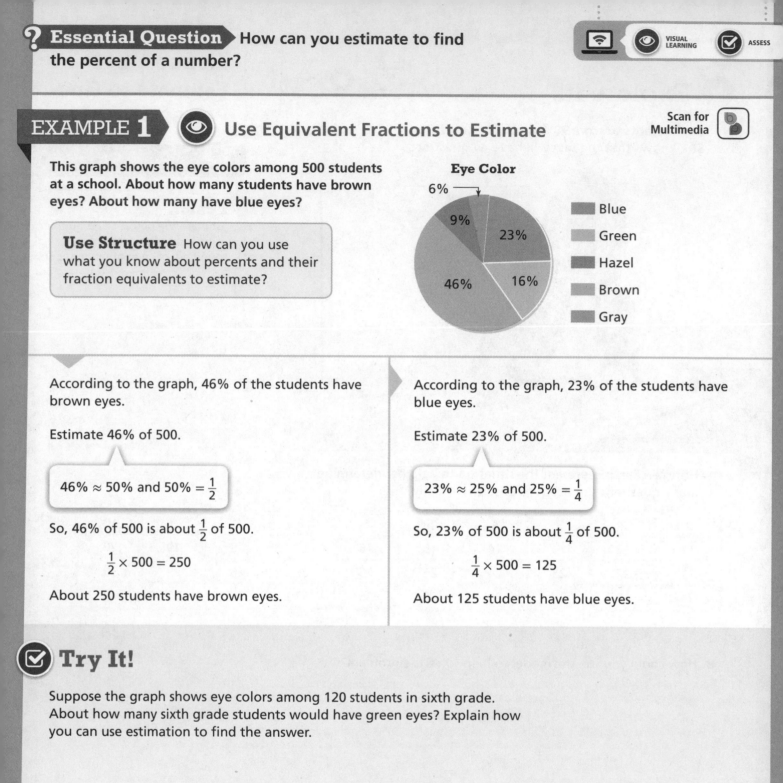

Eye Color

6%
9%
23%
46%
16%

■ Blue
■ Green
■ Hazel
■ Brown
■ Gray

According to the graph, 46% of the students have brown eyes.

Estimate 46% of 500.

$46\% \approx 50\%$ and $50\% = \frac{1}{2}$

So, 46% of 500 is about $\frac{1}{2}$ of 500.

$$\frac{1}{2} \times 500 = 250$$

About 250 students have brown eyes.

According to the graph, 23% of the students have blue eyes.

Estimate 23% of 500.

$23\% \approx 25\%$ and $25\% = \frac{1}{4}$

So, 23% of 500 is about $\frac{1}{4}$ of 500.

$$\frac{1}{4} \times 500 = 125$$

About 125 students have blue eyes.

☑ **Try It!**

Suppose the graph shows eye colors among 120 students in sixth grade. About how many sixth grade students would have green eyes? Explain how you can use estimation to find the answer.

Convince Me! How does understanding fraction equivalents help you estimate how many students in sixth grade have green eyes?

Use the results of the survey shown to the right. About how many high school students plan to get a summer job?

> **Reasoning** You can use rounding or compatible numbers to find a reasonable estimate of how many students plan to get a summer job.

SUMMARY JOBS

> 53% of 94 students surveyed plan to get a summer job.

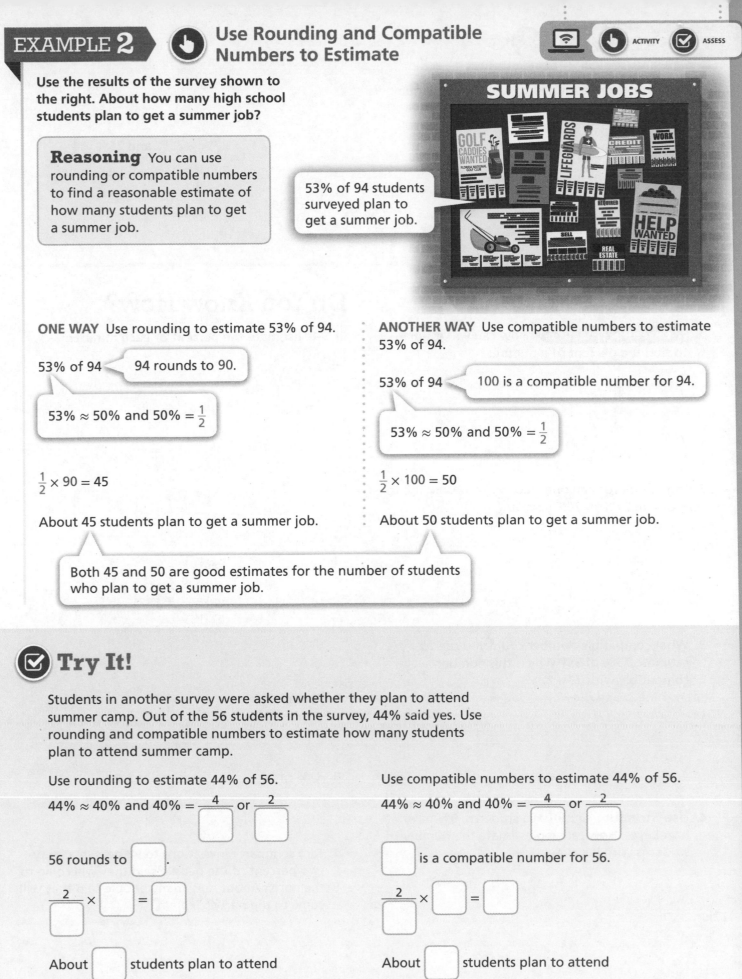

ONE WAY Use rounding to estimate 53% of 94.

53% of 94 ◂ 94 rounds to 90.

53% ≈ 50% and 50% = $\frac{1}{2}$

$\frac{1}{2} \times 90 = 45$

About 45 students plan to get a summer job.

ANOTHER WAY Use compatible numbers to estimate 53% of 94.

53% of 94 ◂ 100 is a compatible number for 94.

53% ≈ 50% and 50% = $\frac{1}{2}$

$\frac{1}{2} \times 100 = 50$

About 50 students plan to get a summer job.

> Both 45 and 50 are good estimates for the number of students who plan to get a summer job.

☑ Try It!

Students in another survey were asked whether they plan to attend summer camp. Out of the 56 students in the survey, 44% said yes. Use rounding and compatible numbers to estimate how many students plan to attend summer camp.

Use rounding to estimate 44% of 56.

44% ≈ 40% and 40% = $\dfrac{4}{\boxed{}}$ or $\dfrac{2}{\boxed{}}$

56 rounds to $\boxed{}$.

$\dfrac{2}{\boxed{}} \times \boxed{} = \boxed{}$

About $\boxed{}$ students plan to attend summer camp.

Use compatible numbers to estimate 44% of 56.

44% ≈ 40% and 40% = $\dfrac{4}{\boxed{}}$ or $\dfrac{2}{\boxed{}}$

$\boxed{}$ is a compatible number for 56.

$\dfrac{2}{\boxed{}} \times \boxed{} = \boxed{}$

About $\boxed{}$ students plan to attend summer camp.

Fraction equivalents, rounding, or compatible numbers can be used to estimate the percent of a number.

$8\% \approx 10\%$ and $10\% = \frac{1}{10}$

$\frac{1}{10} \times 300{,}000 = 30{,}000$

8% of 300,000 is about 30,000.

$27\% \approx 25\%$ and $25\% = \frac{1}{4}$

300 is a compatible number for 297.

$\frac{1}{4} \times 300 = 75$

27% of 297 is about 75.

Do You Understand?

1. **? Essential Question** How can you estimate to find the percent of a number?

2. Is there more than one fraction you could use to estimate 27% of 200? Explain.

3. What compatible number could you use to estimate 75% of 35? Why is this number compatible with 75%?

4. **Use Structure** Out of 195 students, 9% have hazel eyes. How can you estimate the number of students with hazel eyes?

Do You Know How?

In 5–8, estimate the percent of each number.

5. 47% of 77

$47\% \approx \boxed{}$ $77 \approx \boxed{}$

$\boxed{}$ of $\boxed{} = \boxed{}$

6. 18% of 48

$18\% \approx \boxed{}$ $48 \approx \boxed{}$

$\boxed{}$ of $\boxed{} = \boxed{}$

7. 73% of 800

8. 31% of 94

9. Tara sent party invitations to 98 people. Eighty-two percent of the people said they will come to the party. About how many people said they will come to the party? Explain.

Name: _____

Practice & Problem Solving

Leveled Practice In **10–15**, estimate the percent of each number.

10. 74% of 63

74% ≈ [   ]   63 ≈ [   ]

[   ] of [   ] = [   ]

11. 8% of 576

8% ≈ [   ]   576 ≈ [   ]

[   ] of [   ] = [   ]

12. 34% of 55

13. 27% of 284

14. 65% of 89

15. 4% of 802

---

16. There are about 320 million residents in the United States. If 38% of them live in the South, estimate how many live in other areas of the United States.

38% of the U.S. population lives in this region.

17. Lisa and Bill made 60 magnets for a craft fair. They sold 55% of the magnets. Lisa says that they sold about 30 magnets. Bill says that they sold about 36 magnets. Could they both be correct? Explain.

---

18. Make Sense and Persevere Roland has 180 coins in his collection. Approximately 67% of the coins are quarters. About how much money does Roland have in quarters? Explain.

19. Out of 9,799 whistles that a company manufactured, some were rejected for shipment to stores because they did not pass the quality control standards of the company. Estimate the number of whistles that did not pass.

19% of the whistles were rejected.

REJECTED

20. There are 8,249 people registered to vote in the town of Mayfield. About how many people voted in the election? Explain.

21. Higher Order Thinking Lea spent 25% of x hours at her part-time job. What is x if 25% of x is about 30 hours? Explain how you estimated and which property of equality you used to find x.

22. Reasoning Vanessa scored 78% on a test with 120 questions. What benchmark fraction would you use to estimate the number of questions that Vanessa answered correctly? Explain.

23. Jason has saved 41% of what he needs to buy a skateboard. About how much has Jason saved? Explain.

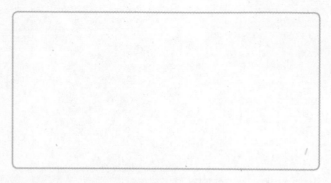

☑ Assessment Practice

24. There were 240 shoppers at an electronics store on opening day. The specials that day allowed 25% of shoppers to receive a free set of earbuds and 20% of shoppers to receive $10 off their first purchase.

PART A

Use an equivalent fraction to determine how many shoppers received a free set of earbuds. Show your work.

PART B

Use an equivalent fraction to determine how many shoppers received $10 off their first purchase. Show your work.

Solve & Discuss It!

📶 🖱 ACTIVITY

Lauren bought a jacket that was on sale for 60% off. She paid 40% of the original price of $75. How much did Lauren pay for the jacket?

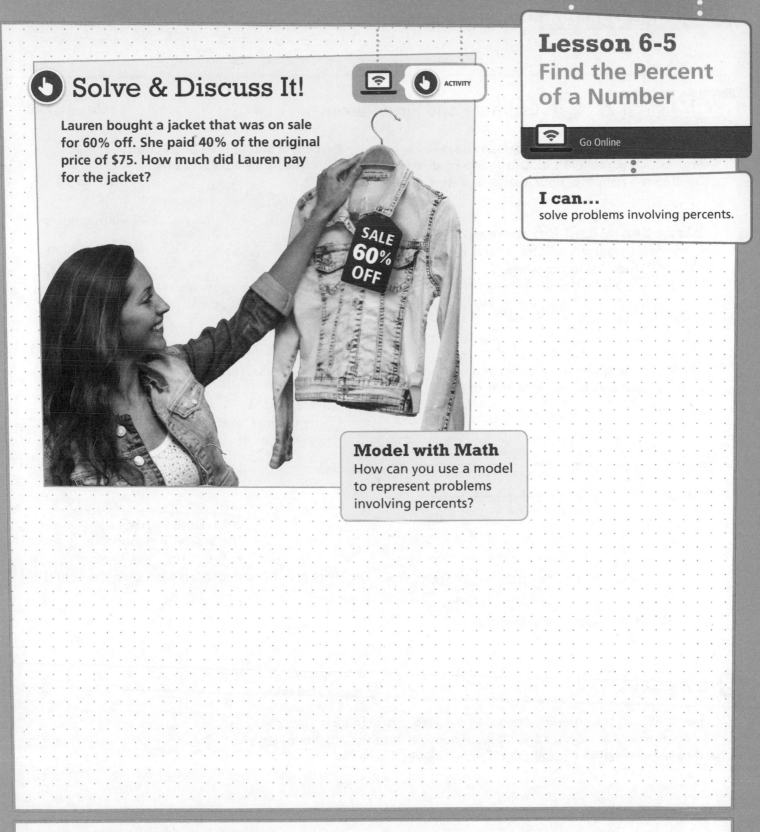

SALE 60% OFF

I can...
solve problems involving percents.

Model with Math
How can you use a model to represent problems involving percents?

Focus on math practices

Generalize When finding the percent of a number, how can you tell whether your answer is reasonable? Will the answer be greater than or less than the original amount? Explain.

EXAMPLE 1 👁 Estimate and Find Percent

Scan for
Multimedia 🅑

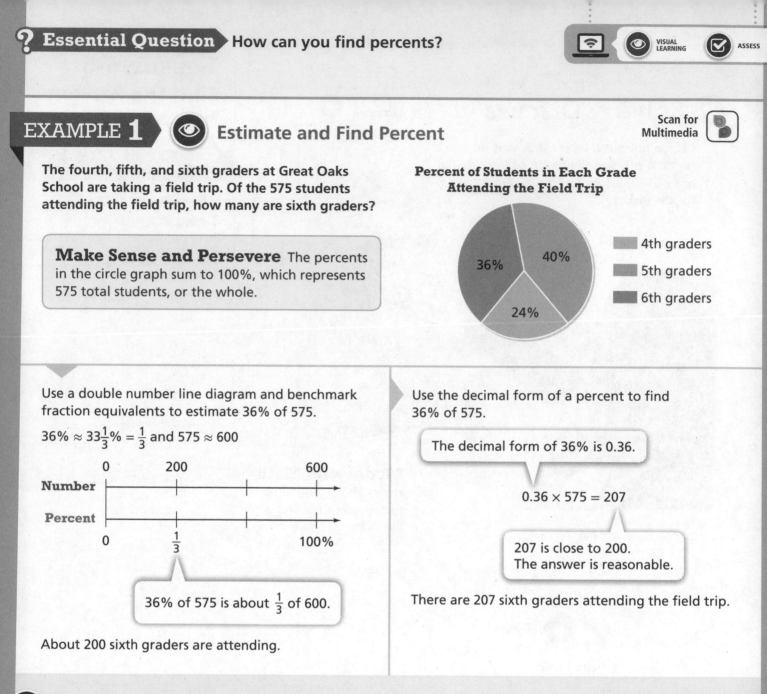

The fourth, fifth, and sixth graders at Great Oaks School are taking a field trip. Of the 575 students attending the field trip, how many are sixth graders?

Make Sense and Persevere The percents in the circle graph sum to 100%, which represents 575 total students, or the whole.

Percent of Students in Each Grade Attending the Field Trip

36% 40% 24%

4th graders
5th graders
6th graders

Use a double number line diagram and benchmark fraction equivalents to estimate 36% of 575.

$36\% \approx 33\frac{1}{3}\% = \frac{1}{3}$ and $575 \approx 600$

| Number | 0 | 200 | | 600 |

| Percent | 0 | $\frac{1}{3}$ | | 100% |

36% of 575 is about $\frac{1}{3}$ of 600.

About 200 sixth graders are attending.

Use the decimal form of a percent to find 36% of 575.

The decimal form of 36% is 0.36.

$0.36 \times 575 = 207$

207 is close to 200. The answer is reasonable.

There are 207 sixth graders attending the field trip.

☑ Try It!

Suppose 68% of the students attending the field trip were boys. How can you use the double number line diagram above to find the number of boys and to check whether your answer is reasonable?

Convince Me! In finding the percent of a number, when might you want to use the fraction form of the percent instead of the decimal form?

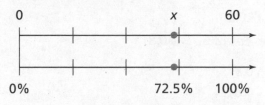 **Find the Part**

D'wayne plans to wallpaper 72.5% of a 60-square-foot wall. How many square feet of the wall does D'wayne plan to wallpaper? Find 72.5% of 60.

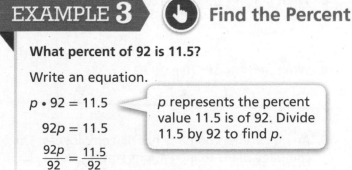

> **Model with Math** You can use a double number line diagram to help write an equation to find the part in a percent problem.

72.5% of a 60 square foot wall

Write an equation.

$x = 0.725 \cdot 60$ ← *x* represents 72.5% of 60. Multiply 72.5% by 60 to find *x*.

$x = 43.5$

So, 43.5 is 72.5% of 60.

D'wayne plans to wallpaper 43.5 square feet.

✅ **Try It!**

What is 0.8% of 35?

EXAMPLE 3  **Find the Percent**

What percent of 92 is 11.5?

Write an equation.

$p \cdot 92 = 11.5$ ← *p* represents the percent value 11.5 is of 92. Divide 11.5 by 92 to find *p*.

$92p = 11.5$

$\dfrac{92p}{92} = \dfrac{11.5}{92}$

$p = 0.125$ or 12.5%

So, 11.5 is 12.5% of 92.

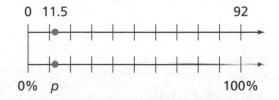

> **Model with Math** You can use a double number line diagram to help write an equation to find the percent of a number.

✅ **Try It!**

What percent of 120 is 72?

Percent equations have a part, a whole, and a percent. You can use the equation to solve for the part, the whole, or the percent.

Find the Part:

What is 12% of 6.75?

$x = 0.12 \cdot 6.75$
$x = 0.81$

12% of 6.75 is 0.81.

Find the Percent:

What percent of 6.75 is 0.81?

$p \cdot 6.75 = 0.81$
$6.75p = 0.81$
$\dfrac{6.75p}{6.75} = \dfrac{0.81}{6.75}$
$p = 0.12$ or 12%

12% of 6.75 is 0.81.

Do You Understand?

1. **? Essential Question** How can you find percents?

2. Describe the equation you use to find the unknown part in a percent problem.

3. Describe the equation you use to find the percent value in a percent problem.

4. **Be Precise** In the expression 34% of 60, what operation does the word "of" mean?

5. **Use Appropriate Tools** How can you use a calculator to find what percent of 180 is 108?

$\dfrac{30}{100} \times 450$

Do You Know How?

In 6 and 7, find the part.

6. What is 26% of 50?

$26\% \times 50$
$=$

7. What is 2.1% of 60?

In 8 and 9, find the percent.

8. What percent of 315 is 126?

9. What percent of 120 is 28.8?

10. An electronics company has 450 employees. The company plans to increase its staff by 30%. How many new employees will the company hire?

11. The original price of a computer game is $45. The price is marked down by $18. What percent of the original price is the markdown?

$\dfrac{18}{45} = \dfrac{x}{100}$

$\dfrac{45x}{45} = \dfrac{1800}{45} \qquad x = 40$

Practice & Problem Solving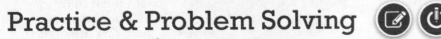

Leveled Practice In **12–17**, find each part or percent.

12. What is 5% of 210?

$x = \boxed{} \times 210$

$x = \boxed{}$

13. What is 8.2% of 500?

$x = \boxed{} \times 500$

$x = \boxed{}$

14. What percent of 32 is 5.6?

$p \cdot 32 = \boxed{}$

$32p = \boxed{}$

$\dfrac{32p}{32} = \dfrac{\boxed{}}{32}$

$p = \boxed{} = \boxed{}\%$

15. What is 35% of 10?

16. What percent of 75 is 33?

17. What is 2.25% of 24?

---

18. The meal tax at a restaurant is 5.5%. What is the meal tax on a dinner that costs $24?

Dinner	$24.00
MEAL TAX, 5.5%	
TOTAL	

Thank You • Please Come Again

19. An electronics store donated a percentage of every sale to charity. The total sales were $7,150, of which the store donated $429. What percent of $7,150 was donated to charity?

In **20–22**, use the circle graph.

There are 180 cars in a parking lot. The colors of the cars are represented in the circle graph.

20. How many blue cars are there?

21. How many red cars are there?

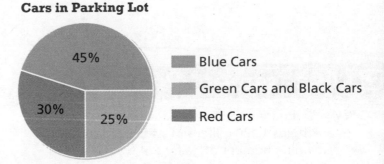

Cars in Parking Lot

45%
30%
25%

■ Blue Cars
■ Green Cars and Black Cars
■ Red Cars

22. Reasoning There are 27 more green cars than black cars in the parking lot. What percentage of the cars in the parking lot are green? What percent are black?

23. The bank contains pennies, nickels, dimes, and quarters. There are 4 more nickels than pennies. How much money does the bank contain?

Of the 50 coins, 10% are pennies and 42% are dimes.

24. Model with Math How can you use the double number line diagram to find what percent of 450 is 270?

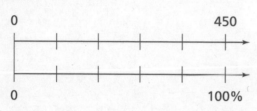

```
0                           450
|---+---+---+---+---+--->

0                          100%
|---+---+---+---+---+--->
```

25. Make Sense and Persevere A movie complex is showing the same movie in three theaters. In theater A, 112 of the 160 seats are filled. In theater B, 84 seats are filled and 56 seats are empty. In theater C, 63 of the 180 seats are empty. Which theater has the greatest percent of its seats filled?

26. Higher Order Thinking Thomas has an album that holds 600 baseball cards. Each page of the album holds 6 cards. If 45% of the album is empty, how many pages are filled with baseball cards?

27. Be Precise Miguel collected aluminum cans for recycling. He collected a total of 150 cans. How many of the cans Miguel collected were not soda cans?

58% of the cans collected were soda cans.

✓ Assessment Practice

28. Ava's aquarium is 95% filled with water. The tank holds 1,120 gallons of water. Which is the remaining number of gallons of water needed to fill the aquarium to the top?

(A) 1,120 gallons

(B) 1,010 gallons

(C) 101 gallons

(D) 56 gallons

29. Students set a goal of collecting 900 cans for the canned food drive. The number of cans they have collected so far is 82% of their goal. How many more cans do the students need to collect to reach their goal?

(A) 162 cans

(B) 180 cans

(C) 720 cans

(D) 738 cans

I can...
find the whole amount when given a part and the percent.

👆 Solve & Discuss It!

📺 👆 ACTIVITY

A school soccer team won 80% of its matches. The team won 40 matches. How many matches did the soccer team play?

Look for Relationships
How can you use a diagram to analyze the relationship between the quantities?

Focus on math practices

Model with Math Write an equation to find the total number of matches played by the soccer team. Let *m* represent the total number of matches.

? Essential Question How can you find the whole in a percent problem?

VISUAL LEARNING   ASSESS

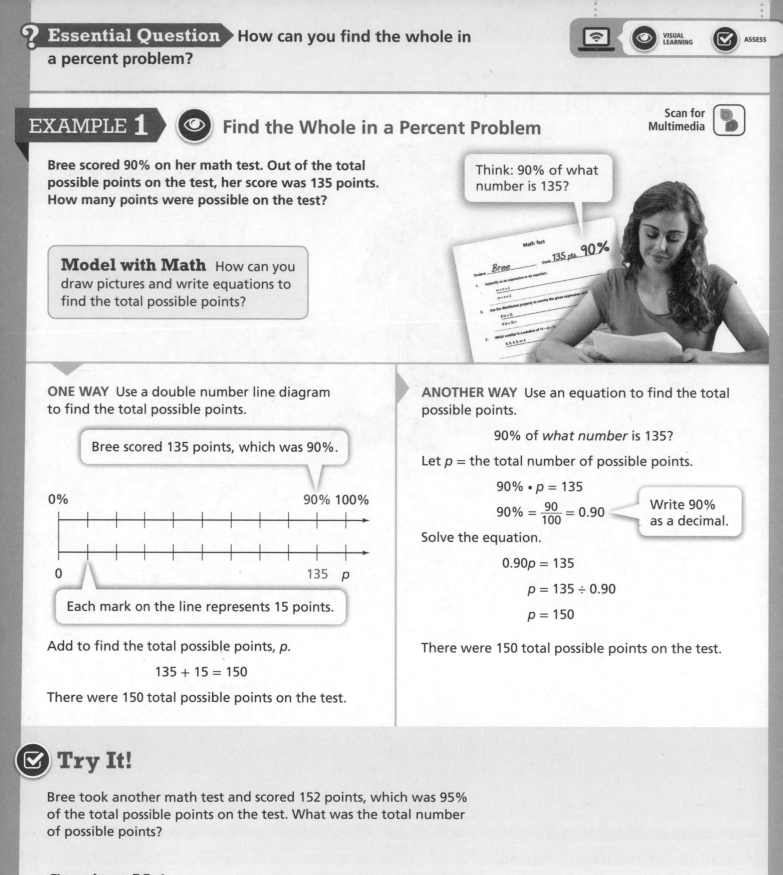

EXAMPLE 1 👁 **Find the Whole in a Percent Problem**

Scan for Multimedia

Bree scored 90% on her math test. Out of the total possible points on the test, her score was 135 points. How many points were possible on the test?

> Think: 90% of what number is 135?

Model with Math How can you draw pictures and write equations to find the total possible points?

ONE WAY Use a double number line diagram to find the total possible points.

> Bree scored 135 points, which was 90%.

0%   90% 100%

0   135 *p*

> Each mark on the line represents 15 points.

Add to find the total possible points, *p*.

$$135 + 15 = 150$$

There were 150 total possible points on the test.

ANOTHER WAY Use an equation to find the total possible points.

90% of *what number* is 135?

Let *p* = the total number of possible points.

$$90\% \cdot p = 135$$

$$90\% = \frac{90}{100} = 0.90$$

> Write 90% as a decimal.

Solve the equation.

$$0.90p = 135$$

$$p = 135 \div 0.90$$

$$p = 150$$

There were 150 total possible points on the test.

☑ Try It!

Bree took another math test and scored 152 points, which was 95% of the total possible points on the test. What was the total number of possible points?

Convince Me! How could you use a double number line diagram to check your answer?

EXAMPLE 2 ▶ Find the Whole When the Percent Is Greater Than 100

The students in one classroom sold tickets to the talent show. They sold 200% of the amount of tickets that they sold last year. How many tickets did the students sell last year? Find the number of which 200% is 40.

One classroom sold a total of 40 tickets.

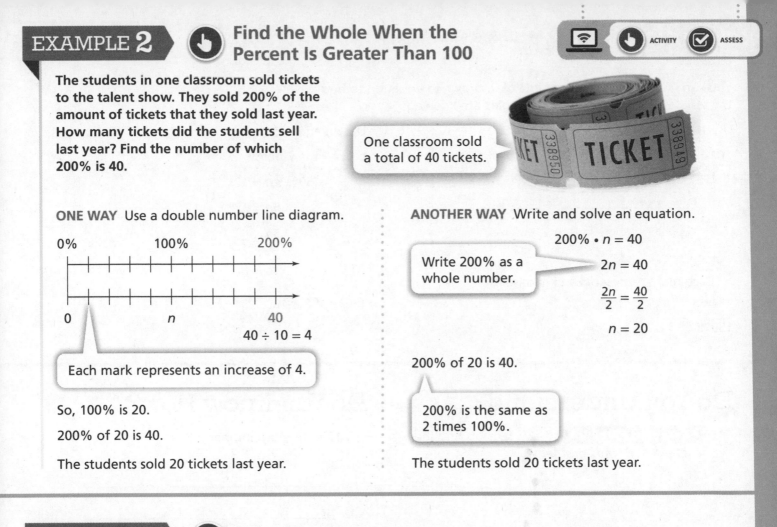

ONE WAY Use a double number line diagram.

0%   100%   200%

0   n 40

$40 \div 10 = 4$

Each mark represents an increase of 4.

So, 100% is 20.

200% of 20 is 40.

The students sold 20 tickets last year.

ANOTHER WAY Write and solve an equation.

$$200\% \cdot n = 40$$

Write 200% as a whole number.

$$2n = 40$$

$$\frac{2n}{2} = \frac{40}{2}$$

$$n = 20$$

200% of 20 is 40.

200% is the same as 2 times 100%.

The students sold 20 tickets last year.

EXAMPLE 3 ▶ Find the Whole When the Percent Is a Decimal

62.5% of what number is 30?

ONE WAY Use a double number line diagram.

0%   62.5%   100%

0   30 n

$30 \div 5 = 6$

Each mark represents an increase of 6.

62.5% of 48 is 30.

ANOTHER WAY Write and solve an equation.

$$62.5\% \cdot n = 30$$

$$0.625n = 30$$

$$\frac{0.625n}{0.625} = \frac{30}{0.625}$$

$$n = 48$$

62.5% of 48 is 30.

✓ Try It!

a. 300% of what number is 180?

b. 0.3% of what number is 24?

You can use a double number line diagram or an equation to find the whole when the percent and a part are known.

Use a diagram.

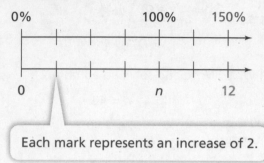

Each mark represents an increase of 2.

150% of 8 is 12.

Use an equation.

Let n = the whole.

$$150\% \cdot n = 12$$
$$1.5n = 12$$
$$\frac{1.5n}{1.5} = \frac{12}{1.5}$$
$$n = 8$$

150% of 8 is 12.

Do You Understand?

1. **? Essential Question** How can you find the whole in a percent problem?

2. When you write an equation for a problem such as *300% of what number is 180*, what do you use to represent the phrase 'what number'?

3. When you find the whole in a percent problem in which the percent is greater than 100%, is the whole less than or greater than the part?

4. **Be Precise** Tony participated in 6 races, or 10% of the events. Do the 6 races represent the part, the percent, or the whole? Tell what the others represent.

Do You Know How?

5. 40% of what number is 80?

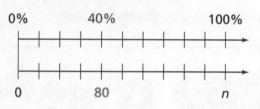

6. 300% of what number is 90?

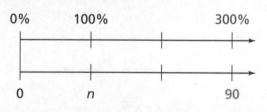

7. 70% of what number is 112?

8. 35% of what number is 28?

9. 7.5% of what number is 15?

Practice & Problem Solving

Leveled Practice In **10–15**, find each whole.

10. 35% of what number is 91?

$$35\% \cdot a = 91$$

$$0.35a = \boxed{}$$

$$\frac{0.35a}{\boxed{}} = \frac{\boxed{}}{\boxed{}}$$

$$a = \boxed{}$$

35% of $\boxed{}$ is 91.

11. 125% of what number is 45?

$$125\% \cdot n = 45$$

$$1.25n = \boxed{}$$

$$\frac{1.25n}{\boxed{}} = \frac{\boxed{}}{\boxed{}}$$

$$n = \boxed{}$$

125% of $\boxed{}$ is 45.

12. 87.5% of what number is 49?

$$87.5\% \cdot y = 49$$

$$\boxed{} y = 49$$

$$\frac{\boxed{} y}{\boxed{}} = \frac{49}{\boxed{}}$$

$$y = \boxed{}$$

87.5% of $\boxed{}$ is 49.

13. 700% of what number is 1,540?

14. 0.7% of what number is 35?

15. 56% of what number is 14?

In **16–18**, use the list of state taxes.

16. Reasoning Otis had a salad for $4.50, a sandwich for $6.25, and a drink at his favorite restaurant. The tax for the entire meal was $0.54. What was the price of the drink?

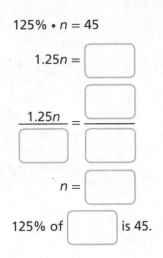

STATE TAXES

Sales tax:	3.5%
Income tax:	5%
Meal tax:	4.5%

17. Jill paid a sales tax of $1.40 when she bought a vest. What was the price of the vest not including the tax?

18. Rachel paid $46 in tax for the money she earned as a camp counselor. How much money did Rachel earn?

19. A restaurant wants to study how well its salads sell. The circle graph shows the sales of salads during the past few days. If 5 of the salads sold were Caesar salads, how many total salads did the restaurant sell?

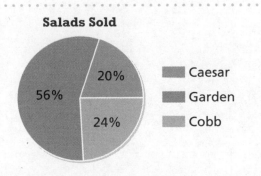

Salads Sold

Caesar 20%
Garden 56%
Cobb 24%

20. Make Sense and Persevere Sydney completed 60% of the math problems assigned for homework. She has 4 more problems to finish. How many math problems were assigned for homework?

$\frac{60}{60} = \frac{60}{100}$ X=61

21. Reasoning Carrie gave her hair stylist a $4.20 tip. The tip was 15% of the cost of the haircut. Write an equation to find h, the cost of the haircut.

22. Use Structure Solve each of the number sentences and describe the pattern.

80% of what number is 80?
60% of what number is 60?
127% of what number is 127?

23. Higher Order Thinking An hour before show time, only 105 people have arrived for a concert. According to ticket sales, 95% of the people have yet to arrive. How many tickets were sold for the concert? Explain.

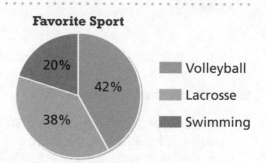

24. Nineteen students named lacrosse as their favorite sport. Explain how to use the circle graph to find the total number of students surveyed.

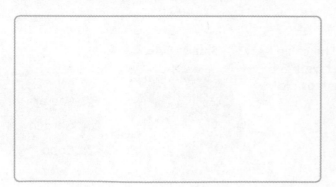

Favorite Sport

- Volleyball
- Lacrosse
- Swimming

20%
42%
38%

 Assessment Practice

25. People use water to cook, clean, and drink every day. It is estimated that 16.8% of the water used each day is for cleaning. If a family uses 67.2 gallons of water per day for cleaning, how many total gallons do they use per day? Explain.

26. Martha has a budget for groceries, fuel, and utilities. She spent 20% of her budget on groceries. If Martha spent $42.00 on groceries, how much is her budget?

ACT 1

1. After watching the video, what is the first question that comes to mind?

2. Write the Main Question you will answer.

3. Predict an answer to this Main Question.

4. Construct Arguments Explain how you arrived at your prediction.

5. What information in this situation would be helpful to know?
   How would you use that information?

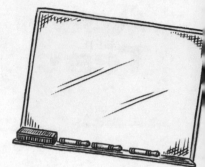

6. **Use Appropriate Tools** What tools can you use to solve the problem? Explain
   how you would use them strategically.

7. **Model with Math** Represent the situation using mathematics. Use your
   representation to answer the Main Question.

8. What is your answer to the Main Question? Does it differ from your
   prediction? Explain.

9. Write the answer you saw in the video.

10. **Reasoning** Does your answer match the answer in the video? If not, what are some reasons that would explain the difference?

11. **Make Sense and Persevere** Would you change your model now that you know the answer? Explain.

Reflect

12. Model with Math Explain how you used a mathematical model to represent the situation. How did the model help you answer the Main Question?

13. Be Precise Why are percents more useful in this situation than the number of correct answers?

14. Reasoning Suppose each test has 3 additional questions, and she gets 2 of them correct. How will that affect the answer?

? Topic Essential Question

What is the meaning of percent? How can percent be estimated and found?

Vocabulary Review

Complete each definition with a vocabulary word.

> **Vocabulary**   compatible numbers   fraction   percent   ratio

1. A ratio of a quantity to 100 is a _____ .

2. A _____ compares two numbers or the number of items in two groups.

3. _____ are numbers that are easier to compute mentally.

Draw a line to match each *fraction*, *decimal*, or *percent* in Column A to the equivalent value in Column B.

Column A	Column B
4. $\frac{40}{50}$	$1\frac{3}{4}$
5. 13%	$1\frac{11}{20}$
6. 1.75	0.13
7. 155%	80%

Use Vocabulary in Writing

Out of 230 students surveyed, 11% chose gymnastics as their favorite sport. Explain how you can estimate the number of students who chose gymnastics. Use vocabulary words in your explanation.

Concept and Skills Review

Understand Percent

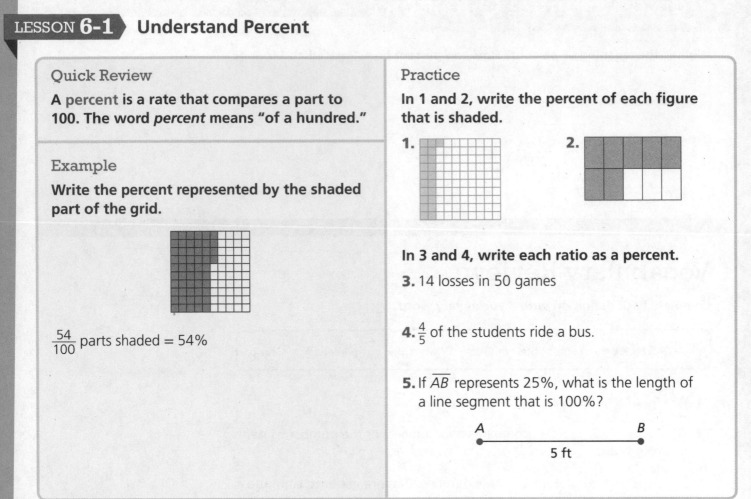

Quick Review

A **percent** is a rate that compares a part to 100. The word *percent* means "of a hundred."

Example

Write the percent represented by the shaded part of the grid.

$\frac{54}{100}$ parts shaded = 54%

Practice

In 1 and 2, write the percent of each figure that is shaded.

1.

2.

In 3 and 4, write each ratio as a percent.

3. 14 losses in 50 games

4. $\frac{4}{5}$ of the students ride a bus.

5. If $\overline{AB}$ represents 25%, what is the length of a line segment that is 100%?

A B

5 ft

Relate Fractions, Decimals, and Percents

Quick Review

Fractions, decimals, and percents are three ways to show parts of a whole. You can write a percent as a fraction with 100 as the denominator. Then you can write that fraction as a decimal.

Example

Write 35% as a fraction and a decimal.

$35\% = \frac{35}{100}$ or $\frac{7}{20}$

$\frac{35}{100} = 0.35$

Practice

In 1–6, write each number using the two other forms of notation: fraction, decimal, or percent.

1. 0.16

2. $\frac{63}{100}$

3. 27%

4. $\frac{7}{8}$

5. 0.55

6. 7%

7. One piece of wheat bread contains 2 g of fiber, or 8% of the amount of fiber that most people need in a day. What is 8% as a decimal and as a fraction?

Quick Review

Percents less than 1% are less than $\frac{1}{100}$, and percents greater than 100% are more than one whole. You can express percents greater than 100 or less than 1 in equivalent forms.

Example

Write 221% as a fraction and as a decimal.

Fraction: $\frac{221}{100}$

Decimal: $\frac{221}{100} = 221 \div 100 = 2.21$

Write $\frac{1}{4}$% as a fraction and as a decimal.

Fraction: $\frac{1}{4}\% = \frac{1}{4} \div 100$

$$= \frac{1}{4} \times \frac{1}{100} = \frac{1}{400}$$

Decimal: $\frac{1}{4}\% = 0.25\%$

$$= \frac{0.25}{100}$$

$$= \frac{25}{10,000}$$

$$= 0.0025$$

Practice

In 1–6, write each percent as a fraction and as a decimal.

1. 140%

2. $\frac{7}{10}$%

3. 375%

4. 0.33%

5. 0.5%

6. 250%

7. The radius of the planet Saturn is 945% of the radius of Earth. What is 945% expressed as a fraction and as a decimal?

Quick Review

Fraction equivalents, rounding, or compatible numbers can be used to estimate the percent of a number.

Example

Estimate 24% of 83.

$24\% \approx 25\%$ and $25\% = \frac{1}{4}$

83 rounds to 80.

$\frac{1}{4} \times 80 = 20$

24% of 83 is about 20.

Practice

In 1–6, estimate the percent of each number.

1. 22% of 96

2. 38% of 58

3. 9% of 89

4. 76% of 41

5. 48% of 71

6. 27% of 62

7. Joanna wants to buy a backpack that costs $37.98. The sales tax rate is 8.75%. Estimate the amount of sales tax that Joanna will pay.

LESSON 6-5 Find the Percent of a Number

Quick Review

Percent equations have a percent value, a whole, and a part.

Example

What is 16% of 73.5?

Let x = the unknown part.

$x = 0.16 \cdot 73.5$ — Write 16% as a decimal.

$x = 11.76$

16% of 73.5 is 11.76.

What percent of 22 is 9.35?

Let p = the percent value.

$p \cdot 22 = 9.35$

$22p = 9.35$

$\dfrac{22p}{22} = \dfrac{9.35}{22}$

$p = 0.425 = 42.5\%$

42.5% of 22 is 9.35.

Practice

Find each part or percent.

1. 9% of 124

2. What percent of 20 is 3?

3. 24% of 35

4. What percent of 110 is 71.5?

5. 43% of 82

6. What percent of 30 is 24?

7. On Tuesday, 620 students attended a middle school. A survey showed that 341 students brought lunch to school that day. What percent of the students brought their lunches?

LESSON 6-6 Find the Whole Given a Part and the Percent

Quick Review

You can use an equation or a double number line diagram to find the whole when given the part and the percent.

Example

80% of what number is 96?

Let n = the whole. Write an equation, rename the percent as a decimal, and solve for n.

$80\% \cdot n = 96$

$0.8n = 96$

$\dfrac{0.8n}{0.8} = \dfrac{96}{0.8}$

$n = 120$

80% of 120 is 96.

Practice

Find each whole.

1. 140% of what number is 308?

2. 62% of what number is 186?

3. 80% of what number is 120?

4. 40% of what number is 10?

5. Desmond paid 8.5% sales tax when he bought a new phone. The sales tax was $12.75. What was the total cost of the phone, including tax?

Crisscrossed

Find each quotient. Write your answers in the cross-number puzzle below. Each digit of your answer goes in its own box.

I can...
divide multidigit numbers.

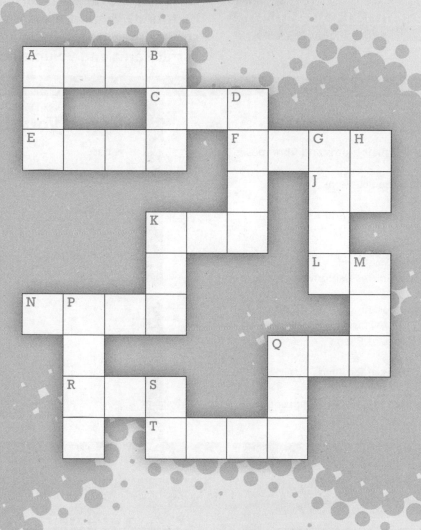

ACROSS

A 94,070 ÷ 46

C 3,828 ÷ 22

E 46,680 ÷ 15

F 61,065 ÷ 45

J 5,136 ÷ 214

K 9,840 ÷ 48

L 2,407 ÷ 29

N 67,870 ÷ 55

Q 9,114 ÷ 62

R 8,268 ÷ 12

T 80,120 ÷ 20

DOWN

A 7,644 ÷ 28

B 22,016 ÷ 43

D 49,980 ÷ 12

G 67,704 ÷ 13

H 10,582 ÷ 143

K 4,148 ÷ 17

M 10,062 ÷ 26

P 63,860 ÷ 31

Q 4,508 ÷ 23

S 7,238 ÷ 77

TOPIC 7

SOLVE AREA, SURFACE AREA, AND VOLUME PROBLEMS

? Topic Essential Question

How can the areas of certain shapes be found? What are the meanings of surface area and volume and how can surface area and volume be found?

Topic Overview

7-1 Find Areas of Parallelograms and Rhombuses

7-2 Solve Triangle Area Problems

7-3 Find Areas of Trapezoids and Kites

7-4 Find Areas of Polygons

7-5 Represent Solid Figures Using Nets

3-Act Mathematical Modeling: That's a Wrap

7-6 Find Surface Areas of Prisms

7-7 Find Surface Areas of Pyramids

7-8 Find Volume with Fractional Edge Lengths

Topic Vocabulary

- base
- edge
- face
- kite
- net
- polyhedron
- vertex

Lesson Digital Resources

INTERACTIVE STUDENT EDITION
Access online or offline.

VISUAL LEARNING ANIMATION
Interact with visual learning animations.

ACTIVITY Use with *Solve & Discuss It, Explore I*
and *Explain It* activities, and to explore Example

VIDEOS Watch clips to support *3-Act Mathematical Modeling Lessons* and *STEM Proje*

 Go online

That's a Wrap

 ## That's a Wrap

How you wrap a gift can say a lot about you. Some people conserve resources by reusing paper bags instead of purchasing wrapping paper. It may not look as nice at first, but you can unleash your crafty side and decorate the gift yourself.

No matter what you use to wrap a gift, you always need to consider the size of the object and how much paper you'll need. Think about this during the 3-Act Mathematical Modeling lesson.

 PRACTICE Practice what you've learned.

 TUTORIALS Get help from *Virtual Nerd*, right when you need it.

 MATH TOOLS Explore math with digital tools.

 GAMES Play Math Games to help you learn.

 KEY CONCEPT Review important lesson content.

A-Z **GLOSSARY** Read and listen to English/Spanish definitions.

 ASSESSMENT Show what you've learned.

Did You Know?

Food packaging is designed to identify products and to attract customers. Packaging also ensures food remains fresh and free from damage and contamination.

Common types of material used for packaging are paper, cardboard, glass, steel, and aluminum. **The best material to use for packaging depends on the contents—for example, soup in a paper bag could be rather messy!**

Manufacturers consider several factors when designing packaging, such as cost, amount of material used, and potential environmental impact. **Steel food cans are the most recycled food package** in the United States.

Packaging engineers consistently look for ways to innovate. **Some food packaging is now self-opening, self-closing, or self-heating. Some packaging is biodegradable. Other advances include edible packaging.**

Your Task: Pack It ▶

Food packaging engineers consider many elements related to both form and function when designing packaging. How do engineers make decisions about package designs as they consider constraints, such as limited dimensions or materials? You and your classmates will use the engineering design process to explore and propose food packaging that satisfies certain criteria.

Review What You Know!

Vocabulary

Choose the best term from the box to complete each definition.

area
parallelogram
perpendicular
polygon
volume

1. A triangle is an example of a three-sided _____ .

2. _____ lines form a right angle.

3. _____ is the number of cubic units needed to fill a solid figure.

4. A _____ has opposite sides that are parallel and the same length.

Evaluate Expressions

Find the value of each expression when $a = 12$, $b = 3$, $c = 4$, and $d = 9$.

5. ac

6. $\frac{1}{2}b$

7. abd

8. $0.5a$

9. $\frac{3}{4}(ad)$

10. $ab + cd$

Multiplication

Find each product.

11. 3.14×12

12. 45.8×5

13. 0.8×2.7

14. $14 \times 7.25 \times 2.5$

15. $1\frac{1}{2} \times \frac{1}{4}$

16. $2\frac{1}{3} \times 2\frac{1}{4} \times 1\frac{3}{8}$

Geometry

17. How are parallelograms and rectangles similar and how are they different?

18. How are the formulas for the area of a rectangle and the area of a triangle alike and different? Explain.

Language Development

Use the graphic organizer to help relate new vocabulary in this topic to terms you studied in previous topics.

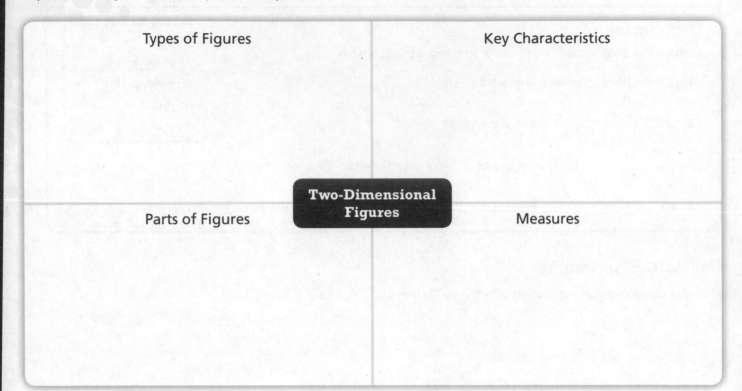

Types of Figures

Key Characteristics

Two-Dimensional Figures

Parts of Figures

Measures

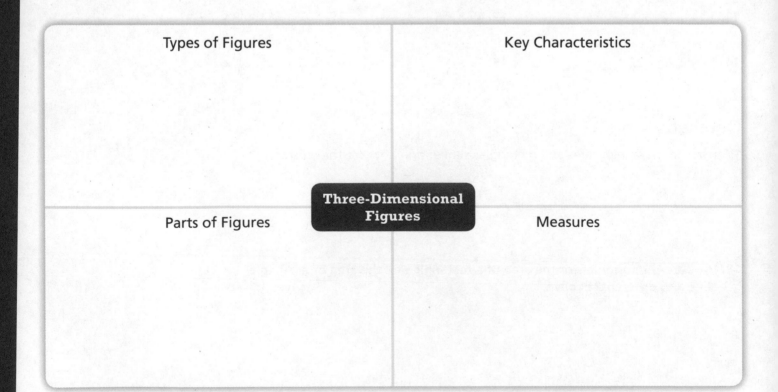

Types of Figures

Key Characteristics

Three-Dimensional Figures

Parts of Figures

Measures

PROJECT
7A

If you could pick the shape of a building to live in, what shape would it be?

PROJECT: COMPARE CUBE-SHAPED BUILDINGS

PROJECT
7B

What are some ways you can use number cubes?

PROJECT: DRAW NETS OF NUMBER CUBES

PROJECT 7C

How far do you think a roll of wrapping paper reaches?

PROJECT: CALCULATE THE AMOUNT OF GIFT WRAP

PROJECT 7D

What sorts of music do you like?

PROJECT: WRITE A RAP BATTLE

Solve & Discuss It!

ACTIVITY

Sofía drew the grid below and plotted the points *A*, *B*, *C*, and *D*. Connect point *A* to *B*, *B* to *C*, *C* to *D*, and *D* to *A*. Then find the area of the shape and explain how you found it. Using the same grid, move points *B* and *C* four units to the right. Connect the points to make a new parallelogram *ABCD*. What is the area of this shape?

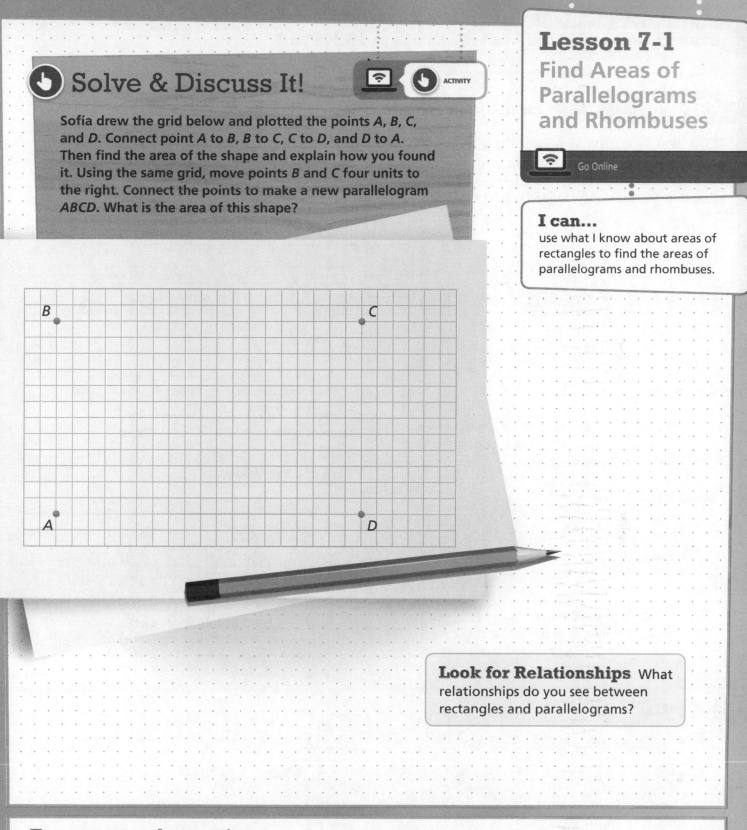

I can...
use what I know about areas of rectangles to find the areas of parallelograms and rhombuses.

Look for Relationships What relationships do you see between rectangles and parallelograms?

Focus on math practices

Generalize How can you find the area of any parallelogram?

? Essential Question How can you use the area formula of a rectangle to find the area formula of a parallelogram?

VISUAL LEARNING   ASSESS

EXAMPLE 1 ◉ **Find the Area Formula of a Parallelogram**

Scan for Multimedia

Look at the parallelogram below. If you move the triangle to the opposite side, you form a rectangle with the same area as the parallelogram. How can you find the area of a parallelogram?

Use Structure To compose a rectangle from a parallelogram, first decompose the parallelogram into a right triangle and a trapezoid.

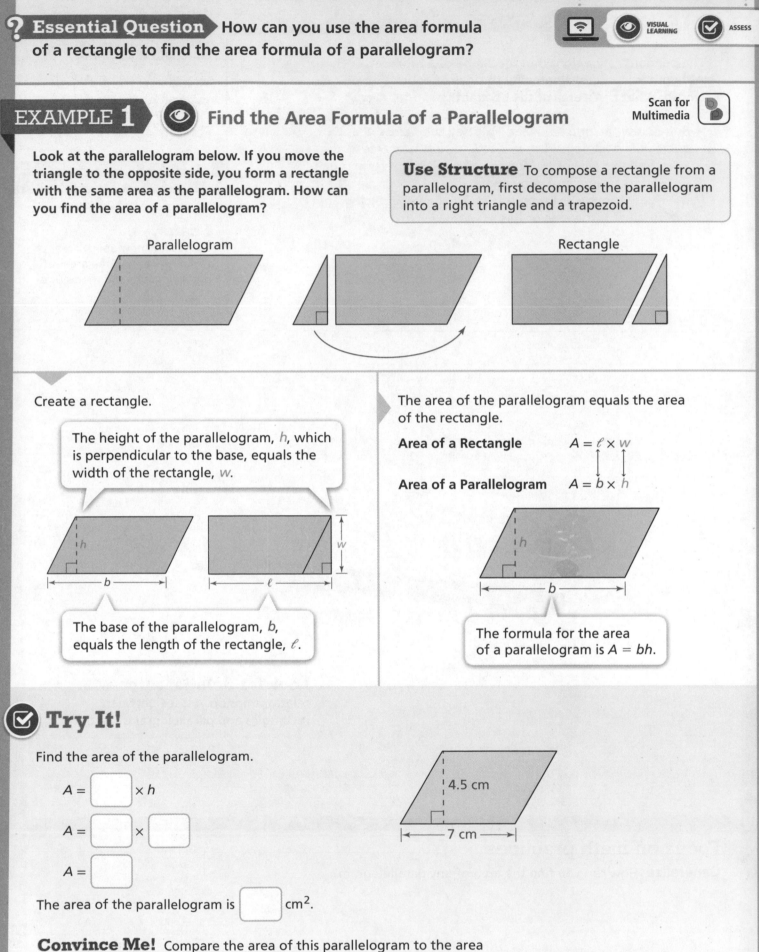

Parallelogram

Rectangle

Create a rectangle.

The height of the parallelogram, *h*, which is perpendicular to the base, equals the width of the rectangle, *w*.

The base of the parallelogram, *b*, equals the length of the rectangle, *ℓ*.

The area of the parallelogram equals the area of the rectangle.

Area of a Rectangle $A = \ell \times w$

Area of a Parallelogram $A = b \times h$

The formula for the area of a parallelogram is $A = bh$.

☑ **Try It!**

Find the area of the parallelogram.

$A = \boxed{} \times h$

$A = \boxed{} \times \boxed{}$

$A = \boxed{}$

4.5 cm

7 cm

The area of the parallelogram is $\boxed{}$ cm².

Convince Me! Compare the area of this parallelogram to the area of a rectangle with a length of 7 cm and a width of 4.5 cm. Explain.

EXAMPLE **2** 🖱 **Find the Area of a Rhombus**

📶 🖱 ACTIVITY ☑ ASSESS

The pendant at the right is in the shape of a rhombus.
A rhombus is a parallelogram with sides of equal
length. What is the area of the pendant?

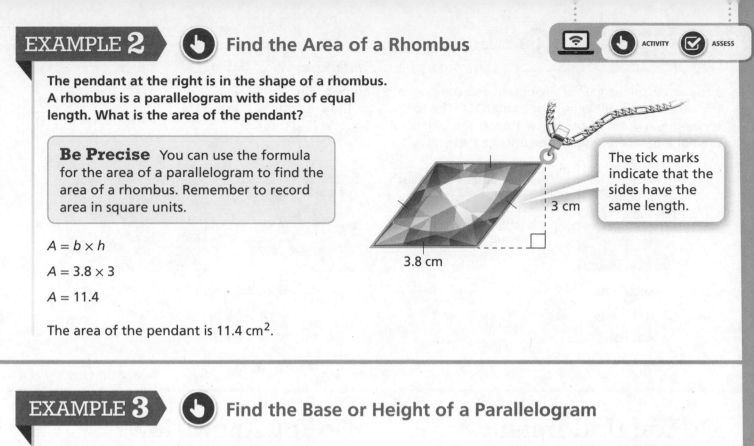

Be Precise You can use the formula
for the area of a parallelogram to find the
area of a rhombus. Remember to record
area in square units.

The tick marks
indicate that the
sides have the
same length.

3 cm

3.8 cm

$A = b \times h$

$A = 3.8 \times 3$

$A = 11.4$

The area of the pendant is 11.4 cm².

EXAMPLE **3** 🖱 **Find the Base or Height of a Parallelogram**

A. The area of the parallelogram is 72 m².
What is the height of the parallelogram?

12 m

$A = b \times h$

$72 = 12 \times h$ ← Substitute 72 for
A and 12 for b.

$6 = h$

The height of the parallelogram is 6 m.

B. The area of the parallelogram
is 135 in.². What is the base
of the parallelogram?

15 in.

b

$A = b \times h$

$135 = b \times 15$ ← Substitute 135 for
A and 15 for h.

$9 = b$

The base of the parallelogram is 9 in.

☑ **Try It!**

a. Find the area of the rhombus.

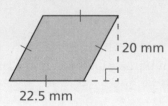

20 mm

22.5 mm

b. The area of the parallelogram is 65 ft².
What is its height?

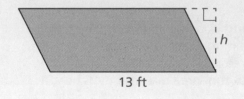

h

13 ft

You can decompose a parallelogram and compose a rectangle to find the area of a parallelogram or a rhombus. The formula for the area of a rectangle, $A = \ell \times w$, can be written as the formula $A = b \times h$ to find the area of a parallelogram or the area of a rhombus.

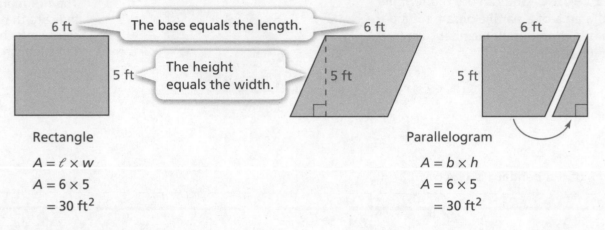

The base equals the length.

The height equals the width.

Rectangle	Parallelogram
$A = \ell \times w$	$A = b \times h$
$A = 6 \times 5$	$A = 6 \times 5$
$= 30\ \text{ft}^2$	$= 30\ \text{ft}^2$

Do You Understand?

1. **? Essential Question** How can you use the area formula of a rectangle to find the area formula of a parallelogram?

2. Ken combined a triangle and a trapezoid to make a parallelogram. If the area of the triangle is 12 in.^{2} and the area of the trapezoid is 24 in.^{2}, what is the area of the parallelogram? Explain.

3. **Critique Reasoning** A parallelogram is 3 meters long and 7 meters high. Liam said that the parallelogram's area is greater than the area of a rectangle with the same dimensions. Is he correct? Explain.

Do You Know How?

In 4–6, use a formula to find the area.

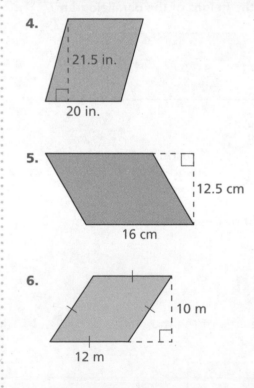

4.
21.5 in.
20 in.

5.
12.5 cm
16 cm

6.
10 m
12 m

7. A rhombus has an area of 440 m^2 and a base of 22 m. What is its height?

Name: _____

Practice & Problem Solving

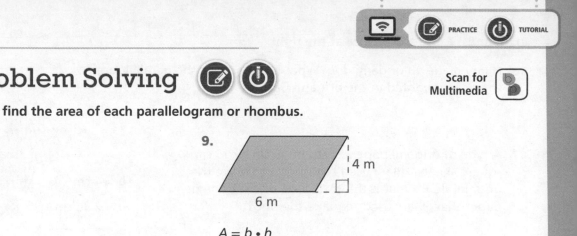

Leveled Practice In 8–11, find the area of each parallelogram or rhombus.

8.

6 yd

2 yd

$A = b \cdot h$

$= \boxed{} \cdot 6$

$= \boxed{} \ \text{yd}^2$

9.

4 m

6 m

$A = b \cdot h$

$= \boxed{} \cdot \boxed{}$

$= \boxed{} \ \text{m}^2$

10.

10 in.

$10\frac{1}{2}$ in.

11.

$2\frac{1}{3}$ yd

9 yd

---

12. The area of the parallelogram is 132 in.². What is the height of the parallelogram?

h

11 in.

13. The area of the rhombus is 52 m². What is the base of the rhombus?

6.5 m

b

---

14. Micah and Jason made parallelogram-shaped stained glass windows with the same area. The height of Micah's window is 9 inches, and its base is 10 inches. The height of Jason's window is 6 inches. What is the base of Jason's window?

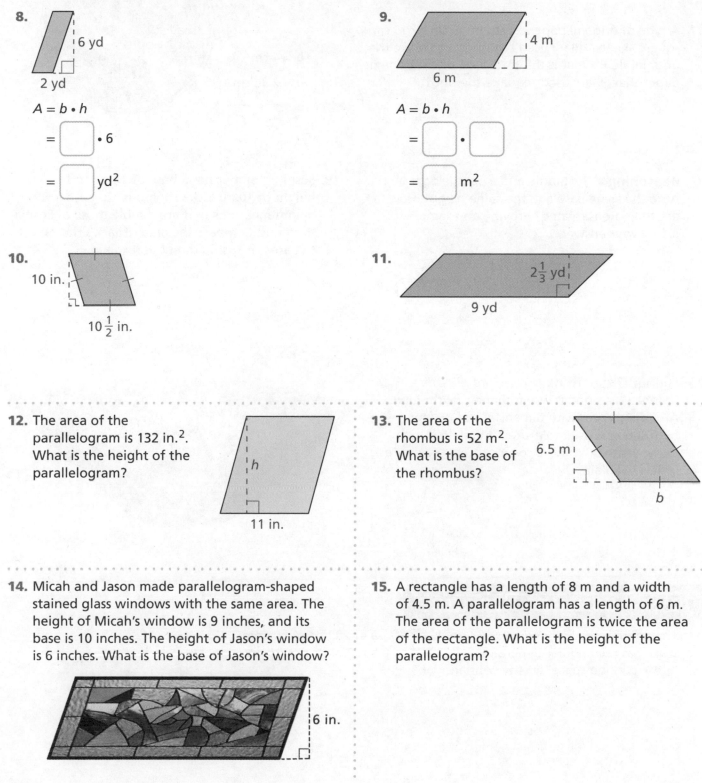

6 in.

15. A rectangle has a length of 8 m and a width of 4.5 m. A parallelogram has a length of 6 m. The area of the parallelogram is twice the area of the rectangle. What is the height of the parallelogram?

In 16 and 17, use the picture at the right.

16. Hilary made an origami dog. What is the area of the parallelogram that is highlighted in the origami figure?

17. A type of origami paper comes in 15 cm by 15 cm square sheets. Hilary used two sheets to make the origami dog. What is the total area of the origami paper that Hilary used to make the dog?

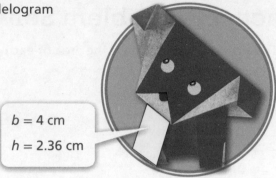

$b = 4$ cm

$h = 2.36$ cm

18. **Reasoning** A rectangle and a parallelogram have the same base and the same height. How are their areas related? Provide an example to justify your answer.

19. Soshi's rhombus has a base of 12 in. and a height of 10 in. Jack's rhombus has base and height measures that are double those of Soshi's rhombus. Compare the area of Jack's rhombus to the area of Soshi's rhombus. Explain.

20. **Higher Order Thinking** The infield of a baseball diamond is in the shape of a rhombus. An infield cover with dimensions of 85 feet by 100 feet is used to protect the field during rainy weather. Will the cover protect the entire infield? Explain.

90 feet 90 feet
90 feet 90 feet

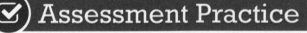 Assessment Practice

21. The parking space shown at the right has an area of 209 ft². A custom truck has rectangular dimensions of 13.5 ft by 8.5 ft. Can the truck fit in the parking space? Justify your answer.

19 ft

b ft

Solve & Discuss It!

ACTIVITY

Connect point *A* to *B*, *B* to *C*, *C* to *D*, and *D* to *A*. Then draw a diagonal line connecting opposite vertices in the figure and find the area of each triangle formed.

I can...
find the areas of triangles.

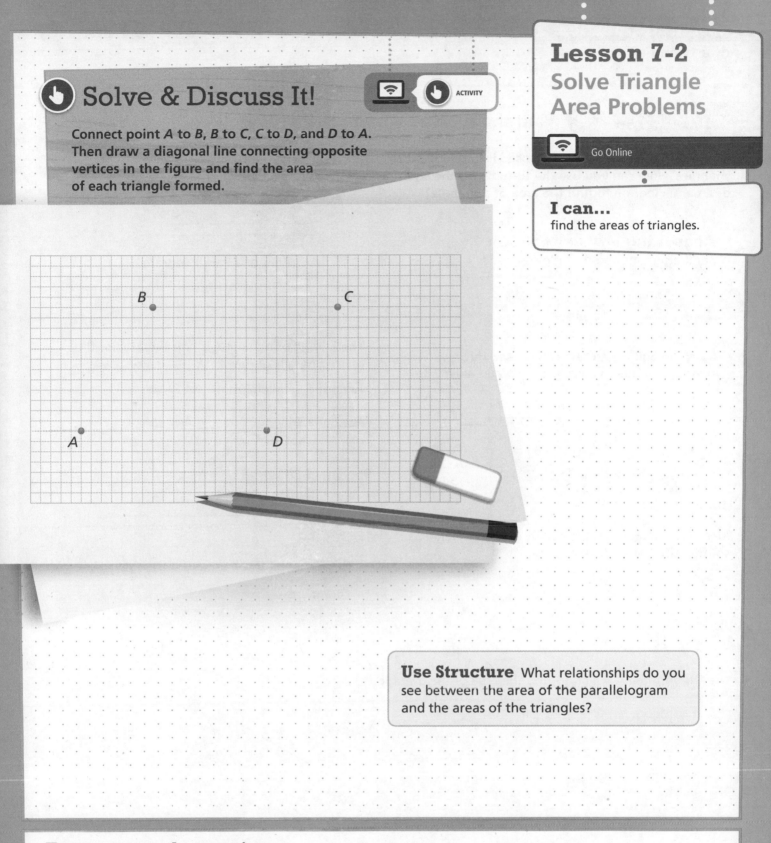

Use Structure What relationships do you see between the area of the parallelogram and the areas of the triangles?

Focus on math practices
Generalize What is a rule for finding the area of any triangle?

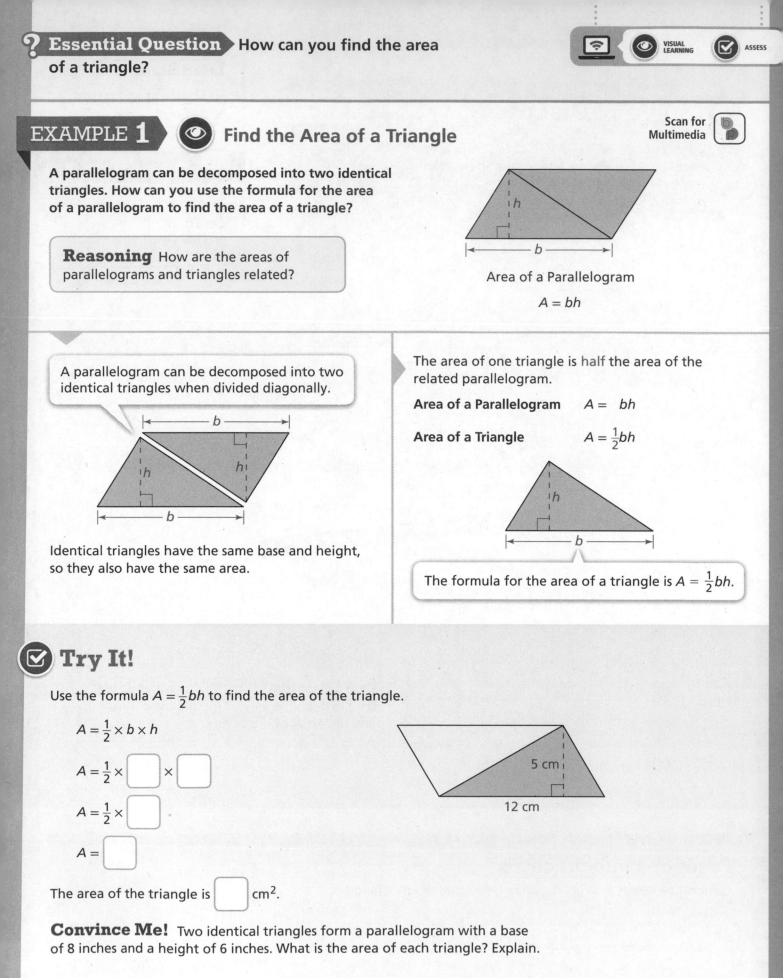

VISUAL LEARNING

ASSESS

EXAMPLE 1 👁 **Find the Area of a Triangle**

Scan for Multimedia

A parallelogram can be decomposed into two identical triangles. How can you use the formula for the area of a parallelogram to find the area of a triangle?

Reasoning How are the areas of parallelograms and triangles related?

Area of a Parallelogram

$$A = bh$$

A parallelogram can be decomposed into two identical triangles when divided diagonally.

Identical triangles have the same base and height, so they also have the same area.

The area of one triangle is half the area of the related parallelogram.

Area of a Parallelogram $A = bh$

Area of a Triangle $A = \frac{1}{2}bh$

The formula for the area of a triangle is $A = \frac{1}{2}bh$.

☑ **Try It!**

Use the formula $A = \frac{1}{2}bh$ to find the area of the triangle.

$A = \frac{1}{2} \times b \times h$

$A = \frac{1}{2} \times \boxed{} \times \boxed{}$

$A = \frac{1}{2} \times \boxed{}$

$A = \boxed{}$

5 cm

12 cm

The area of the triangle is $\boxed{}$ cm².

Convince Me! Two identical triangles form a parallelogram with a base of 8 inches and a height of 6 inches. What is the area of each triangle? Explain.

EXAMPLE 2

ACTIVITY   ASSESS

EXAMPLE 2 ▶ 👆 Find the Area of a Right Triangle

The side of a birdhouse is in the shape of a right triangle.
What is the area of the side of the birdhouse?

Draw a triangle and compose a square.

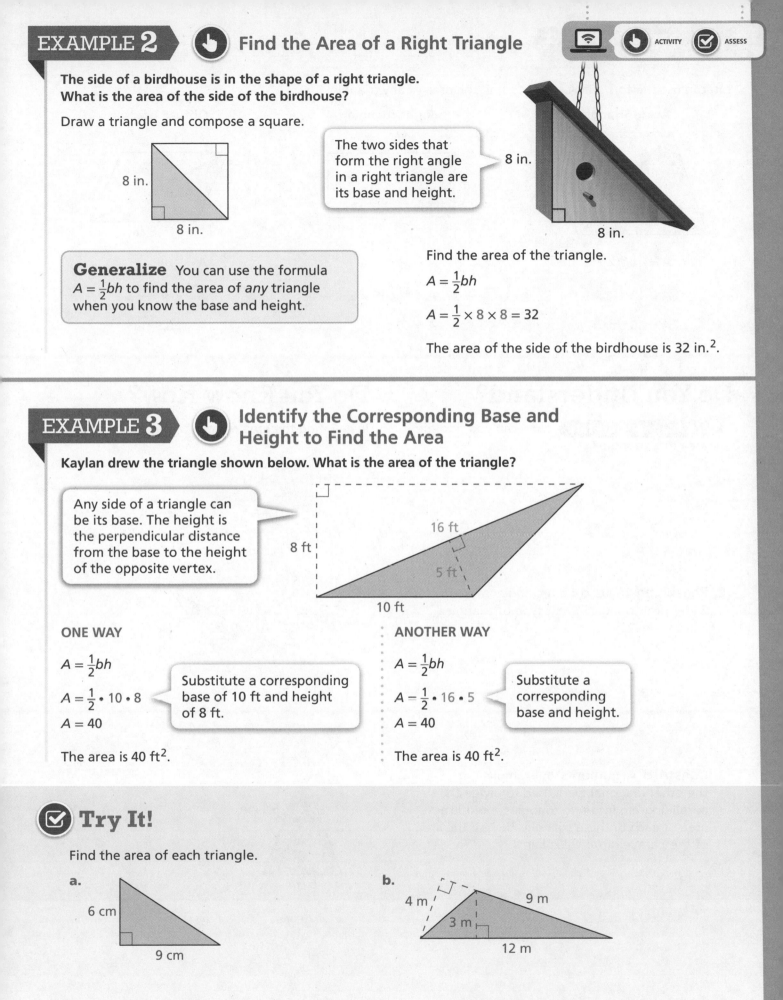

8 in.

8 in.

The two sides that form the right angle in a right triangle are its base and height.

8 in.

8 in.

8 in.

Generalize You can use the formula $A = \frac{1}{2}bh$ to find the area of *any* triangle when you know the base and height.

Find the area of the triangle.

$$A = \frac{1}{2}bh$$

$$A = \frac{1}{2} \times 8 \times 8 = 32$$

The area of the side of the birdhouse is 32 in.^{2}.

EXAMPLE 3 ▶ 👆 Identify the Corresponding Base and Height to Find the Area

Kaylan drew the triangle shown below. What is the area of the triangle?

Any side of a triangle can be its base. The height is the perpendicular distance from the base to the height of the opposite vertex.

16 ft

8 ft

5 ft

10 ft

ONE WAY

$$A = \frac{1}{2}bh$$

$$A = \frac{1}{2} \cdot 10 \cdot 8$$

$$A = 40$$

Substitute a corresponding base of 10 ft and height of 8 ft.

The area is 40 ft^2.

ANOTHER WAY

$$A = \frac{1}{2}bh$$

$$A = \frac{1}{2} \cdot 16 \cdot 5$$

$$A = 40$$

Substitute a corresponding base and height.

The area is 40 ft^2.

☑ Try It!

Find the area of each triangle.

a.

6 cm

9 cm

b.

4 m

9 m

3 m

12 m

You can use the formula $A = \frac{1}{2}bh$ to find the area of any triangle.

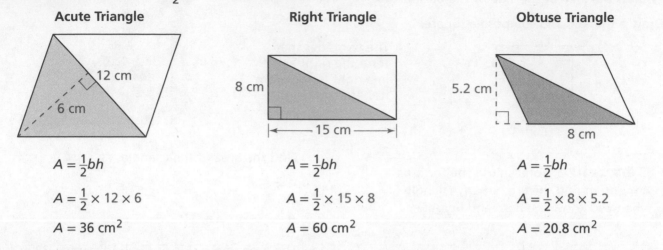

Acute Triangle

12 cm

6 cm

$A = \frac{1}{2}bh$

$A = \frac{1}{2} \times 12 \times 6$

$A = 36 \text{ cm}^2$

Right Triangle

8 cm

15 cm

$A = \frac{1}{2}bh$

$A = \frac{1}{2} \times 15 \times 8$

$A = 60 \text{ cm}^2$

Obtuse Triangle

5.2 cm

8 cm

$A = \frac{1}{2}bh$

$A = \frac{1}{2} \times 8 \times 5.2$

$A = 20.8 \text{ cm}^2$

Do You Understand?

1. **? Essential Question** How can you find the area of a triangle?

2. **Reasoning** If you cut a rectangle into 2 identical triangles, what type of triangles will they be?

3. **Construct Arguments** In Example 1, if the other diagonal were used to divide the parallelogram into two triangles, would the area of each of these triangles be half the area of the parallelogram? Explain.

Do You Know How?

In 4–6, find the area of each triangle.

4.

2 ft

4 ft

5.

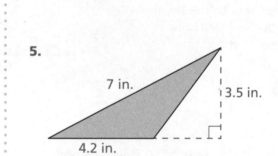

7 in.

3.5 in.

4.2 in.

6.

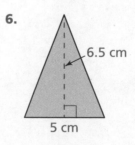

6.5 cm

5 cm

Name: _____

Practice & Problem Solving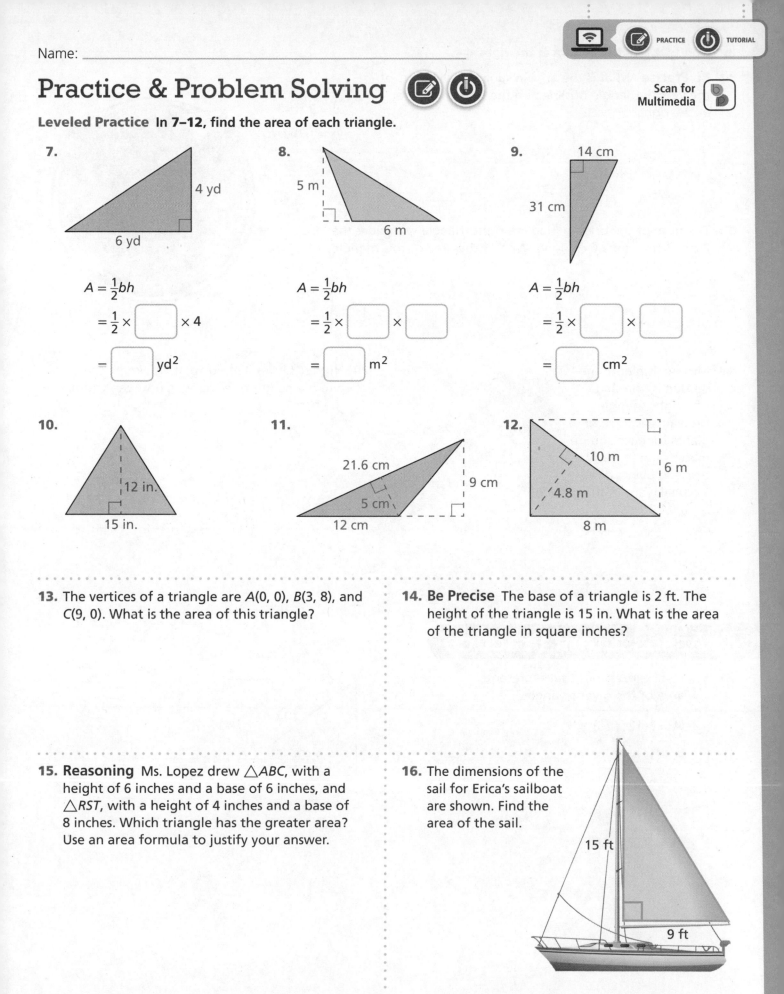

Leveled Practice In **7–12**, find the area of each triangle.

7.

4 yd

6 yd

$A = \frac{1}{2}bh$

$= \frac{1}{2} \times \boxed{} \times 4$

$= \boxed{}$ yd^2

8.

5 m

6 m

$A = \frac{1}{2}bh$

$= \frac{1}{2} \times \boxed{} \times \boxed{}$

$= \boxed{}$ m^2

9.

14 cm

31 cm

$A = \frac{1}{2}bh$

$= \frac{1}{2} \times \boxed{} \times \boxed{}$

$= \boxed{}$ cm^2

10.

12 in.

15 in.

11.

21.6 cm

5 cm

9 cm

12 cm

12.

10 m

4.8 m

6 m

8 m

---

13. The vertices of a triangle are $A(0, 0)$, $B(3, 8)$, and $C(9, 0)$. What is the area of this triangle?

14. Be Precise The base of a triangle is 2 ft. The height of the triangle is 15 in. What is the area of the triangle in square inches?

15. Reasoning Ms. Lopez drew $\triangle ABC$, with a height of 6 inches and a base of 6 inches, and $\triangle RST$, with a height of 4 inches and a base of 8 inches. Which triangle has the greater area? Use an area formula to justify your answer.

16. The dimensions of the sail for Erica's sailboat are shown. Find the area of the sail.

15 ft

9 ft

In 17 and 18, use the picture at the right.

17. **Be Precise** What is the area in square millimeters of the yellow triangle outlined on the origami figure at the right?

$b = 3$ cm

$h = 1.76$ cm

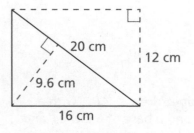

18. The nose of the origami dog is a right triangle with sides that are 2 cm, 3 cm, and 3.6 cm long. What is the area of this triangle?

19. Michael is planting a garden in the shape of a right triangle. He wants 4 tickseed plants for each square meter of area. How many tickseed plants does Michael want in the garden?

7 m

24 m

25 m

20. **Higher Order Thinking** If you know the area and the height of a triangle, how can you find the base?

☑ Assessment Practice

21. Select all expressions that represent the area of the given triangle.

☐ $A = \frac{1}{2}(12 \times 16)$

☐ $A = 12 \times 16$

☐ $A = 9.6 \times 20$

☐ $A = \frac{1}{2}(16 \times 9.6)$

☐ $A = \frac{1}{2}(20 \times 9.6)$

20 cm

12 cm

9.6 cm

16 cm

Explain It!

ACTIVITY

The European basketball key was changed from a trapezoid shape to a rectangle in 2010. The diagram shows the shape of the key before 2010 outlined in blue.

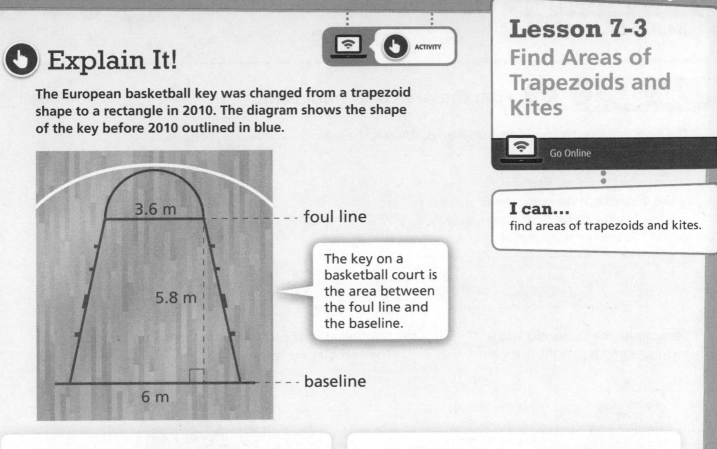

3.6 m

---- foul line

The key on a basketball court is the area between the foul line and the baseline.

5.8 m

---- baseline

6 m

I can...
find areas of trapezoids and kites.

A. Construct Arguments Tim finds the area of the key by multiplying the base by the height. Does his strategy make sense?

B. Use Structure How could Tim find the area of the trapezoid by decomposing it into shapes he knows? What is the area of the key?

Focus on math practices

Use Structure How can you find the area of this kite? Explain.

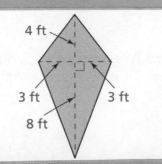

4 ft

3 ft   3 ft

8 ft

413

? **Essential Question** How can you find the areas of trapezoids and kites?

VISUAL LEARNING   ASSESS

EXAMPLE 1 👁 Find the Area of a Trapezoid

Scan for Multimedia

The pasture is in the shape of a trapezoid. What is the area of the pasture?

Be Precise What are the properties of a trapezoid and how can they help you to find the area of a trapezoid?

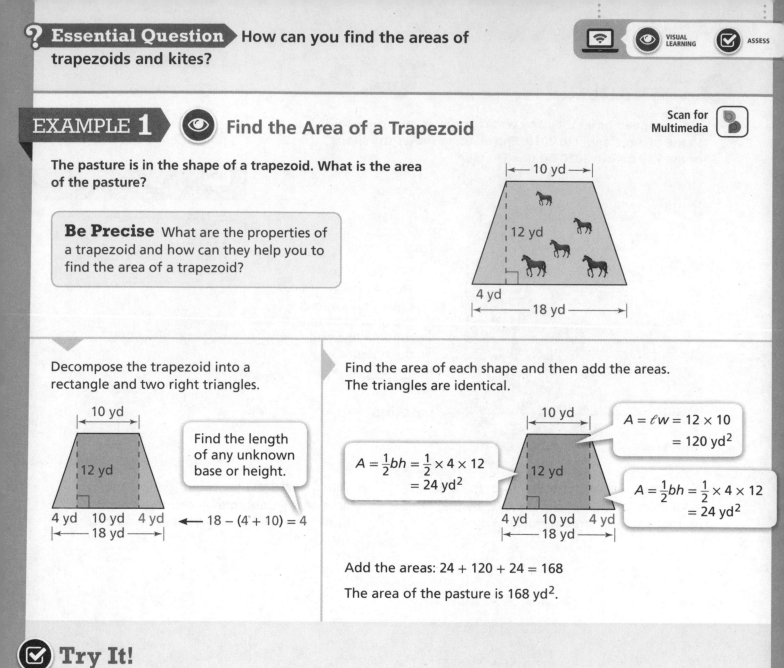

Decompose the trapezoid into a rectangle and two right triangles.

Find the length of any unknown base or height.

18 − (4 + 10) = 4

Find the area of each shape and then add the areas. The triangles are identical.

$A = \ell w = 12 \times 10$
$= 120 \text{ yd}^2$

$A = \frac{1}{2}bh = \frac{1}{2} \times 4 \times 12$
$= 24 \text{ yd}^2$

$A = \frac{1}{2}bh = \frac{1}{2} \times 4 \times 12$
$= 24 \text{ yd}^2$

Add the areas: 24 + 120 + 24 = 168

The area of the pasture is 168 yd².

✓ **Try It!**

How would you decompose this trapezoid to find its area? Find the area of the trapezoid.

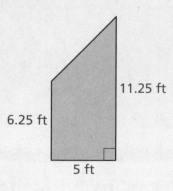

Convince Me! How is finding the area of the trapezoid in Example 1 different from finding the area of the trapezoid in the Try It!?

EXAMPLE 2

Find the Area of a Different Trapezoid

ACTIVITY ASSESS

A builder needs to cut one stone in the shape of a trapezoid to fit in the space. What is the area of the front side of that stone?

> **Look for Relationships** When you decompose a trapezoid into a rectangle and two triangles, the triangles are not always identical.

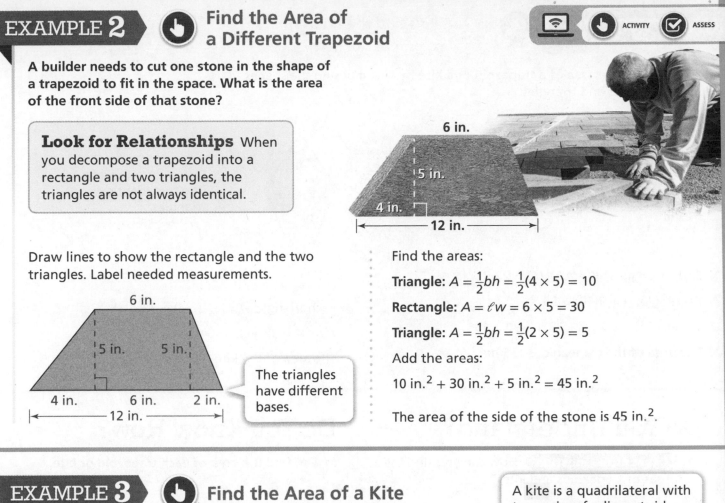

6 in.

5 in.

4 in.

12 in.

Draw lines to show the rectangle and the two triangles. Label needed measurements.

6 in.

5 in.   5 in.

4 in.   6 in.   2 in.

12 in.

> The triangles have different bases.

Find the areas:

Triangle: $A = \frac{1}{2}bh = \frac{1}{2}(4 \times 5) = 10$

Rectangle: $A = \ell w = 6 \times 5 = 30$

Triangle: $A = \frac{1}{2}bh = \frac{1}{2}(2 \times 5) = 5$

Add the areas:

$10 \text{ in.}^2 + 30 \text{ in.}^2 + 5 \text{ in.}^2 = 45 \text{ in.}^2$

The area of the side of the stone is 45 in.^{2}.

EXAMPLE 3

Find the Area of a Kite

> A kite is a quadrilateral with two pairs of adjacent sides that are equal in length.

Jackson has a rectangular piece of cloth that has an area of 298 cm^2. Does Jackson have enough cloth to make the kite shown?

STEP 1 Decompose the kite into two identical triangles. Find the area of the triangles.

$A = \frac{1}{2}bh$

$A = \frac{1}{2} \cdot 30 \cdot 10$

$A = 150 \text{ cm}^2$

Each triangle has an area of 150 cm^2. The area of the kite is 300 cm^2.

STEP 2 Find the area of the kite. Compare the area of the kite to the area of the cloth.

$2 \times 150 \text{ cm}^2 = 300 \text{ cm}^2$

$300 \text{ cm}^2 > 298 \text{ cm}^2$

Jackson does not have enough cloth to make the kite.

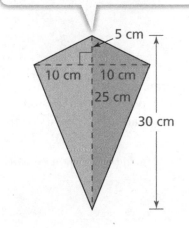

5 cm

10 cm 10 cm

25 cm

30 cm

✓ **Try It!**

Find the area of the trapezoid and the area of the kite.

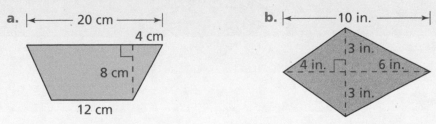

a.
20 cm
4 cm
8 cm
12 cm

b.
10 in.
3 in.
4 in.   6 in.
3 in.

You can find the area of a trapezoid or a kite by decomposing the shapes into rectangles and triangles.

Trapezoid

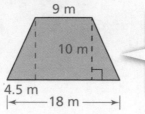

Decompose the trapezoid into two triangles and a rectangle. Find the length of the unknown triangle base.

Kite

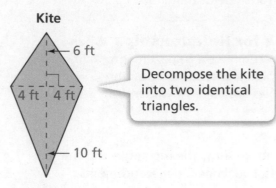

Decompose the kite into two identical triangles.

Each triangle: $A = \frac{1}{2}(4.5)(10) = 22.5$

Rectangle: $A = 9(10) = 90$

Trapezoid: $A = 22.5 + 22.5 + 90 = 135$

The area of the trapezoid is 135 m².

Each triangle: $A = \frac{1}{2}(16)(4) = 32$

Kite: $A = 32 + 32 = 64$

The area of the kite is 64 ft².

Do You Understand?

1. **? Essential Question** How can you find the areas of trapezoids and kites?

2. Draw a line to divide the pasture in Example 1 into two triangles. What are the measures of the bases and the heights of the two triangles?

3. **Construct Arguments** In Example 3, how could you use 4 triangles to find the kite's area?

Do You Know How?

In 4–6, find the area of each trapezoid or kite.

4.

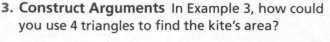

5.

6.

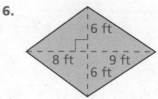

Practice & Problem Solving

Leveled Practice In **7–12**, find the area of each trapezoid or kite.

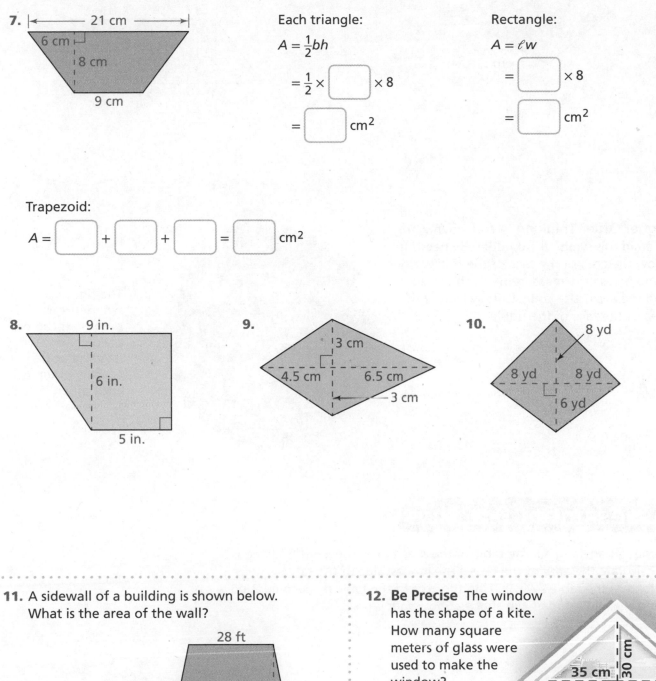

7.

21 cm

6 cm

8 cm

9 cm

Each triangle:

$A = \frac{1}{2}bh$

$= \frac{1}{2} \times \boxed{} \times 8$

$= \boxed{}$ cm²

Rectangle:

$A = \ell w$

$= \boxed{} \times 8$

$= \boxed{}$ cm²

Trapezoid:

$A = \boxed{} + \boxed{} + \boxed{} = \boxed{}$ cm²

8.

9 in.

6 in.

5 in.

9.

3 cm

4.5 cm   6.5 cm

3 cm

10.

8 yd

8 yd   8 yd

6 yd

11. A sidewall of a building is shown below. What is the area of the wall?

28 ft

30 ft

6 ft

40 ft

12. Be Precise The window has the shape of a kite. How many square meters of glass were used to make the window?

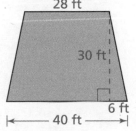

35 cm   30 cm

35 cm

40 cm

13. The area of the kite is 30 m². What is the value of x? Explain.

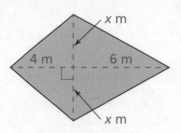

x m

4 m   6 m

x m

14. Make Sense and Persevere Hunter drew two identical trapezoids and composed them to form a parallelogram. Use the area of the parallelogram to find the area of one trapezoid. Explain.

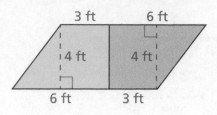

3 ft   6 ft

4 ft   4 ft

6 ft   3 ft

15. Higher Order Thinking A craftsman wants to build this symmetrical fiddle. He needs to know the area of the face of the fiddle. How could he use the measurements shown to find the area? Use your strategy to find the area of the face of the fiddle.

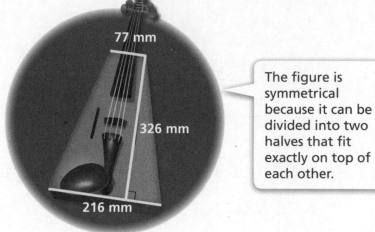

77 mm

326 mm

216 mm

The figure is symmetrical because it can be divided into two halves that fit exactly on top of each other.

✓ Assessment Practice

16. Marique is making a large table in the shape of a trapezoid. She needs to calculate the area of the table. The longest side of the table is twice as long as the table's width. Find the area of the table by decomposing the trapezoid into familiar shapes. Show your work.

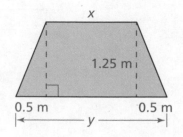

x

1.25 m

0.5 m   0.5 m

y

Solve & Discuss It!

📶 ⏻ ACTIVITY

Gabrielle wants to cover the floors of a room and a hallway in her dollhouse. She measured the room and hallway and sketched the floor plan below. How much felt does Gabrielle need?

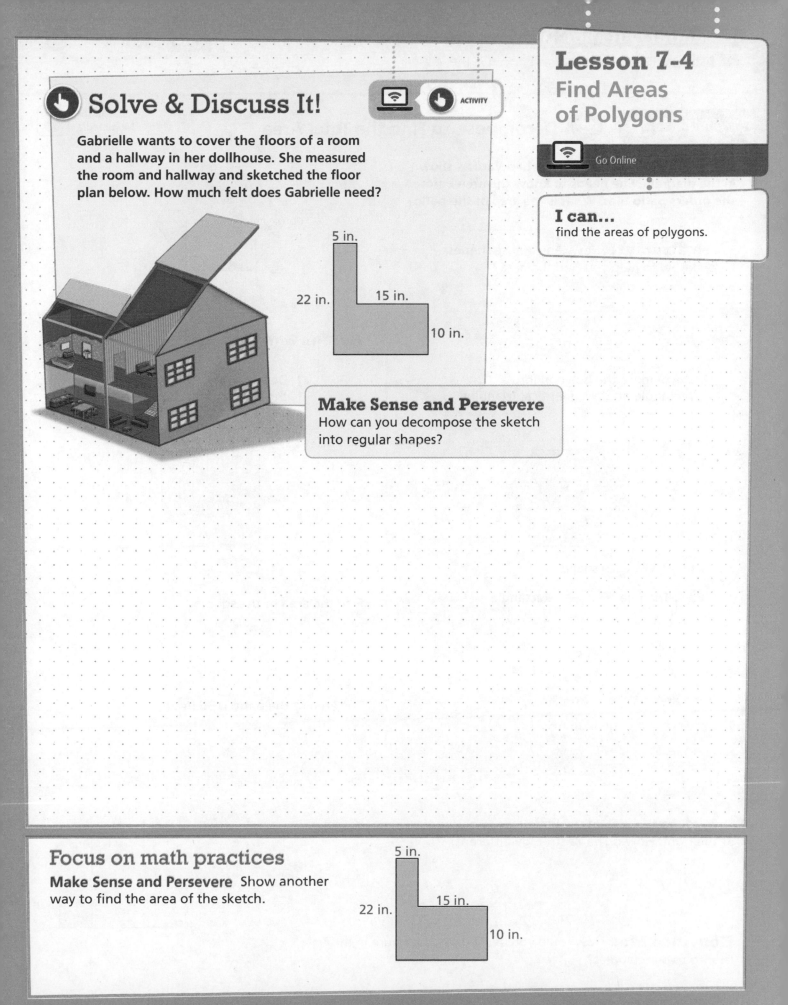

5 in.

22 in.   15 in.

10 in.

I can...
find the areas of polygons.

Make Sense and Persevere
How can you decompose the sketch into regular shapes?

Focus on math practices
Make Sense and Persevere Show another way to find the area of the sketch.

5 in.

22 in.   15 in.

10 in.

? **Essential Question** How can you find the areas of polygons?

VISUAL LEARNING ASSESS

EXAMPLE 1 👁 **Decompose to Find the Total Area**

Scan for Multimedia

Denise is building a patio in her backyard as shown in the diagram. She needs to know the area before she orders patio tiles. What is the area of the patio?

> **Use Structure** How can you use shapes you know to help you find the area?

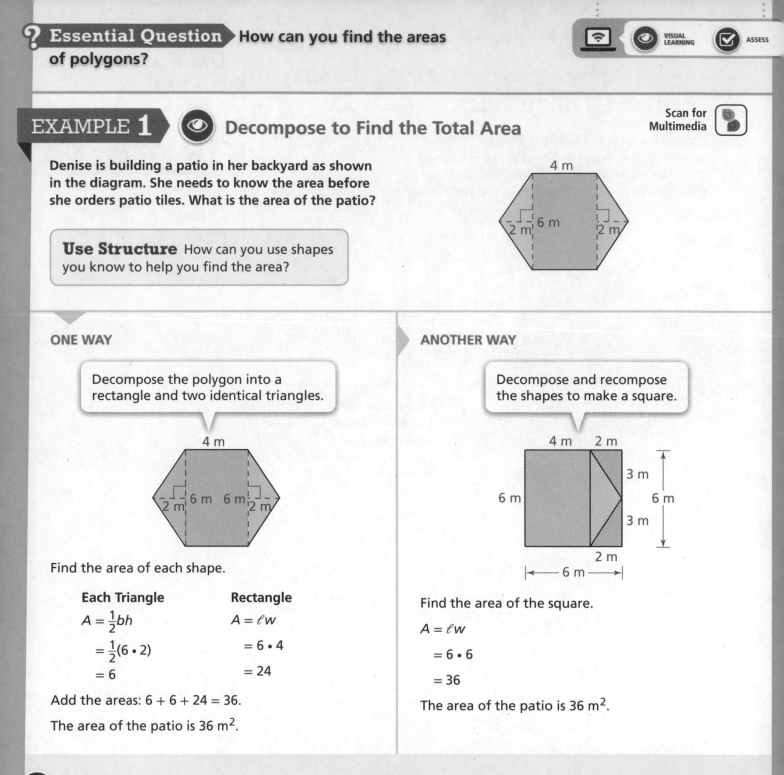

ONE WAY

> Decompose the polygon into a rectangle and two identical triangles.

Find the area of each shape.

Each Triangle	**Rectangle**
$A = \frac{1}{2}bh$	$A = \ell w$
$= \frac{1}{2}(6 \cdot 2)$	$= 6 \cdot 4$
$= 6$	$= 24$

Add the areas: $6 + 6 + 24 = 36$.

The area of the patio is 36 m².

ANOTHER WAY

> Decompose and recompose the shapes to make a square.

Find the area of the square.

$A = \ell w$

$= 6 \cdot 6$

$= 36$

The area of the patio is 36 m².

✅ **Try It!**

Shari found the area of the patio by composing the shapes as shown at the right. How is Shari's strategy different?

Convince Me! How could you decompose the figure in the Try It! into two rectangles?

EXAMPLE **2** ▶ 👆 **Subtract to Find the Total Area**

📶 👆 ACTIVITY ✅ ASSESS

The Robinsons are planning to resurface the path that surrounds their garden, as shown. What is the area of the path?

> **Make Sense and Persevere** The area of the path can be found by subtracting the area of the garden from the total area of the garden and the path.

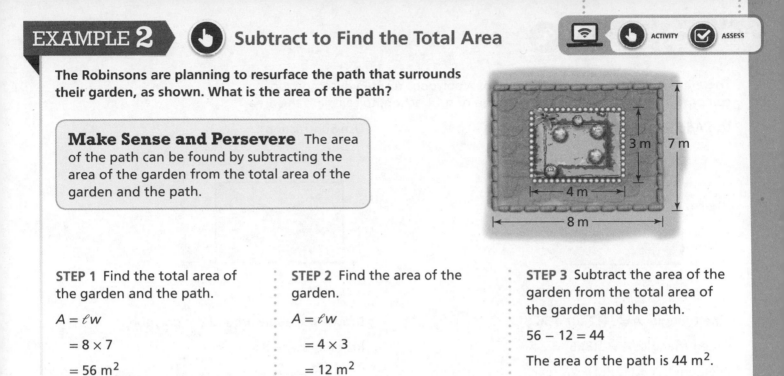

STEP 1 Find the total area of the garden and the path.

$A = \ell w$

$\quad = 8 \times 7$

$\quad = 56 \text{ m}^2$

STEP 2 Find the area of the garden.

$A = \ell w$

$\quad = 4 \times 3$

$\quad = 12 \text{ m}^2$

STEP 3 Subtract the area of the garden from the total area of the garden and the path.

$56 - 12 = 44$

The area of the path is 44 m².

EXAMPLE **3** ▶ 👆 **Find the Area of a Polygon on the Coordinate Plane**

The floor plan for a new stage at a school is sketched on a coordinate plane. A flooring expert recommends bamboo flooring for the stage floor. How much bamboo flooring, in square meters, does the school need?

STEP 1 Decompose the polygon. Find the needed dimensions.

STEP 2 Find the area of each part.

Each square represents 1 square meter.

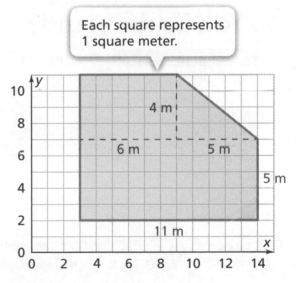

Right Triangle

$A = \frac{1}{2}bh$

$\quad = \frac{1}{2} \cdot 5 \cdot 4$

$\quad = 10$

Rectangles

$A = \ell w$

$\quad = 6 \cdot 4$

$\quad = 24$

$A = \ell w$

$\quad = 11 \cdot 5$

$\quad = 55$

Add the areas: $10 + 24 + 55 = 89$

The school needs 89 m² of bamboo flooring.

✅ **Try It!**

Find the area of the shaded region in square units.

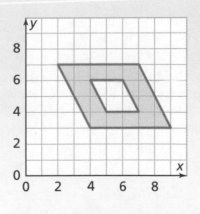

There are many ways to find the area of a polygon. You can decompose or compose shapes, or you can use addition or subtraction, to calculate the area.

Use Addition

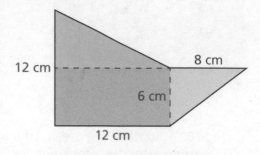

Blue triangle: $A = \frac{1}{2}(12)(6) = 36$

Green triangle: $A = \frac{1}{2}(8)(6) = 24$

Rectangle: $A = (12)(6) = 72$

$36 + 24 + 72 = 132$

The area of the polygon is 132 cm².

Use Subtraction

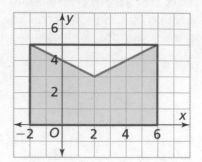

Draw a rectangle around the polygon.

Rectangle: $A = 8 \times 5 = 40$

Triangle: $A = \frac{1}{2} \times 8 \times 2 = 8$

$40 - 8 = 32$

The area of the polygon is 32 square units.

Do You Understand?

1. **? Essential Question** How can you find the areas of polygons?

2. Describe a way in which you can use subtraction to find the area of the shape in Exercise 4.

3. **Model with Math** Describe how to break the floor plan in Example 3 into a trapezoid and a rectangle. Use coordinates to describe the line you can draw.

Do You Know How?

In 4 and 5, find the area of each polygon.

4.

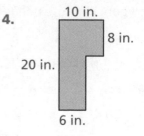

5. A polygon with vertices at (6, 2), (9, 5), (12, 2), (12, −4), and (6, −4)

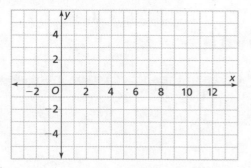

Practice & Problem Solving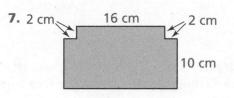

In 6–9, find the area of each polygon or shaded region.

6.

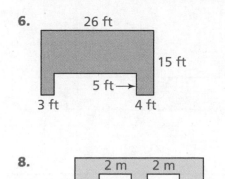

26 ft
15 ft
5 ft→
3 ft   4 ft

7.

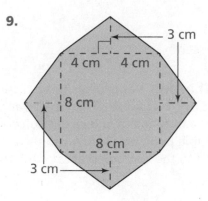

2 cm   16 cm   2 cm
10 cm

8.

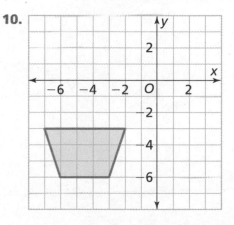

2 m   2 m
4 m
2 m   2 m
8 m

9.

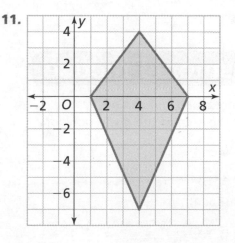

3 cm
4 cm   4 cm
8 cm
8 cm
3 cm

In 10 and 11, find the area in square units of each polygon.

10.

11.

12. Be Precise Diego is designing an exercise room. How many square feet of rubber flooring will he need to cover the floor? The product is sold in whole square yards. How many square yards should Diego buy? Explain.

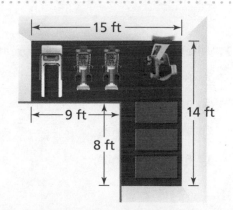

15 ft
9 ft
8 ft
14 ft

In 13 and 14, use the diagram at the right.

13. David drew this diagram of a picture frame that he is going to make. Each square represents 1 square inch. What is the area of the picture frame?

14. **Use Structure** How could you find the area of the picture frame without decomposing the frame into smaller shapes?

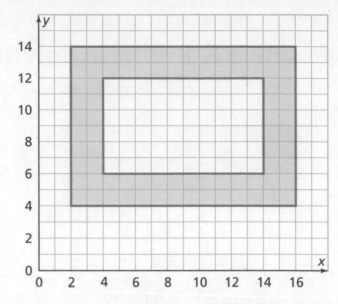

15. **Higher Order Thinking** Isabella has three rectangular cards that are 4 inches by 5 inches. How can she arrange the cards, without overlapping, to make one larger polygon with the smallest possible perimeter? How will the area of the polygon compare to the combined area of the three cards?

✓ Assessment Practice

16. Select all expressions that can be used to find the area of the given polygon.

☐ $(2 \times 5) + (6 \times 4)$

☐ $(5 \times 2) + 2 \cdot \frac{1}{2}(3 \times 4)$

☐ $(6 \times 5) - (3 \times 4)$

☐ $(6 \times 9) - (3 \times 4)$

☐ $(5 \times 2) + \frac{1}{2}[(2 + 2 + 2) \times 4]$

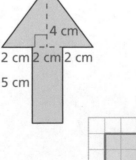

17. What is the area of the polygon at the right?

Ⓐ 86 square units

Ⓑ 78 square units

Ⓒ 70 square units

Ⓓ 68 square units

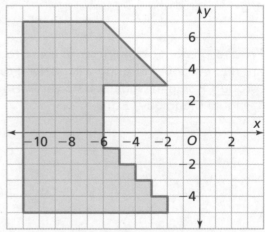

Name: _____

1. **Vocabulary** How many pairs of opposite sides are parallel in a trapezoid? How is this different from a parallelogram? *Lesson 7-3*

2. Calculate the area of each figure at the right. Which figure has the greatest area? *Lessons 7-1, 7-2, and 7-3*

   Ⓐ triangle

   Ⓑ parallelogram

   Ⓒ trapezoid

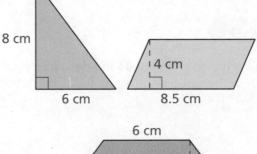
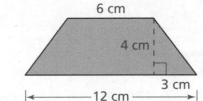

3. An earring has the shape of a rhombus. The height is 5.2 mm and the area of the earring is 39 mm². What is the length of each side of the earring? *Lesson 7-1*

4. Shane wrapped the kite at the right with paper. How many square inches of paper did Shane use to cover the front and back? *Lesson 7-3*

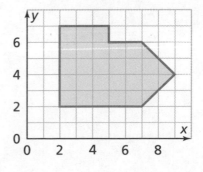

5. Explain one way to find the area of the polygon at the right. Then find the area in square units. *Lesson 7-4*

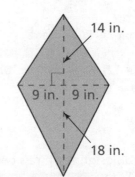

How well did you do on the mid-topic checkpoint? Fill in the stars.

MID-TOPIC
PERFORMANCE TASK

Kira hires a contractor to build a new deck in her backyard. A design for the deck is shown.

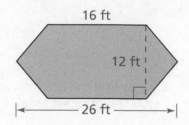

16 ft

12 ft

26 ft

PART A

Kira found the area of the deck by decomposing it into two identical trapezoids. Describe another strategy you could use to find the area of the deck.

PART B

Which expression can you use to find the area of the deck? Select all that apply.

☐ $(16 \times 12) + 2(\frac{1}{2} \times 12 \times 5)$

☐ $(26 \times 12) + 2(\frac{1}{2} \times 12 \times 5)$

☐ $(26 \times 12) - 4(\frac{1}{2} \times 6 \times 5)$

☐ $(16 \times 6) + 2(\frac{1}{2} \times 6 \times 5) + (16 \times 6) + 2(\frac{1}{2} \times 6 \times 5)$

☐ $(16 \times 12) + 2(\frac{1}{2} \times 12 \times 10)$

PART C

A second design for Kira's deck is shown at the right. Find the areas of the two deck designs. Which design will give Kira the deck with the greater area? Explain.

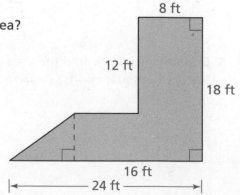

8 ft

12 ft

18 ft

16 ft

24 ft

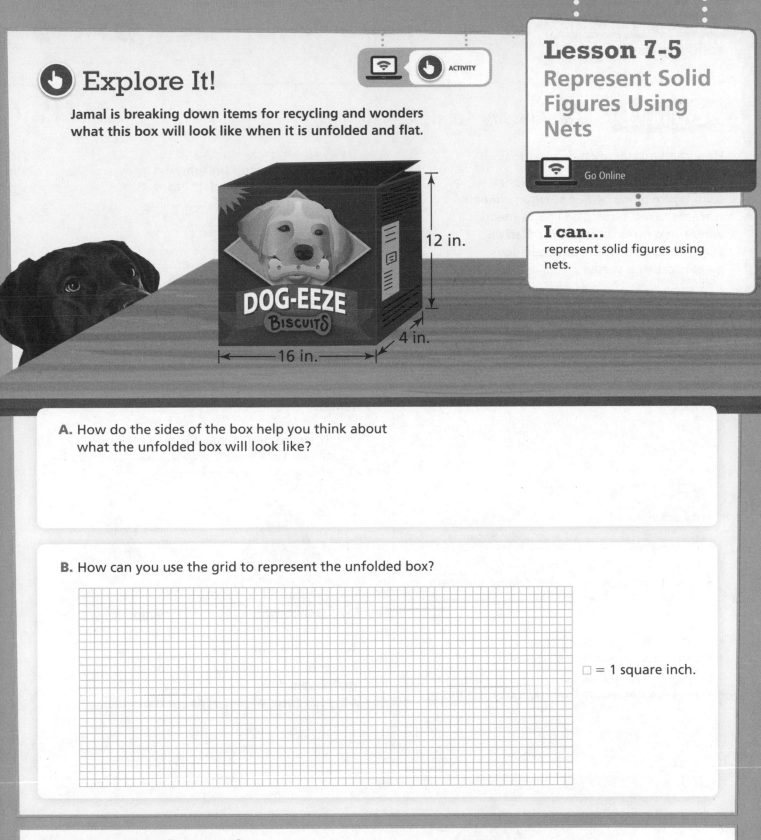

Explore It!

Jamal is breaking down items for recycling and wonders what this box will look like when it is unfolded and flat.

ACTIVITY

DOG-EEZE BISCUITS

12 in.

4 in.

16 in.

I can...
represent solid figures using nets.

A. How do the sides of the box help you think about what the unfolded box will look like?

B. How can you use the grid to represent the unfolded box?

☐ = 1 square inch.

Focus on math practices

Reasoning Is there another way to represent the unfolded box on the grid? Explain.

VISUAL LEARNING   ASSESS

EXAMPLE 1 👁 Classify Solids

Scan for Multimedia

How can you classify a polyhedron?

A polyhedron is a three-dimensional solid figure made of flat polygon-shaped surfaces called faces. The line segment where two faces intersect is called an edge. The point where several edges meet is called a vertex.

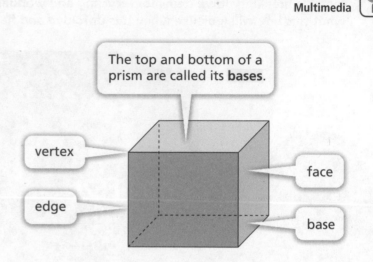

The top and bottom of a prism are called its **bases**.

vertex

edge

face

base

Prisms

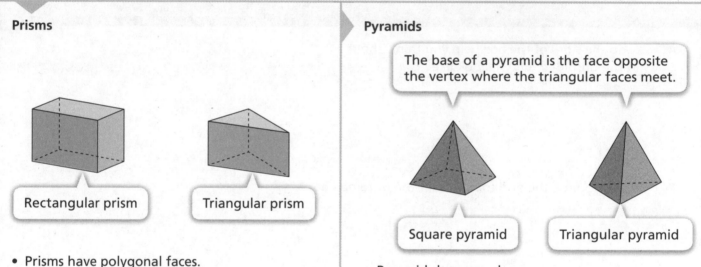

Rectangular prism

Triangular prism

- Prisms have polygonal faces.
- Prisms have two identical, parallel, polygon-shaped bases.
- Prisms are named by the shape of their bases.

Pyramids

The base of a pyramid is the face opposite the vertex where the triangular faces meet.

Square pyramid

Triangular pyramid

- Pyramids have one base.
- Pyramids are named by the shape of their bases.
- All other faces of pyramids are triangular.

☑ Try It!

Classify this solid figure.

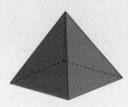

Convince Me! What attributes of a solid figure should you identify to classify it as a polyhedron?

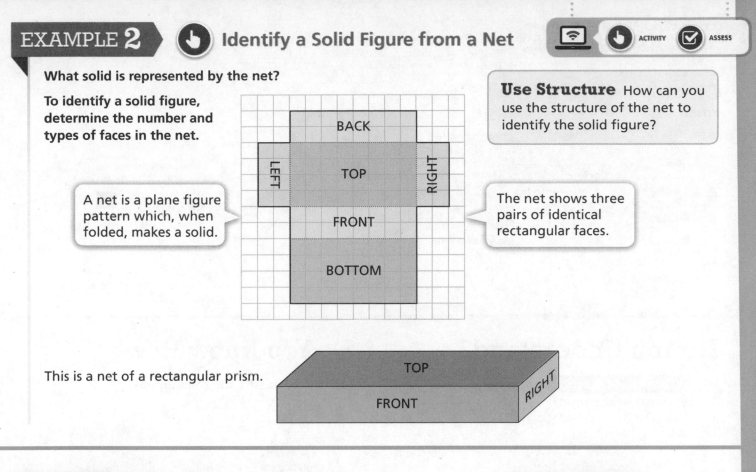

EXAMPLE 2 Identify a Solid Figure from a Net

ACTIVITY   ASSESS

What solid is represented by the net?

To identify a solid figure, determine the number and types of faces in the net.

A net is a plane figure pattern which, when folded, makes a solid.

Use Structure How can you use the structure of the net to identify the solid figure?

The net shows three pairs of identical rectangular faces.

This is a net of a rectangular prism.

EXAMPLE 3 Draw a Net of a Solid Figure

How can you draw a net of a rectangular prism that has a height of 2 units and bases that are 4 units long and 2 units wide?

STEP 1 Draw one base of the prism.

STEP 2 Above and below the base, draw a rectangle with the same width as the base and a height of 2 units.

STEP 3 Draw three additional rectangles, in line with the base, that have the same length as the base and a width of 2 units.

Be Precise How can you determine whether the dimensions in the net match the dimensions of the rectangular prism?

☑ Try It!

Identify the solid from its net.

Shape of polygonal faces: _____

Shape of base(s): _____

This is a net of a _____ .

You can use nets to represent solid figures.

Prism

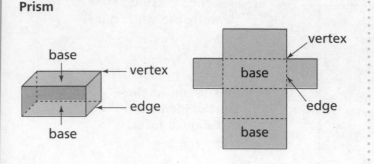

Pyramid

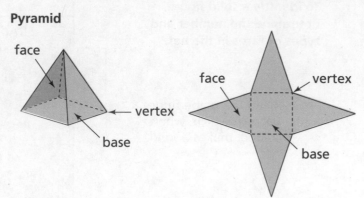

Do You Understand?

1. **? Essential Question** How do you classify and represent solid figures?

2. **Use Structure** Explain the difference between a vertex and an edge.

3. **Be Precise** Explain the difference between a pyramid and a prism.

4. Describe the net of a triangular prism.

Do You Know How?

In 5 and 6, classify the solid figures.

5.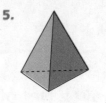

6.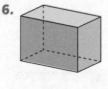

In 7 and 8, identify each solid from its net.

7.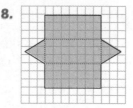

8.

9. Draw a net of a rectangular prism that has a height of 2 units and bases that are 3 units long and 1 unit wide.

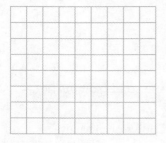

Practice & Problem Solving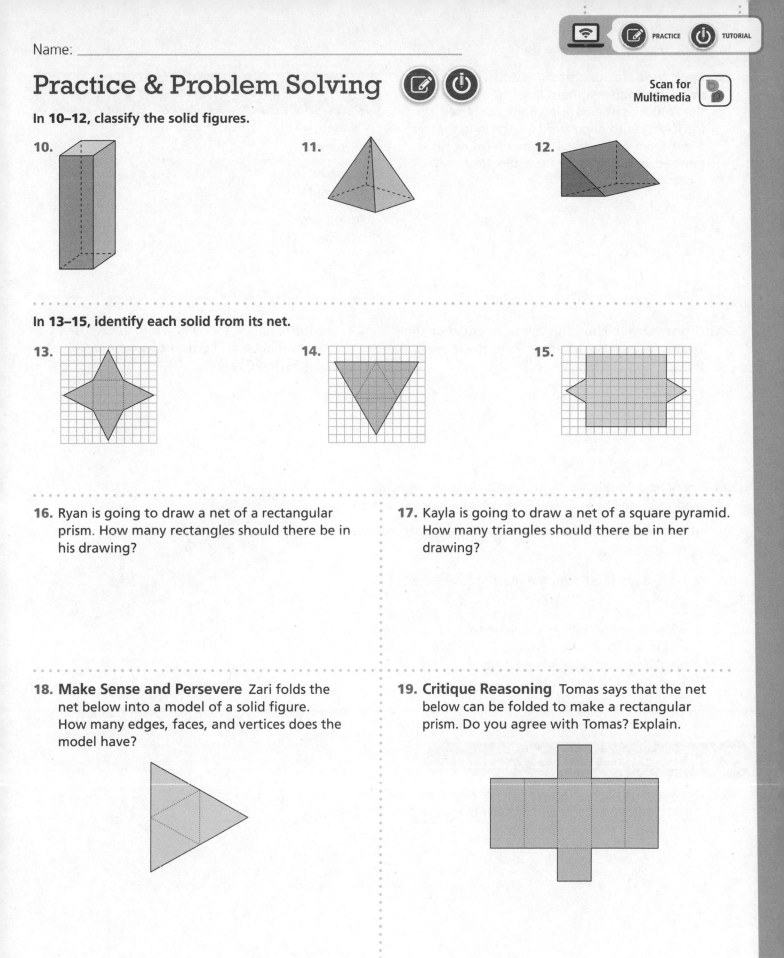

In 10–12, classify the solid figures.

10.

11.

12.

In 13–15, identify each solid from its net.

13.

14.

15.

16. Ryan is going to draw a net of a rectangular prism. How many rectangles should there be in his drawing?

17. Kayla is going to draw a net of a square pyramid. How many triangles should there be in her drawing?

18. Make Sense and Persevere Zari folds the net below into a model of a solid figure. How many edges, faces, and vertices does the model have?

19. Critique Reasoning Tomas says that the net below can be folded to make a rectangular prism. Do you agree with Tomas? Explain.

In 20–22, use the table at the right.

20. **Look for Relationships** The Swiss mathematician Leonhard Euler (OY-ler) and the French mathematician René Descartes (dã KART) both discovered a pattern in the numbers of edges, vertices, and faces of polyhedrons. Complete the table. Describe a pattern in the table.

Polyhedron	Faces (F)	Vertices (V)	F + V	Edges (E)
Triangular Pyramid				
Rectangular Pyramid				
Triangular Prism				
Rectangular Prism				

21. **Higher Order Thinking** Write an equation that relates the number of edges, E, to the number of faces, F, and vertices, V.

22. Use the equation that you wrote in Exercise 21 to find the number of vertices of a cube, which has 12 edges and 6 faces.

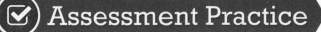

23. Corey bought the mailing tube shown at the right to mail a poster of the Gators Little League baseball team.

    a. The mailing tube has the shape of which polyhedron?

    b. How many faces does the mailing tube have?

    c. When Corey bought the mailing tube, it was unfolded and looked like a net. What polygons would Corey have seen in the unfolded mailing tube?

☑ Assessment Practice

24. Draw a net of a square pyramid for which the base is 2 units long and the height of each triangular face is 5 units.

3-ACT MATH ▷ ▷ ▷

That's a Wrap

 ACT 1

1. After watching the video, what is the first question that comes to mind?

2. Write the Main Question you will answer.

3. Construct Arguments Predict an answer to this Main Question. Explain your prediction.

4. On the number line below, write a number that is too small to be the answer. Write a number that is too large.

Too small   **Too large**

←———————————————————————→

⬚   ⬚

5. Plot your prediction on the same number line.

6. What information in this situation would be helpful to know? How would you use that information?

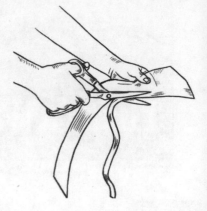

7. **Use Appropriate Tools** What tools can you use to solve the problem? Explain how you would use them strategically.

8. **Model with Math** Represent the situation using mathematics. Use your representation to answer the Main Question.

9. What is your answer to the Main Question? Is it higher or lower than your prediction? Explain why.

10. Write the answer you saw in the video.

11. Reasoning Does your answer match the answer in the video? If not, what are some reasons that would explain the difference?

12. Make Sense and Persevere Would you change your model now that you know the answer? Explain.

Reflect

13. **Model with Math** Explain how you used a mathematical model to represent the situation. How did the model help you answer the Main Question?

14. **Look for Relationships** Explain how the dimensions of the gift are related to the area of its net.

15. **Critique Reasoning** A classmate says that if all dimensions of the gift were doubled, you would need twice as many squares. Do you agree? Justify his reasoning or explain his error.

Solve & Discuss It!

ACTIVITY

Marianne orders boxes to pack gifts. When they arrive, she finds flat pieces of cardboard as shown below. Marianne needs to cover each face of the boxes with green paper. What is the least amount of paper needed to cover each box? Explain.

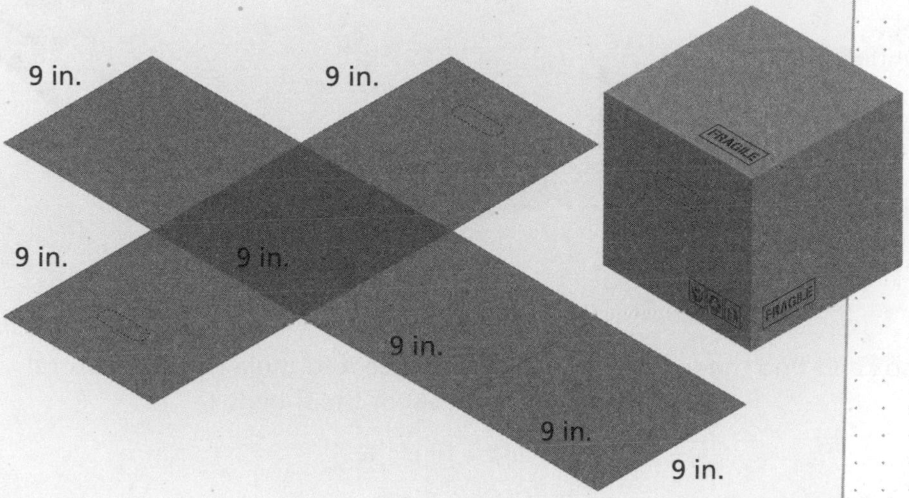

9 in. 9 in.

9 in. 9 in.

9 in.

9 in.

9 in.

Make Sense and Persevere What solid figure does this net represent?

Focus on math practices

Make Sense and Persevere Suppose Marianne has only one large sheet of green paper that is 15 inches by 30 inches. Is the area of this sheet of paper great enough to cover all of the faces of one box? Explain.

VISUAL LEARNING   ASSESS

EXAMPLE 1 ● Find the Surface Area of a Rectangular Prism

Scan for Multimedia

Kelly wants to cover a shoebox with decorative paper without overlapping the paper. How much paper will she need to cover the box?

Use Appropriate Tools Would a net help you find the surface area (*SA*) of the rectangular prism?

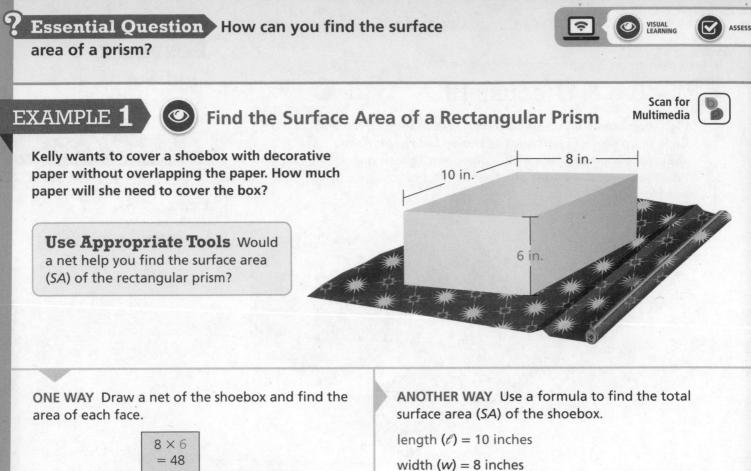

ONE WAY Draw a net of the shoebox and find the area of each face.

$$8 \times 6 = 48$$

| 10×6 = 60 | 10×8 = 80 | 10×6 = 60 | 10×8 = 80 |

$$8 \times 6 = 48$$

Add the areas. Kelly needs 376 square inches of paper to cover the box.

ANOTHER WAY Use a formula to find the total surface area (*SA*) of the shoebox.

length (ℓ) = 10 inches

width (*w*) = 8 inches

height (*h*) = 6 inches

$SA = 2(\ell w) + 2(wh) + 2(\ell h)$

$\quad = 2(10 \cdot 8) + 2(8 \cdot 6) + 2(10 \cdot 6)$

$\quad = 2(80) + 2(48) + 2(60)$

$\quad = 376$

The area of each face in the net is calculated in the formula.

Kelly needs 376 square inches of paper to cover the box.

☑ **Try It!**

Use the net and the formula to find the surface area of the prism.

$SA = 2(\ell w) + 2(wh) + 2(\ell h)$

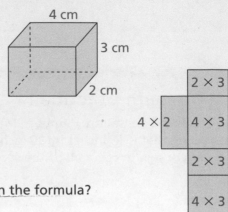

Convince Me! Why are ℓw, wh, and ℓh each multiplied by 2 in the formula?

EXAMPLE 2 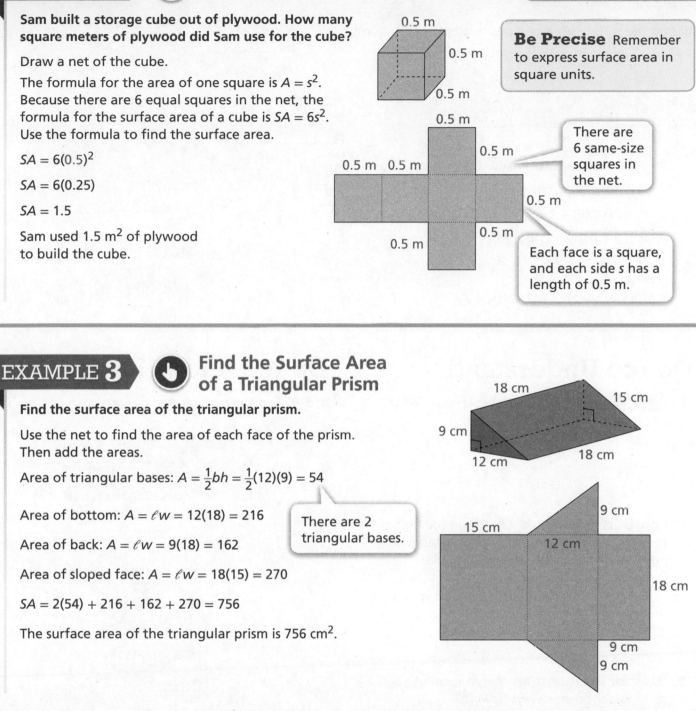 **Find the Surface Area of a Cube**

Sam built a storage cube out of plywood. How many square meters of plywood did Sam use for the cube?

Draw a net of the cube.

The formula for the area of one square is $A = s^2$. Because there are 6 equal squares in the net, the formula for the surface area of a cube is $SA = 6s^2$. Use the formula to find the surface area.

$SA = 6(0.5)^2$

$SA = 6(0.25)$

$SA = 1.5$

Sam used 1.5 m² of plywood to build the cube.

> **Be Precise** Remember to express surface area in square units.

> There are 6 same-size squares in the net.

> Each face is a square, and each side s has a length of 0.5 m.

0.5 m
0.5 m
0.5 m
0.5 m
0.5 m
0.5 m 0.5 m
0.5 m
0.5 m
0.5 m

EXAMPLE 3 **Find the Surface Area of a Triangular Prism**

Find the surface area of the triangular prism.

Use the net to find the area of each face of the prism. Then add the areas.

Area of triangular bases: $A = \frac{1}{2}bh = \frac{1}{2}(12)(9) = 54$

Area of bottom: $A = \ell w = 12(18) = 216$

Area of back: $A = \ell w = 9(18) = 162$

Area of sloped face: $A = \ell w = 18(15) = 270$

$SA = 2(54) + 216 + 162 + 270 = 756$

The surface area of the triangular prism is 756 cm².

> There are 2 triangular bases.

18 cm
15 cm
9 cm
12 cm
18 cm

9 cm
15 cm
12 cm
18 cm
9 cm
9 cm

✓ Try It!

Find the surface area of each prism.

a.
4.2 cm
4.2 cm
4.2 cm

b.
5 ft
5 ft
4 ft
7 ft
6 ft

To find the surface area of a prism, use a net or a formula.

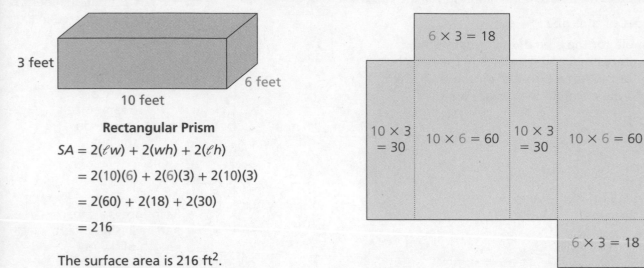

Rectangular Prism

$SA = 2(\ell w) + 2(wh) + 2(\ell h)$

$= 2(10)(6) + 2(6)(3) + 2(10)(3)$

$= 2(60) + 2(18) + 2(30)$

$= 216$

The surface area is 216 ft².

Do You Understand?

1. **Essential Question** How can you find the surface area of a prism?

2. **Construct Arguments** Could you use the formula for the surface area of a rectangular prism to find the surface area of a cube? Explain.

3. **Look for Relationships** Which faces of a rectangular prism always have the same area?

4. **Generalize** What does it mean to find surface area?

Do You Know How?

In 5–7, find the surface area of each prism.

5.

6.

7.

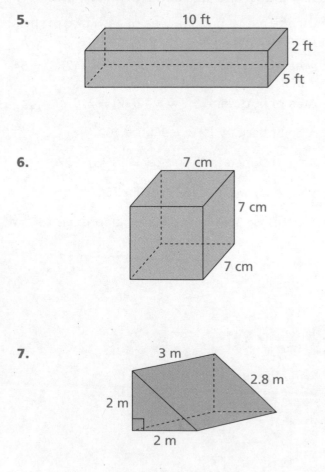

Practice & Problem Solving 📝 ⏻

In 8–13, find the surface area of each prism.

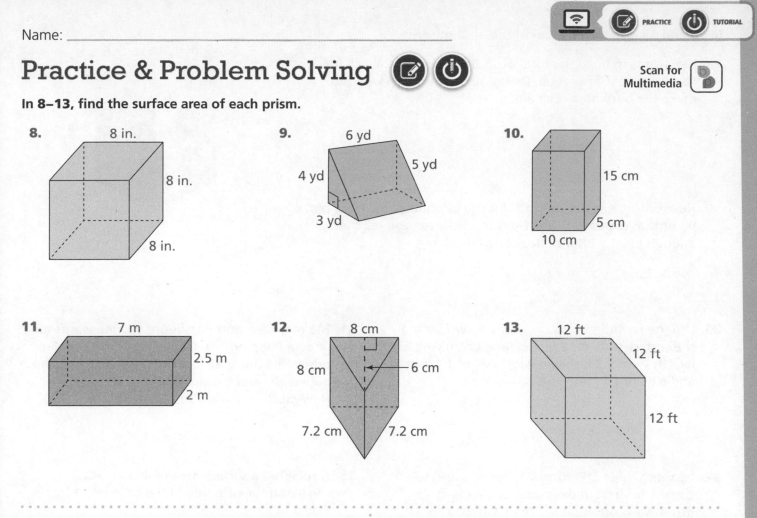

8. 8 in. / 8 in. / 8 in.

9. 6 yd / 5 yd / 4 yd / 3 yd

10. 15 cm / 5 cm / 10 cm

11. 7 m / 2.5 m / 2 m

12. 8 cm / 8 cm / 6 cm / 7.2 cm / 7.2 cm

13. 12 ft / 12 ft / 12 ft

14. Critique Reasoning Jacob says that the surface area of the cube is less than 1,000 cm². Do you agree with Jacob? Explain.

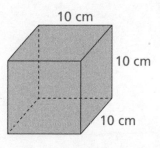

10 cm / 10 cm / 10 cm

15. You want to wrap a paperweight shaped like the triangular prism shown. How many square inches of wrapping paper do you need to completely cover the prism?

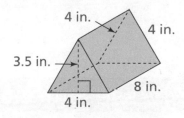

4 in. / 4 in. / 3.5 in. / 8 in. / 4 in.

16. Sasha has 2 blocks of clay shaped like the rectangular prism below. She joins them to form a rectangular prism with a length of 12 inches. What is the surface area of the larger prism?

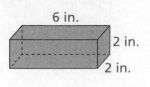

6 in. / 2 in. / 2 in.

17. A rectangular prism has a length of 12 cm, a height of 6 cm, and a width of 4 cm. Use the formula $SA = 2(\ell w) + 2(wh) + 2(\ell h)$ to find the surface area of the rectangular prism.

In 18 and 19, use the diagram of the birdhouse.

18. Kali wants to build this birdhouse. She bought a 24-inch by 48-inch sheet of plywood. Does Kali have enough wood to make the birdhouse? Explain.

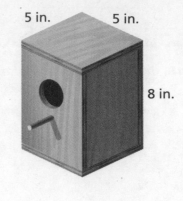

5 in.   5 in.

8 in.

19. **Reasoning** Kali decides to paint the birdhouse. She has a pint of paint that covers 32.5 ft^2 of surface. How can you tell that Kali has enough paint without calculating?

---

20. Use the formula $SA = 2\ell w + 2\ell h + 2wh$ to find the surface area for a rectangular prism with a length, ℓ, of 2.3 inches; a width, w, of 1.1 inches; and a height, h, of 3 inches.

21. **Make Sense and Persevere** Justine wants to wrap a shipping box shaped like a rectangular prism. The box is 28 inches tall and has a square base with sides that each measure 2 inches. How much paper will Justine use?

---

22. **Higher Order Thinking** Margaret wants to cover a footrest in the shape of a rectangular prism with cotton fabric. The footrest is 18 inches by 12 inches by 10 inches. Margaret has 1 square yard of fabric. Can she completely cover the footrest? Explain.

23. A cube has a surface area of 486 in.^{2}. Can the length of each side of the cube be 11 in.? Explain.

☑ Assessment Practice

24. Using nets, find the surface area, in square feet, of a rectangular prism with a height of 2 feet, a length of 4.2 feet, and a width of 2.5 feet.

25. The surface area of a cube is 273.375 square feet. The net of the prism is shown.

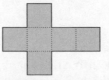

What are the possible dimensions of the cube in feet?

Ⓐ 6, 6, 6

Ⓑ 6, 6.75, 6.75

Ⓒ 6.5, 6.5, 6.5

Ⓓ 6.75, 6.75, 6.75

👆 **Solve & Discuss It!**

📶 👆 ACTIVITY

The fence in Marci's front yard has decorative tops, in the shape of square pyramids, every 6 feet. Marci paints each face of each top a different color before attaching the tops to the fence. What is the total surface area that she paints on each decorative top?

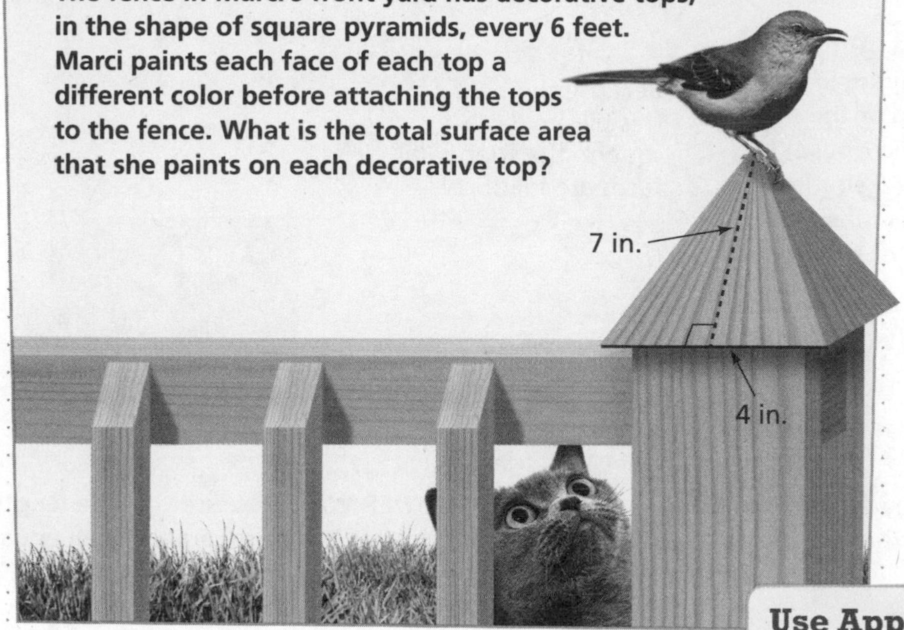

7 in.

4 in.

I can...
draw a net of a pyramid and use it to find the pyramid's surface area.

Use Appropriate Tools
What tools can you use to help solve this problem?

Focus on math practices

Use Structure Suppose the side lengths of the square base of each decorative top are increased by 2 inches. What is the total surface area of each top?

? **Essential Question** How can you find the surface area of a pyramid?

VISUAL LEARNING   ASSESS

EXAMPLE 1 👁 Find the Surface Area of a Square Pyramid

Scan for Multimedia

Maxwell made a model of a house using a cube for the bottom and a square pyramid for the top. He wants to paint the top of the house blue to match the bottom of the house. One tube of craft paint covers about 20 square inches. How many tubes of paint does Maxwell need to cover all the faces of the top of his model?

Because the base of this pyramid is a square, the triangular faces are identical.

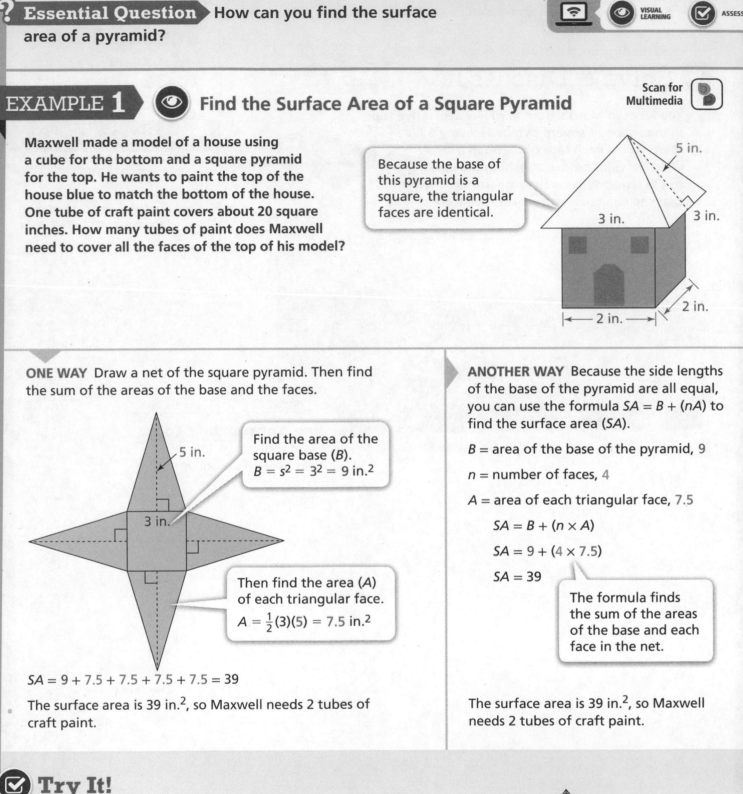

ONE WAY Draw a net of the square pyramid. Then find the sum of the areas of the base and the faces.

Find the area of the square base (B).
$B = s^2 = 3^2 = 9$ in.^{2}

Then find the area (A) of each triangular face.
$A = \frac{1}{2}(3)(5) = 7.5$ in.^{2}

$SA = 9 + 7.5 + 7.5 + 7.5 + 7.5 = 39$

The surface area is 39 in.^{2}, so Maxwell needs 2 tubes of craft paint.

ANOTHER WAY Because the side lengths of the base of the pyramid are all equal, you can use the formula $SA = B + (nA)$ to find the surface area (SA).

B = area of the base of the pyramid, 9

n = number of faces, 4

A = area of each triangular face, 7.5

$$SA = B + (n \times A)$$
$$SA = 9 + (4 \times 7.5)$$
$$SA = 39$$

The formula finds the sum of the areas of the base and each face in the net.

The surface area is 39 in.^{2}, so Maxwell needs 2 tubes of craft paint.

☑ Try It!

Find the surface area of the square pyramid. Draw a net to find the areas of the base and each face of the pyramid.

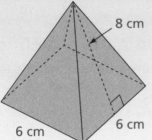

Convince Me! For the pyramid in the Try It!, what values would you use for B, n, and A in the formula $SA = B + (nA)$?

EXAMPLE 2 ▶ 🖑 **Find the Surface Area of a Triangular Pyramid**

🛜 🖑 ACTIVITY ☑ ASSESS

Tamara made a small gift box that has the shape of a triangular pyramid. The faces of the box are identical equilateral triangles. How many square centimeters of cardboard did Tamara use for the box?

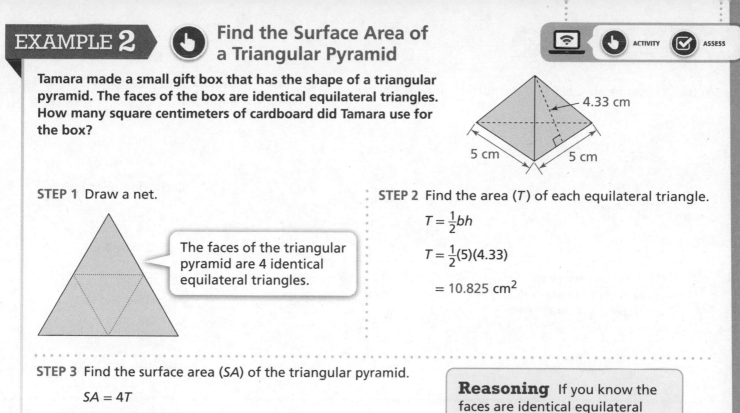

4.33 cm

5 cm   5 cm

STEP 1 Draw a net.

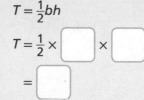

The faces of the triangular pyramid are 4 identical equilateral triangles.

STEP 2 Find the area (T) of each equilateral triangle.

$$T = \frac{1}{2}bh$$

$$T = \frac{1}{2}(5)(4.33)$$

$$= 10.825 \text{ cm}^2$$

STEP 3 Find the surface area (SA) of the triangular pyramid.

$$SA = 4T$$

$$SA = 4 \times 10.825$$

$$= 43.3 \text{ cm}^2$$

Tamara used 43.3 cm² of cardboard for the box.

Reasoning If you know the faces are identical equilateral triangles, then you just find the area of one triangle and multiply by 4.

☑ **Try It!**

Draw a net and find the surface area of the triangular pyramid.

Find the area (T) of each equilateral triangle.

$$T = \frac{1}{2}bh$$

$$T = \frac{1}{2} \times \boxed{} \times \boxed{}$$

$$= \boxed{}$$

The area of each equilateral triangle is $\boxed{}$ m².

There are 4 identical faces.

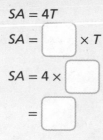

3.5 m

4 m   4 m

The faces are equilateral triangles.

Find the surface area (SA) of the triangular pyramid.

$$SA = 4T$$

$$SA = \boxed{} \times T$$

$$SA = 4 \times \boxed{}$$

$$= \boxed{}$$

The surface area of the triangular pyramid is $\boxed{}$ m².

You can use a net to help find the surface area of a pyramid.

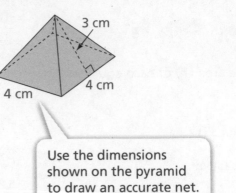

Use the dimensions shown on the pyramid to draw an accurate net.

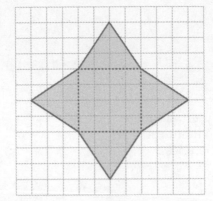

Square base:

$B = s^2$

$= 4 \cdot 4 = 16$

Each triangular face:

$A = \frac{1}{2}bh$

$= \frac{1}{2} \cdot 4 \cdot 3 = 6$

Surface area:

$SA = 16 + 4 \times 6$

$= 16 + 24$

$= 40$

The surface area is 40 cm².

Do You Understand?

1. **Essential Question** How can you find the surface area of a pyramid?

2. **Look for Relationships** How does finding the area of one face of a triangular pyramid that is made up of equilateral triangles help you find the surface area of the triangular pyramid?

3. **Make Sense and Persevere** In the formula $SA = 4T$, for the surface area of a triangular pyramid in which the faces are equilateral triangles, what does the variable T represent?

Do You Know How?

4. Each side of the base of a square pyramid is 4 inches and the height of each triangular face is 3 inches. Draw a net for this pyramid and find its surface area.

5. The faces of this triangular pyramid are equilateral triangles. Draw a net of the pyramid and use it to find the surface area.

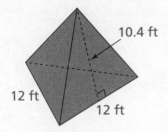

Practice & Problem Solving 🖉 ⏻

Leveled Practice In 6 and 7, find the surface area of each pyramid. The faces
of each triangular pyramid are equilateral triangles.

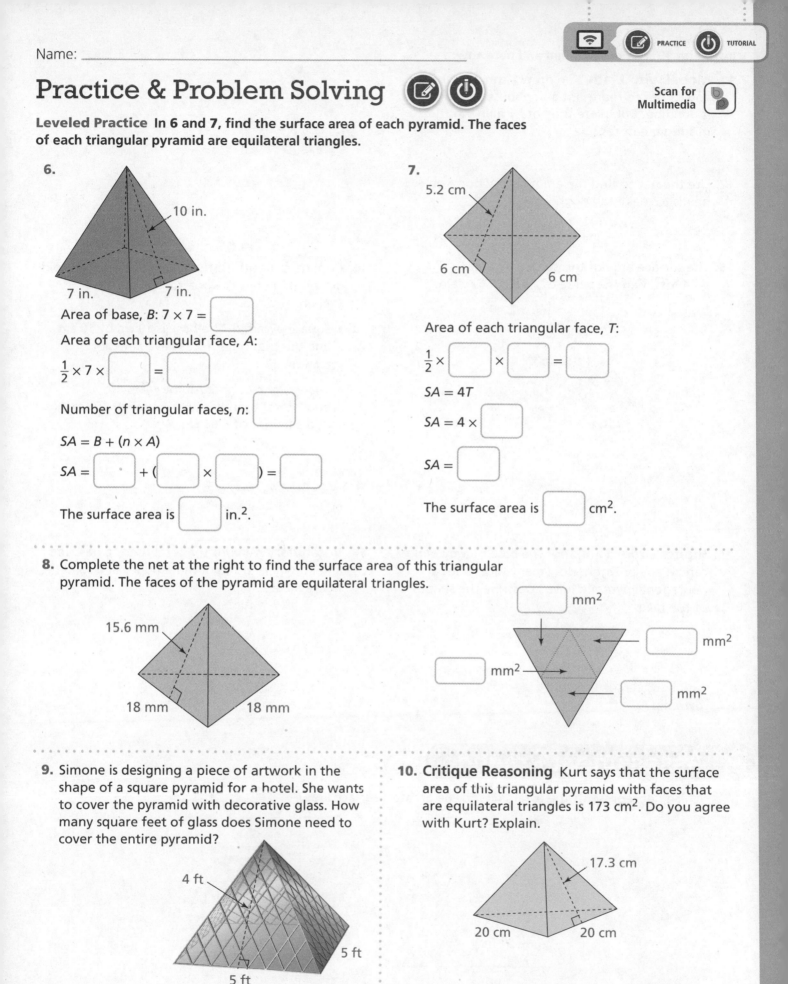

6.

10 in.

7 in.   7 in.

Area of base, B: $7 \times 7 =$ ☐

Area of each triangular face, A:

$\frac{1}{2} \times 7 \times$ ☐ $=$ ☐

Number of triangular faces, n: ☐

$SA = B + (n \times A)$

$SA =$ ☐ $+ ($ ☐ $\times$ ☐ $) =$ ☐

The surface area is ☐ in.²

7.

5.2 cm

6 cm   6 cm

Area of each triangular face, T:

$\frac{1}{2} \times$ ☐ $\times$ ☐ $=$ ☐

$SA = 4T$

$SA = 4 \times$ ☐

$SA =$ ☐

The surface area is ☐ cm².

8. Complete the net at the right to find the surface area of this triangular
pyramid. The faces of the pyramid are equilateral triangles.

15.6 mm

18 mm   18 mm

☐ mm²

☐ mm²

☐ mm²

☐ mm²

9. Simone is designing a piece of artwork in the
shape of a square pyramid for a hotel. She wants
to cover the pyramid with decorative glass. How
many square feet of glass does Simone need to
cover the entire pyramid?

4 ft

5 ft

5 ft

10. Critique Reasoning Kurt says that the surface
area of this triangular pyramid with faces that
are equilateral triangles is 173 cm². Do you agree
with Kurt? Explain.

17.3 cm

20 cm   20 cm

In 11 and 12, use the pyramid and net shown.

11. **Model with Math** Ken drew a square pyramid and its net to represent a doghouse that he is building. Complete the net by filling in the missing measures.

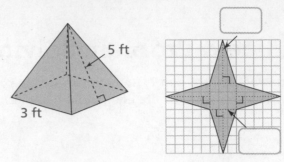

12. Use the net to find the amount of wood Ken needs to make the doghouse.

---

13. The surface area of this square pyramid is 644 ft². Can the value of x be 20? Explain.

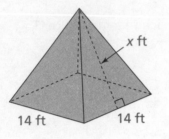

14 ft   14 ft

14. **Construct Arguments** Which of these pyramids do you think has the greater surface area? Explain.

- Square pyramid: The base is 10 cm by 10 cm and the triangular faces have a height of 8.66 cm.

- Triangular pyramid: All the faces are equilateral triangles with a base of 10 cm and a height of 8.66 cm.

---

15. **Higher Order Thinking** The base of a pyramid can be any polygon. How many faces does a pentagonal pyramid have? Describe the shapes of the faces.

16. **Vocabulary** What is the term used to describe a point where three or more edges of a solid figure meet?

✅ Assessment Practice

17. Which net represents the pyramid with the greatest surface area?

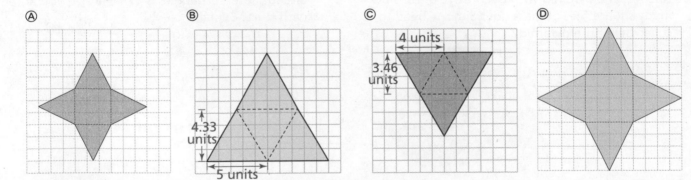

Ⓐ

Ⓑ 4.33 units   5 units

Ⓒ 4 units   3.46 units

Ⓓ

✋ Solve & Discuss It!

📶 ✋ ACTIVITY

A rectangular prism has the dimensions shown. What is the volume of this rectangular prism?

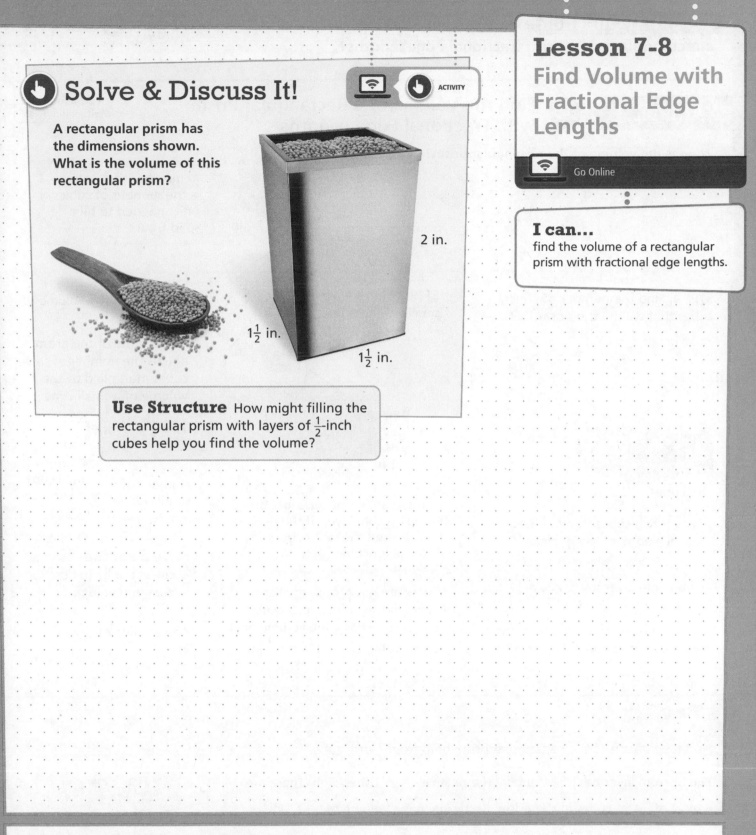

2 in.

$1\frac{1}{2}$ in.

$1\frac{1}{2}$ in.

Use Structure How might filling the rectangular prism with layers of $\frac{1}{2}$-inch cubes help you find the volume?

I can...
find the volume of a rectangular prism with fractional edge lengths.

Focus on math practices

Look for Relationships You know how to use the formula $V = \ell wh$ to find the volume of a rectangular prism. How might you use the formula to find the volume of the prism above?

VISUAL LEARNING · ASSESS

EXAMPLE 1 · Find the Volume of a Rectangular Prism with Fractional Edge Lengths

Scan for Multimedia

What is the volume of the rectangular prism?

$1\frac{1}{2}$ in. $2\frac{1}{2}$ in. $2\frac{1}{2}$ in.

Remember that volume is the number of cubic units needed to fill a solid figure.

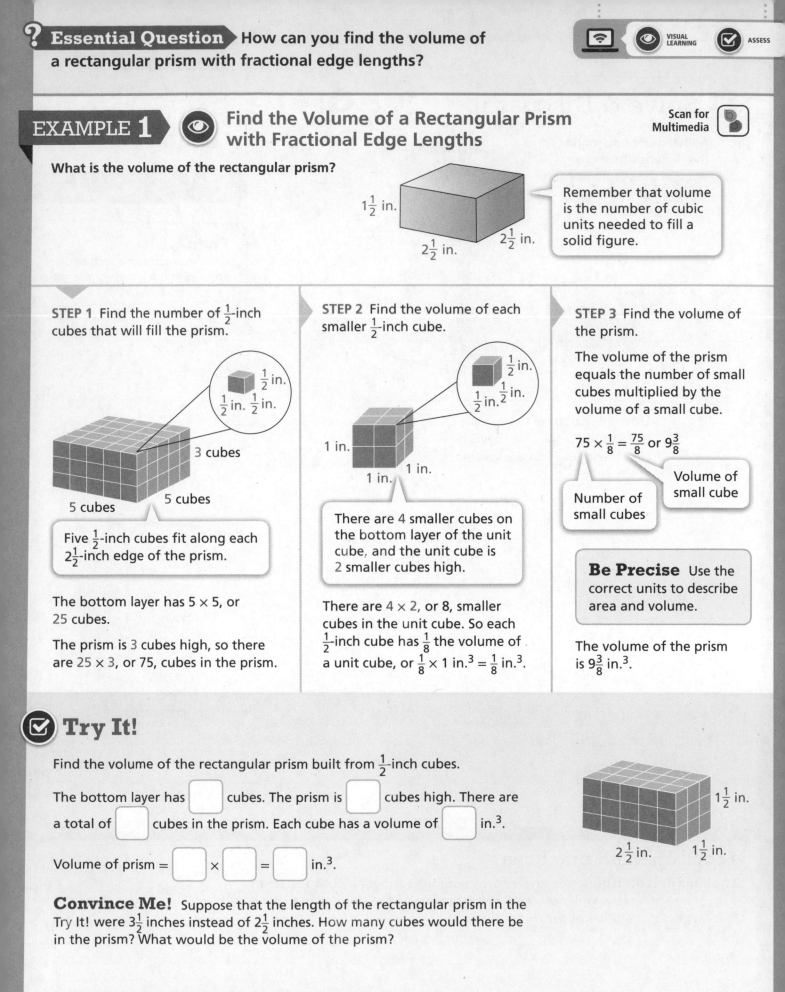

STEP 1 Find the number of $\frac{1}{2}$-inch cubes that will fill the prism.

$\frac{1}{2}$ in. $\frac{1}{2}$ in. $\frac{1}{2}$ in.

3 cubes

5 cubes

5 cubes

Five $\frac{1}{2}$-inch cubes fit along each $2\frac{1}{2}$-inch edge of the prism.

The bottom layer has 5 × 5, or 25 cubes.

The prism is 3 cubes high, so there are 25 × 3, or 75, cubes in the prism.

STEP 2 Find the volume of each smaller $\frac{1}{2}$-inch cube.

$\frac{1}{2}$ in. $\frac{1}{2}$ in. $\frac{1}{2}$ in.

1 in.

1 in. 1 in.

There are 4 smaller cubes on the bottom layer of the unit cube, and the unit cube is 2 smaller cubes high.

There are 4 × 2, or 8, smaller cubes in the unit cube. So each $\frac{1}{2}$-inch cube has $\frac{1}{8}$ the volume of a unit cube, or $\frac{1}{8} \times 1$ in.$^3 = \frac{1}{8}$ in.^{3}.

STEP 3 Find the volume of the prism.

The volume of the prism equals the number of small cubes multiplied by the volume of a small cube.

$75 \times \frac{1}{8} = \frac{75}{8}$ or $9\frac{3}{8}$

Number of small cubes

Volume of small cube

Be Precise Use the correct units to describe area and volume.

The volume of the prism is $9\frac{3}{8}$ in.^{3}.

✓ Try It!

Find the volume of the rectangular prism built from $\frac{1}{2}$-inch cubes.

The bottom layer has ☐ cubes. The prism is ☐ cubes high. There are a total of ☐ cubes in the prism. Each cube has a volume of ☐ in.^{3}.

Volume of prism = ☐ × ☐ = ☐ in.^{3}.

$1\frac{1}{2}$ in. $2\frac{1}{2}$ in. $1\frac{1}{2}$ in.

Convince Me! Suppose that the length of the rectangular prism in the Try It! were $3\frac{1}{2}$ inches instead of $2\frac{1}{2}$ inches. How many cubes would there be in the prism? What would be the volume of the prism?

EXAMPLE **2** ▶ 👆 **Use a Formula to Find the Volume of a Rectangular Prism**

ACTIVITY ✓ ASSESS

Sean bought the fish tank shown. What is the volume of Sean's fish tank?

Look for Relationships The volume V of any prism equals the area of the base, B, times the height of the prism, h. $V = Bh$. In a rectangular prism, $B = \ell \times w$.

Use the formula $V = \ell wh$ to find the volume of the fish tank.

$V = 3\frac{1}{3} \times 1 \times 1\frac{1}{3}$

Substitute the values for the length, width, and height. Rename mixed numbers as fractions to solve.

$V = \frac{10}{3} \times \frac{1}{1} \times \frac{4}{3}$

$V = \frac{40}{9}$ or $4\frac{4}{9}$

The volume of the fish tank is $4\frac{4}{9}$ ft^3.

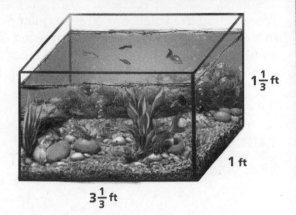

$1\frac{1}{3}$ ft

1 ft

$3\frac{1}{3}$ ft

EXAMPLE **3** 👆 **Use a Formula to Find the Volume of a Cube**

Adah has a ring box in the shape of a cube. What is the volume of Adah's ring box?

Because a cube is a rectangular prism, its volume is also the product of its length, width, and height. Since the length, width, and height of a cube are equivalent, let s represent the length of each edge.

Volume $= s \times s \times s = s^3$

$V = \left(2\frac{1}{2}\right)^3 = 2\frac{1}{2} \times 2\frac{1}{2} \times 2\frac{1}{2}$

Rename mixed numbers as fractions to solve.

$V = \frac{5}{2} \times \frac{5}{2} \times \frac{5}{2}$

$V = \frac{125}{8}$ or $15\frac{5}{8}$

The volume of the ring box is $15\frac{5}{8}$ in.^{3}.

$2\frac{1}{2}$ in.

$2\frac{1}{2}$ in.

$2\frac{1}{2}$ in.

The length, width, and height of a cube are the same.

✓ **Try It!**

Find the volume of each rectangular prism.

a.

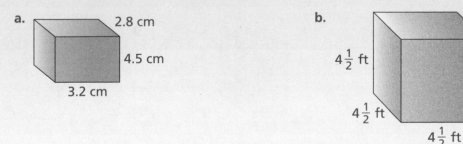

2.8 cm

4.5 cm

3.2 cm

b.

$4\frac{1}{2}$ ft

$4\frac{1}{2}$ ft

$4\frac{1}{2}$ ft

You can find the volume of a rectangular prism with fractional edge lengths by determining the number of same-sized cubes with unit fraction edge lengths needed to completely fill the prism, then multiplying that number of cubes by the volume of each cube. You can also apply a formula.

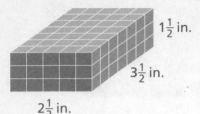

$3\frac{1}{2}$ in.

$1\frac{1}{2}$ in.

$2\frac{1}{2}$ in.

Each $\frac{1}{2}$-inch cube has a volume of $\frac{1}{8}$ in.³.

Prism Dimensions:

Five $\frac{1}{2}$-inch cubes wide

Seven $\frac{1}{2}$-inch cubes long

Three $\frac{1}{2}$-inch cubes tall

$5 \times 7 \times 3 =$ One hundred five $\frac{1}{2}$-inch cubes

$V = 105 \times \frac{1}{8} = 13\frac{1}{8}$

The volume of the prism is $13\frac{1}{8}$ in.³.

$1\frac{1}{2}$ in.

2 in.

$3\frac{1}{4}$ in.

$V = \ell wh$

$V = 3\frac{1}{4} \times 2 \times 1\frac{1}{2}$

$V = \frac{13}{4} \times \frac{2}{1} \times \frac{3}{2}$

$V = \frac{78}{8}$ or $9\frac{3}{4}$

The volume of the prism is $9\frac{3}{4}$ in.³.

Do You Understand?

1. **? Essential Question** How can you find the volume of a rectangular prism with fractional edge lengths?

2. How is finding the volume of a rectangular prism with fractional edge lengths similar to finding the volume of a rectangular prism with whole number edge lengths?

3. **Construct Arguments** How can you use the number of $\frac{1}{2}$-inch cubes in a rectangular prism to find the number of unit cubes in the rectangular prism?

Do You Know How?

In **4 and 5**, tell how many of each size of cube can fill a 1-inch cube.

4. Edge $= \frac{1}{3}$ inch

5. Edge $= \frac{1}{4}$ inch

In **6–9**, find the volume of each rectangular prism.

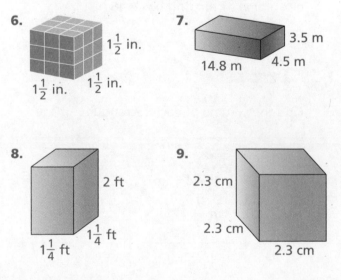

6. $1\frac{1}{2}$ in. $1\frac{1}{2}$ in. $1\frac{1}{2}$ in.

7. 3.5 m 14.8 m 4.5 m

8. 2 ft $1\frac{1}{4}$ ft $1\frac{1}{4}$ ft

9. 2.3 cm 2.3 cm 2.3 cm

Practice & Problem Solving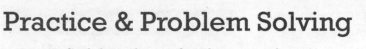

Scan for Multimedia

In 10–13, find the volume of each rectangular prism.

10.

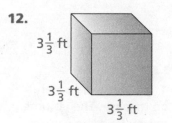

1.2 m
6.5 m
4 m

11.

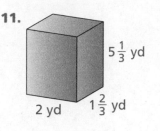

$5\frac{1}{3}$ yd

2 yd $1\frac{2}{3}$ yd

12.

$3\frac{1}{3}$ ft

$3\frac{1}{3}$ ft

$3\frac{1}{3}$ ft

13.

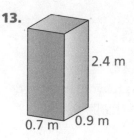

2.4 m

0.7 m   0.9 m

---

14. A clear box has the shape of a rectangular prism and is filled with sand. Find the volume of the box.

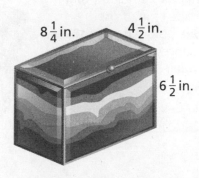

$8\frac{1}{4}$ in. $4\frac{1}{2}$ in.

$6\frac{1}{2}$ in.

15. Use Structure A rectangular prism has a length of $2\frac{1}{2}$ yd, a width of $1\frac{1}{2}$ yd, and a height of $1\frac{1}{2}$ yd. You use cubes with fractional edge lengths of $\frac{1}{2}$ yd to find the volume. How many cubes are there for each of the length, width, and height of the prism? What is the volume of the prism?

---

16. A gift box has the shape of a cube. The length of each side is 10.5 cm. What is the volume of the gift box?

17. A school locker has a length of 1 ft, a width of 18 in., and a height of $2\frac{1}{2}$ ft. What is the volume of the locker in cubic feet?

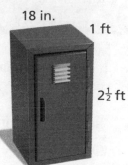

18 in.
1 ft
$2\frac{1}{2}$ ft

In 18 and 19, use the table.

18. **Use Structure** Sandy has two boxes with the dimensions shown. She wants to use the box with the greater volume to ship a gift to her friend. Which box should Sandy use? Explain.

	Length	Width	Height
Box A	$7\frac{1}{2}$ in.	2 in.	$11\frac{1}{2}$ in.
Box B	9 in.	$2\frac{1}{4}$ in.	$8\frac{1}{2}$ in.

19. Sandy finds a third box, box C, that has a length of 8 inches, a width of $2\frac{3}{4}$ inches, and a height of $10\frac{1}{2}$ inches. If Sandy wants to use the box with the greatest volume, should she use box C? Explain.

20. The volume of a large crate is 84 yd^3. It is $2\frac{2}{3}$ yd wide and $4\frac{2}{3}$ yd high. What is the length of the crate?

21. **Higher Order Thinking** A box covers an area of $8\frac{3}{4}$ in.^{2} when resting on its base. The volume of the box is $74\frac{3}{8}$ in.^{3}. Can you find the surface area of the box? Explain.

22. **Make Sense and Persevere** A gold bar is similar in shape to a rectangular prism. A standard mint bar is approximately 7 in. × $3\frac{5}{8}$ in. × $1\frac{3}{4}$ in. If the value of gold is $1,313 per ounce, about how much is one gold bar worth? Use the formula $w \approx 11.15n$, where w is the weight in ounces and n is the volume in cubic inches, to find the weight in ounces. Explain how you found your answer.

✅ Assessment Practice

23. Which rectangular prism with the given dimensions has the same volume as the prism shown?

   Ⓐ 1 in., 3.5 in., 4.25 in.

   Ⓑ 1.25 in., 3.5 in., 4 in.

   Ⓒ 1.75 in., 3 in., 3.5 in.

   Ⓓ 2 in., 2.25 in., 4 in.

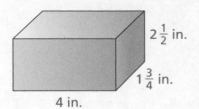

$2\frac{1}{2}$ in.

$1\frac{3}{4}$ in.

4 in.

❓ Topic Essential Question

How can the areas of certain shapes be found? What are the meanings of surface area and volume and how can surface area and volume be found?

Vocabulary Review

Write the vocabulary term that best represents each item.

Vocabulary   net   rhombus   trapezoid   vertex   volume

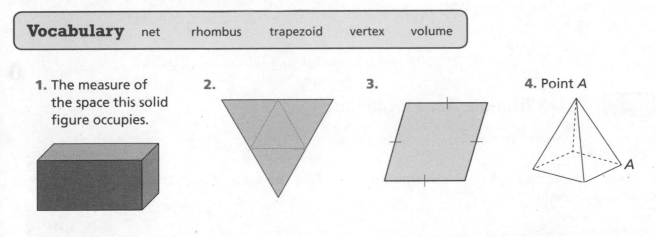

1. The measure of the space this solid figure occupies.

2.

3.

4. Point *A*

Use Vocabulary in Writing

Describe how to find the area of the quadrilateral. Use vocabulary words in your explanation.

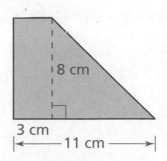

8 cm

3 cm

11 cm

Concepts and Skills Review

Find Areas of Parallelograms and Rhombuses

Quick Review

You can use the formula $A = bh$ to find the area of a parallelogram or a rhombus.

Example

Find the area of the parallelogram.

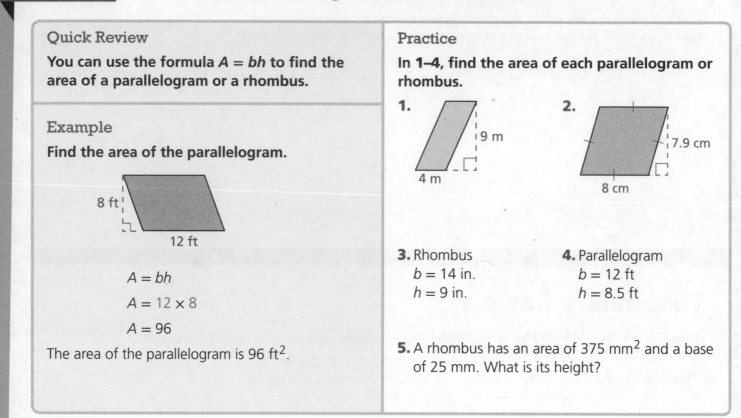

$A = bh$

$A = 12 \times 8$

$A = 96$

The area of the parallelogram is 96 ft².

Practice

In **1–4**, find the area of each parallelogram or rhombus.

1.

2.

3. Rhombus
   $b = 14$ in.
   $h = 9$ in.

4. Parallelogram
   $b = 12$ ft
   $h = 8.5$ ft

5. A rhombus has an area of 375 mm² and a base of 25 mm. What is its height?

Solve Triangle Area Problems

Quick Review

You can use the formula $A = \frac{1}{2}bh$ to find the area of any triangle.

Example

Find the area of the triangle.

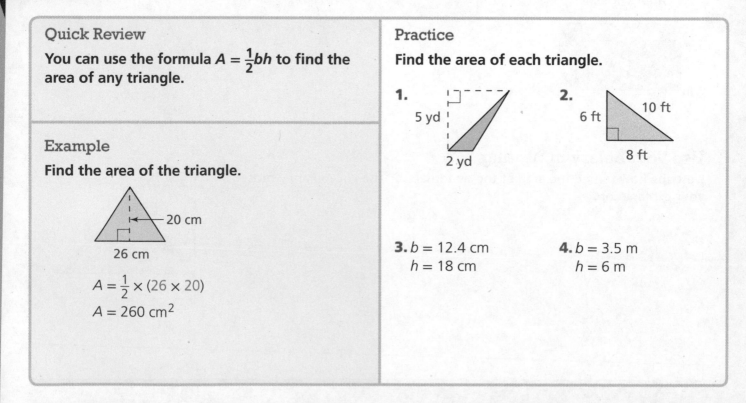

$A = \frac{1}{2} \times (26 \times 20)$

$A = 260$ cm²

Practice

Find the area of each triangle.

1.

2.

3. $b = 12.4$ cm
   $h = 18$ cm

4. $b = 3.5$ m
   $h = 6$ m

Quick Review

You can find the area of a trapezoid by decomposing it into a rectangle and one or more triangles. You can find the area of a kite by decomposing it into triangles.

Example

Find the area of the trapezoid and the kite.

8 yd
8 yd
1 yd   8 yd   1 yd
|←—— 10 yd ——→|

$\frac{1}{2}(1 \times 8) = 4$

$\frac{1}{2}(1 \times 8) = 4$

$8 \times 8 = 64$

$4 + 4 + 64 = 72 \text{ yd}^2$

3 ft
8 ft   4 ft
3 ft

$\frac{1}{2}[(8 + 4) \times 3] = 18$

$\frac{1}{2}[(8 + 4) \times 3] = 18$

$18 + 18 = 36 \text{ ft}^2$

Practice

Find the area of each trapezoid or kite.

1.
6 cm
11 cm
5 cm

2.
13 m
6 m
12 m
1 m

3.
4 in.
4 in.   4 in.
8 in.

4.
4 in.
2 in. 2 in.
10 in.

Quick Review

To find the area of a polygon, you can decompose or compose shapes, then use addition or subtraction to calculate the area.

Example

Find the area of the polygon.

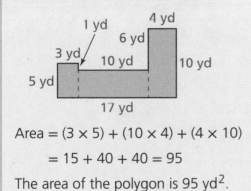

1 yd
4 yd
6 yd
3 yd
10 yd
10 yd
5 yd
17 yd

Area = $(3 \times 5) + (10 \times 4) + (4 \times 10)$

$= 15 + 40 + 40 = 95$

The area of the polygon is 95 yd².

Practice

1. Find the area of the polygon.

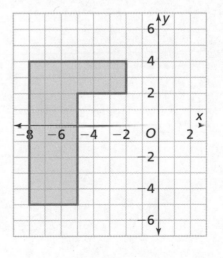

Represent Solid Figures Using Nets

Quick Review
You can use nets to represent solid figures.

Example
Classify the solid figure and draw a net to represent it.

This figure has two congruent parallel bases, so it is a prism. The bases are rectangles, so it is a **rectangular prism**.

Net of rectangular prism:

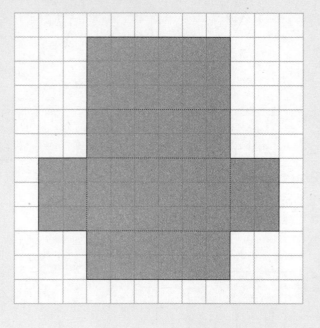

Practice
In 1 and 2, classify the solid figures.

1. 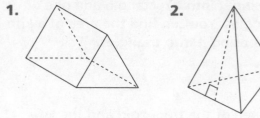 2.

3. Draw a net of the pyramid shown.

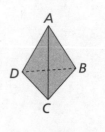

In 4 and 5, identify each solid from its net.

4.

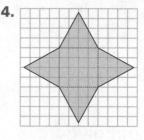

5.

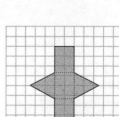

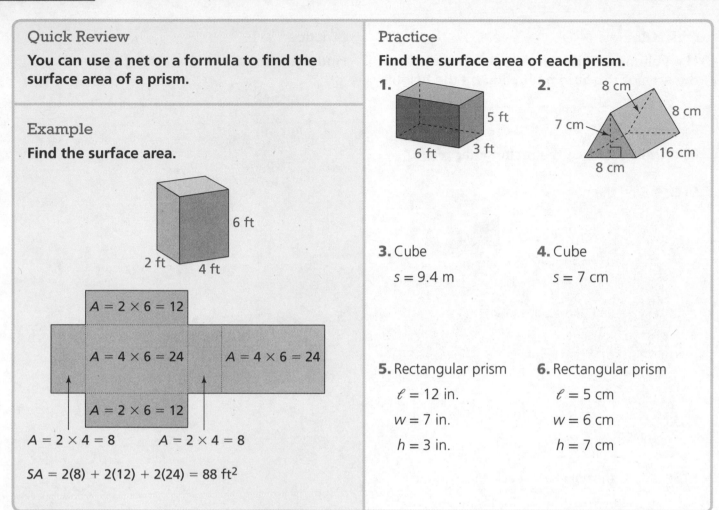

Quick Review

You can use a net or a formula to find the surface area of a prism.

Example

Find the surface area.

6 ft

2 ft   4 ft

A = 2 × 6 = 12

A = 4 × 6 = 24   A = 4 × 6 = 24

A = 2 × 6 = 12

A = 2 × 4 = 8   A = 2 × 4 = 8

SA = 2(8) + 2(12) + 2(24) = 88 ft²

Practice

Find the surface area of each prism.

1.
5 ft
6 ft   3 ft

2.
8 cm
7 cm   8 cm
8 cm   16 cm

3. Cube
s = 9.4 m

4. Cube
s = 7 cm

5. Rectangular prism
ℓ = 12 in.
w = 7 in.
h = 3 in.

6. Rectangular prism
ℓ = 5 cm
w = 6 cm
h = 7 cm

LESSON 7-7 Find Surface Areas of Pyramids

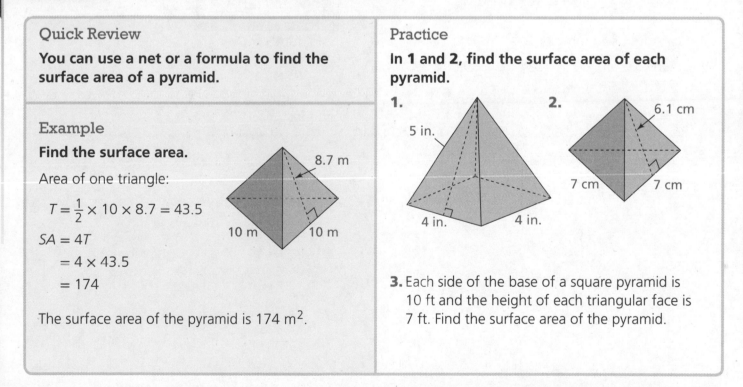

Quick Review

You can use a net or a formula to find the surface area of a pyramid.

Example

Find the surface area.

Area of one triangle:

$T = \frac{1}{2} \times 10 \times 8.7 = 43.5$

8.7 m

10 m   10 m

SA = 4T

= 4 × 43.5

= 174

The surface area of the pyramid is 174 m².

Practice

In **1** and **2**, find the surface area of each pyramid.

1.
5 in.
4 in.   4 in.

2.
6.1 cm
7 cm   7 cm

3. Each side of the base of a square pyramid is 10 ft and the height of each triangular face is 7 ft. Find the surface area of the pyramid.

Find Volume with Fractional Edge Lengths

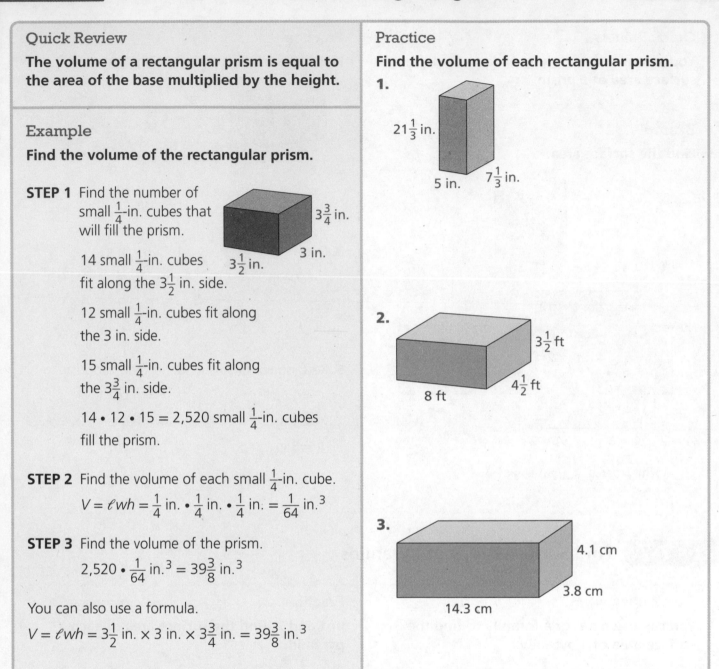

Quick Review

The volume of a rectangular prism is equal to the area of the base multiplied by the height.

Example

Find the volume of the rectangular prism.

STEP 1 Find the number of small $\frac{1}{4}$-in. cubes that will fill the prism.

14 small $\frac{1}{4}$-in. cubes fit along the $3\frac{1}{2}$ in. side.

12 small $\frac{1}{4}$-in. cubes fit along the 3 in. side.

15 small $\frac{1}{4}$-in. cubes fit along the $3\frac{3}{4}$ in. side.

$14 \cdot 12 \cdot 15 = 2{,}520$ small $\frac{1}{4}$-in. cubes fill the prism.

STEP 2 Find the volume of each small $\frac{1}{4}$-in. cube.

$V = \ell wh = \frac{1}{4}$ in. $\cdot \frac{1}{4}$ in. $\cdot \frac{1}{4}$ in. $= \frac{1}{64}$ in.^{3}

STEP 3 Find the volume of the prism.

$2{,}520 \cdot \frac{1}{64}$ in.$^3 = 39\frac{3}{8}$ in.^{3}

You can also use a formula.

$V = \ell wh = 3\frac{1}{2}$ in. $\times 3$ in. $\times 3\frac{3}{4}$ in. $= 39\frac{3}{8}$ in.^{3}

Practice

Find the volume of each rectangular prism.

1.

$21\frac{1}{3}$ in.

5 in. $7\frac{1}{3}$ in.

2.

$3\frac{1}{2}$ ft

$4\frac{1}{2}$ ft

8 ft

3.

4.1 cm

3.8 cm

14.3 cm

Hidden Clue

For each ordered pair, simplify the two coordinates. Then locate and label the corresponding point on the graph. Draw line segments to connect the points in alphabetical order. Connect *L* to *E* to complete the picture, then use the completed picture to help answer the riddle below.

I can...
multiply and divide multidigit decimals.

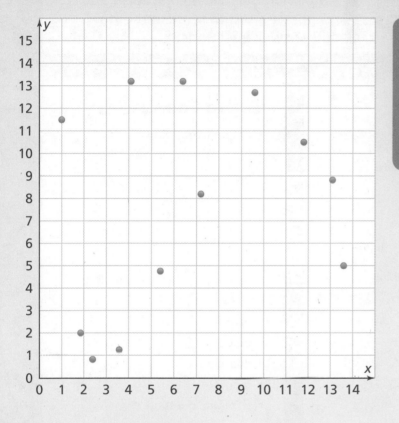

What goes up when rain comes down?

A (1.2 × 1.55, 2.7 ÷ 1.35)   ,

B (1.25 × 1.92, 0.48 ÷ 0.6)   ,

C (5.04 ÷ 1.4, 0.5 × 2.5)   ,

D (2.16 × 2.5, 11.9 ÷ 2.5)   ,

E (16.56 ÷ 2.3, 5.125 × 1.6)   ,

F (6.12 ÷ 0.45, 6.25 × 0.8)   ,

G (2.62 × 5, 12.32 ÷ 1.4)   ,

H (29.5 × 0.4, 3.675 ÷ 0.35)   ,

I (12.48 ÷ 1.3, 10.16 × 1.25)   ,

J (20 × 0.32, 59.4 ÷ 4.5)   ,

K (7.79 ÷ 1.9, 40 × 0.33)   ,

L (25 × 0.04, 48.3 ÷ 4.2)   ,

TOPIC 8

DISPLAY, DESCRIBE, AND SUMMARIZE DATA

? Topic Essential Question

How can data be described by a single number? How can tables and graphs be used to represent data and answer questions?

Topic Overview

Topic Vocabulary

- absolute deviation
- box plot
- data distribution
- frequency table
- histogram
- interquartile range (IQR)
- mean
- mean absolute deviation (MAD)
- median
- mode
- outlier
- quartile
- range
- statistical question

Lesson Digital Resources

INTERACTIVE STUDENT EDITION
Access online or offline.

VISUAL LEARNING ANIMATION
Interact with visual learning animations.

ACTIVITY Use with *Solve & Discuss It, Explore It,* and *Explain It* activities, and to explore Examples

VIDEOS Watch clips to support *3-Act Mathematical Modeling Lessons* and *STEM Proje*

Go online

Vocal Range

Vocal Range

Have you ever disagreed with the judge on a reality TV show? Reality TV competitions rely on the different opinions of the judges to make the show more exciting. There are lots of factors to consider when comparing two contestants on a show. Think about this during the 3-Act Mathematical Modeling lesson.

 PRACTICE Practice what you've learned.

 TUTORIALS Get help from *Virtual Nerd*, right when you need it.

 MATH TOOLS Explore math with digital tools.

 GAMES Play Math Games to help you learn.

 KEY CONCEPT Review important lesson content.

 GLOSSARY Read and listen to English/Spanish definitions.

ASSESSMENT Show what you've learned.

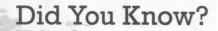
Did You Know?

Earthquakes are caused by the sudden release of energy in the Earth's crust when friction between tectonic plates causes rocks to break along fault lines.

RING OF FIRE

PACIFIC OCEAN

Nearly 80% of Earth's largest earthquakes occur along the "Ring of Fire." Many tectonic plates meet in this horseshoe-shaped region around the Pacific Ocean.

The 1964 Alaskan earthquake magnitude of 9.2 was the strongest recorded in North America. It sent tsunamis as far away as Peru, New Zealand, and Japan.

Earthquakes can cause significant damage to roadways, bridges, buildings, and other structures.

The shape of a pagoda is known for resisting damage from earthquakes.

Your Task: Shake It Up ▶

Engineers design sturdy bridges, buildings, dams and other structures that can withstand earthquakes. They also devise detection devices to predict earthquakes. You and your classmates will gather and display data about earthquake frequency and magnitude. You will analyze the data and determine what constraints engineers must consider when designing roadways, bridges, homes, and other structures.

Review What You Know!

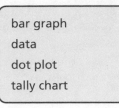

Vocabulary

Choose the best term from the box to complete each sentence.

bar graph
data
dot plot
tally chart

1. _____ are pieces of gathered information.

2. Display data as marks above a number line in a _____.

3. Use the lengths of bars to show and compare data in a _____.

Summarize Data

Use the number of text messages Henry sent each day: 6, 12, 2, 6, 3, 4, 2, 5, 6.

4. What is the least value?

5. What is the greatest value?

6. What numbers are repeated?

7. How many text messages did Henry send in all?

Display Data

8. The table shows the time students spend doing chores each day. Draw a dot plot to show the data.

Minutes Doing Chores Each Day
20, 25, 45, 20, 30, 40, 30, 25, 20, 15, 35, 40

Analyze Data

Use the graph to answer the questions about a student's test performance.

9. How many more points were earned on Test 3 than on Test 1?

10. Which two tests have the least difference in score? What is the difference?

11. What is the greatest difference between two scores? How do you know?

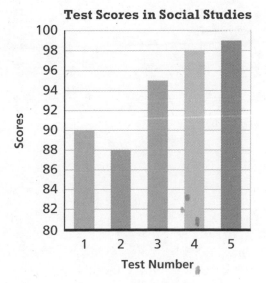

Language Development

Complete the graphic organizer. Write the definition of each measure in your own words.

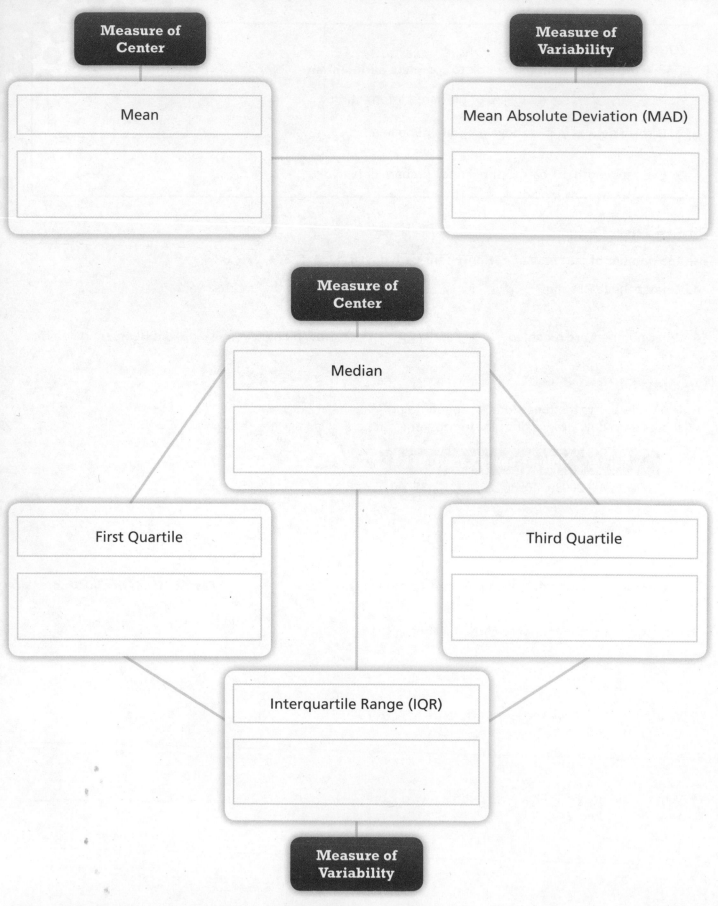

Measure of Center

Mean

Measure of Variability

Mean Absolute Deviation (MAD)

Measure of Center

Median

First Quartile

Third Quartile

Interquartile Range (IQR)

Measure of Variability

PROJECT
8A

If you recorded a video blog, what would it be about?

PROJECT: EXPLORE VIDEO BLOGS

PROJECT
8B

How many different breakfast cereals have you tasted?

PROJECT: INVESTIGATE CEREALS

PROJECT 8C

How far could you bike before needing to rest?

PROJECT: ANALYZE A TIME TRIAL

PROJECT 8D

If you could change something at your school, what would it be?

PROJECT: SURVEY YOUR SCHOOL

Solve & Discuss It!

ACTIVITY

Ms. Jackson wrote a question on the board. Then she collected student responses to the question and recorded them in a tally chart. What question could she have asked? Is there more than one possible response to the question? Explain.

Books	
0	III
1	HHHT
2	HHHT I
3	IIII
4	II
5	I

I can...
identify and write statistical questions.

Make Sense and Persevere
What other questions could you ask that would result in a variety of numerical answers?

Focus on math practices

Reasoning Suppose Ms. Jackson wants to know the amount of time her students spent outdoors the previous afternoon. What question might she ask each student to gather the data?

? **Essential Question** ▷ How are statistical questions different from other questions?

VISUAL LEARNING   ASSESS

EXAMPLE 1 👁 **Recognize a Statistical Question**

Scan for Multimedia

Mr. Borden asked his students a question and recorded the data in a table. What question did Mr. Borden ask?

- What is the area of an $8\frac{1}{2}" \times 11"$ sheet of notebook paper?

- How many sheets of paper did you use last week?

- Did Bill use notebook paper to write his book report?

> **Make Sense and Persevere** How does thinking about possible answers to the questions help you determine which questions are statistical?

Sheets of Paper Used Last Week

Number of Sheets	Number of Students
5	I
10	I
15	II
20	IIII
25	ⅢⅠ
30	Ⅲ

A **statistical question** always has variability in the responses. This is, it has a range of responses.

The question *How many sheets of paper did you use last week?* can have a range of answers so it is a statistical question.

The questions *What is the area of an $8\frac{1}{2}" \times 11"$ sheet of notebook paper?* and *Did Bill use notebook paper to write his book report?* have only one answer, so they are not statistical questions.

Mr. Borden asked, *How many sheets of paper did you use last week?*

You can display the answers to Mr. Borden's question in a bar graph.

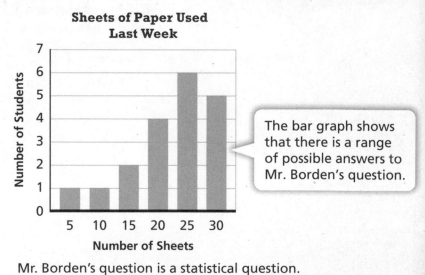

Sheets of Paper Used Last Week

The bar graph shows that there is a range of possible answers to Mr. Borden's question.

Mr. Borden's question is a statistical question.

☑ **Try It!**

Is the question *What was the high temperature on March 8 of last year?* a statistical question? Explain.

Convince Me! How could you change the question above to make it a statistical question?

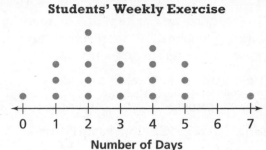

ACTIVITY   ASSESS

Lucia surveyed the students in her class and made a dot plot of the results. What question could Lucia have asked?

Look at the title and labels on the dot plot.

> **Model with Math** A dot plot can be used to display the answers to a statistical question.

Students' Weekly Exercise

```
                    •
              •     •     •
        •     •     •     •     •
        •     •     •     •     •
  •     •     •     •     •     •           •
◄───┼─────┼─────┼─────┼─────┼─────┼─────┼─────┼───►
    0     1     2     3     4     5     6     7
```
Number of Days

The dot plot shows the number of days different students exercise each week. The statistical question Lucia could have asked is *How many days do you exercise each week?*

☑ **Try It!**

What is another statistical question Lucia might ask about the exercise the students in her class do each week?

EXAMPLE **3** 👆 **Use Data to Identify a Statistical Question with Two Answers**

Dante surveyed students to see how they feel about a proposal to choose a new school mascot. The frequency table shows the results. What question did Dante likely ask? Is this a statistical question?

Dante likely asked a question such as *Do you want a new mascot?* There are only two answers, Yes or No. Because there is more than one possible answer, this is a statistical question.

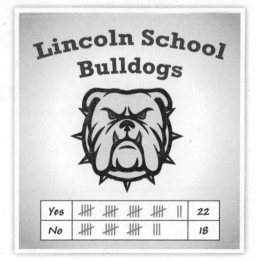

Lincoln School Bulldogs

Yes	⳦ ⳦ ⳦ ⳦ ‖	22
No	⳦ ⳦ ⳦ ⳾	18

☑ **Try It!**

How could Dante change his statistical question so that there would be more than two possible answers?

To recognize and write statistical questions, determine whether the question has only one answer or several different answers. Statistical questions have a variety of different answers.

How many nickels are in a dollar?	**Not statistical**
Which former U.S. president appears on a nickel?	**Not statistical**
How many nickels do students carry in their backpacks?	Statistical

Do You Understand?

1. **? Essential Question** How are statistical questions different from other questions?

2. **Generalize** How does examining the answers to a question help you determine if the question is a statistical question?

3. Write a question about movies that your classmates saw last month. Is the question you wrote a statistical question? Justify your response.

4. Choose which is a statistical question: *What are the ages of the students in this class?* or *How many pennies equal 1 dollar?* Explain.

Do You Know How?

5. Determine which of the questions below are statistical questions.

   a. In which months are the birthdays of everyone in your class?

   b. Does Sue wear glasses?

   c. Who is the current president of the United States?

   d. How tall are the students in Grade 6?

   e. What is the least populated state?

   f. How many fish are in the pond?

6. Mr. Borden asked his students, *How far from school do you live?* Is his question a statistical question? Explain.

7. Mr. Borden also asked his students, *How do you get to school each day?* Is this question statistical? Explain.

Name: _____

Practice & Problem Solving

In **8** and **9**, write a statistical question that you could ask to gather data on each topic.

8. Number of pets classmates own

9. Heights of different household plants

10. Kim asked her classmates, *How many siblings do you have?* She collected the following responses: 0, 1, 2, 1, 2, 0, 3, 1, 0, 5, 5, 1, 3, 1, 0, 2, 4, 1, 3, 0. Make a dot plot to display the data.

11. Sergei asked his classmates, *Will you take Spanish or French next year?* He collected these responses: 15 classmates chose Spanish and 13 chose French. Make a frequency table to display the data.

12. Is the following a statistical question? Explain. *How many plays do students see in a year?*

13. Is the following a statistical question? Explain. *How do shoppers in a town pay for groceries?*

In **14** and **15**, use the dot plot at the right.

14. **Make Sense and Persevere** What statistical question could have been asked to collect the data shown in the dot plot?

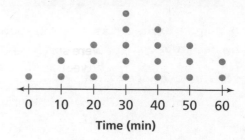

Time Spent on Homework

15. **Higher Order Thinking** If the data in the dot plot show how many minutes students spent on homework the previous night, how many hours in all did these students spend doing homework? Did a typical student from this group spend more or fewer than 20 minutes on homework?

16. **Vocabulary** Wyatt says that a *statistical question* must have a numerical answer. Do you agree with Wyatt? Explain.

17. **Reasoning** Ms. Miller asks parents, *Do you support switching to a new lunch vendor for our school program?* How many different responses could she get? Is this a statistical question?

☑ Assessment Practice

18. Ms. Williams asked each student in her class these two questions:

    • *How many digits are in a phone number, including the area code?*

    • *In a typical week, on how many days do you spend some time watching television?*

    Which of the questions that Ms. Williams asked is a statistical question? Explain.

19. Select all of the statistical questions.

    ☐ What is your favorite color?

    ☐ Does Carmen wear braces?

    ☐ How many books did you read last week?

    ☐ Which U.S. state has the largest land area?

    ☐ Should the basketball team purchase new uniforms?

Lesson 8-2
Summarize Data
Using Mean,
Median, Mode,
and Range

Go Online

Solve & Discuss It!

Eight students were surveyed about the number of hours they spend each week reading for fun. Order their responses from least to greatest values. What do you notice about the number of hours these students spent reading each week?

I can...
identify the mean, median, mode, and range of a data set.

Hours spent reading
for fun each week:
11, 4, 7, 13, 3, 7, 12, 5

Look for Relationships
How does ordering the responses from least to greatest help you analyze the data set?

Focus on math practices

Critique Reasoning Jamal says that the middle value in a data set is the number that occurs most often. Evan disagrees. Why does Jamal say what he says and why does Evan disagree? Explain.

VISUAL LEARNING   ASSESS

EXAMPLE 1 — Use the Mean to Describe a Data Set

Scan for Multimedia

Carla is in a bowling league. The league is ranking the teams by average score. What is the mean, or average, final score of the five bowlers on Carla's team?

The **mean**, or average, is the sum of all the values in a data set divided by the total number of data values in the set.

> **Generalize** You can summarize a data set by using a mean.

	9	10	FINAL SCORE
Desmond	86 7 2	95 6 3 –	95
Ramon	80 4 2	87 7 0 –	87
Kaitlin	77 5 1	84 4 3 –	84
Maria	74 2 4	81 5 2 –	81
Carla	75 3 3	83 6 2 –	83

Team Average   n

To find the mean, equally share the final scores among the five bowlers.

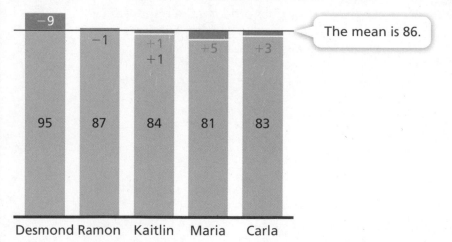

The mean is 86.

To calculate the mean, add the scores in the data set. Then divide the sum by the number of values in the data set.

$$\begin{array}{r} 95 \\ 87 \\ 84 \\ 81 \\ + 83 \\ \hline 430 \end{array} \qquad \begin{array}{r} 86 \\ 5\overline{)430} \\ -40 \\ \hline 30 \\ -30 \\ \hline 0 \end{array}$$

The mean, or average, final score is 86.

A mean is a measure of center. A measure of center summarizes a data set with a single value.

☑ Try It!

The next week, Maria bowls a 151-point game. The other bowlers match their scores. What is the new mean final score for the team? Explain.

Convince Me! How did the mean final score change from the Example to the Try It!?

EXAMPLE 2 ▶ 👆 **Use the Median to Describe a Data Set**

Trey and Sarah each download songs to their music libraries. Their players list each type of music and the total playing time in minutes for each type. How can Trey and Sarah each summarize their data sets using the median?

The **median** is a measure of center. It is the middle data value. To find the median, order the values from least to greatest, then find the middle value.

Trey's Music Library

Music Type	Minutes
Blues	62
Classical	72
Country	61
Gospel	67
Jazz	67
Movie Soundtrack	63
Popular	59

Sarah's Music Library

Music Type	Minutes
Rock	37
Rap	42
Hip Hop	38
Bluegrass	46
New Age	51
Opera	35

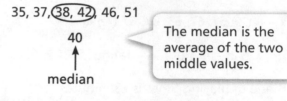

Find the median for Trey's data set.

59, 61, 62, (63), 67, 67, 72

↑
median

Trey's median playing time is 63 minutes.

Find the median for Sarah's data set.

35, 37, (38, 42), 46, 51

40

↑
median

💬 The median is the average of the two middle values.

Sarah's median playing time is 40 minutes.

EXAMPLE 3 ▶ 👆 **Use the Mode to Describe a Data Set**

Look at Trey's and Sarah's music libraries. How can Trey and Sarah each summarize their data sets using the mode?

The **mode** is a measure of center. It is the value that occurs most often. A data set can have one mode, no mode, or more than one mode.

Find the mode for Trey's data set.

59, 61, 62, 63, (67, 67), 72

↑↑
mode

The value 67 appears twice. Every other value only appears once.

Trey's mode playing time is 67 minutes.

Find the mode for Sarah's data set.

35, 37, 38, 42, 46, 51

💬 No values repeat in Sarah's data set.

There is no mode playing time in Sarah's data set.

☑ **Try It!**

Nadia's grades on four quizzes were 95, 75, 85, and 95. Find the mean, median, and mode for Nadia's grades.

EXAMPLE 4

EXAMPLE 4 👆 Use the Range to Describe a Data Set

Look at Trey's and Sarah's music libraries. What is the range of the playing times in each of their data sets?

The **range** is a measure of variability. A measure of variability describes how the values in a data set vary with a single number. The range is the difference of the greatest value and the least value.

Trey's Music Library

Music Type	Minutes
Blues	62
Classical	72
Country	61
Gospel	67
Jazz	67
Movie Soundtrack	63
Popular	59

Sarah's Music Library

Music Type	Minutes
Rock	37
Rap	42
Hip Hop	38
Bluegrass	46
New Age	51
Opera	35

Find the range for Trey's data set.

least value → ⑤⑨ 61, 62, 63, 67, 67, ㉒ ← greatest value

72 − 59 = ⑬ ← range

The range of playing times is 13 minutes.

Find the range for Sarah's data set.

least value → ㉟ 37, 38, 42, 46, ㊿① ← greatest value

51 − 35 = ⑯ ← range

The range of playing times is 16 minutes.

EXAMPLE 5 👆 Use the Mean, Median, Mode, and Range to Describe a Data Set

Seven people waited in line for the "Whirl and Twirl" carnival ride. Find the mean, median, mode, and range of the wait times for the carnival ride. What do the mean, median, and mode tell you about the wait times? What does the range, as a measure of variability, tell you about the wait times?

Mean: 13

Median: 13

Modes: 12 and 15

Range: 5

Carnival Ride Wait Times

Person	Wait time (min.)
A	12
B	12
C	15
D	10
E	14
F	15
G	13

The mean, median, and mode each give a measure of the typical wait time for the ride. The mean and median wait times were 13 minutes. Two pairs each waited 12 or 15 minutes. The range uses a single number to describe how the wait times vary. The wait times vary by 5 minutes.

 Try It!

Find the mean, median, mode, and range for the following set of data.

4, 6, 8, 3, 2, 1, 0, 12, 9

You can summarize a set of data using a measure of center, such as the mean, median, or mode, or a measure of variability, such as the range.

Mean

$(7 + 10 + 16 + 9 + 12 + 21 + 14 + 8 + 13 + 15) \div 10 = 12.5$

Median

7, 8, 9, 10, 12, 13, 14, 15, 16, 21

$(12 + 13) \div 2 = 12.5$

Mode

7, 8, 9, 10, 12, 13, 14, 15, 16, 21

There is no mode.

Range

7, 8, 9, 10, 12, 13, 14, 15, 16, 21

$21 - 7 = 14$

The average number of hours of TV watched each week is 12.5 hours.
The range of hours watched is 14 hours.

Number of Hours of TV Watched in a Week	
Juan	7
Tyrone	10
Abigail	16
Lateisha	9
Helen	12
Albert	21
Tim	14
Josh	8
Anita	13
Henry	15

Do You Understand?

1. **? Essential Question** How can you use a single measure to describe a data set?

2. Maddie scored 3 goals, 2 goals, and 4 goals during her last three soccer games. How can you find the mean, or average, number of goals Maddie scored?

3. **Use Structure** Why is it important to order the data when finding the median?

Do You Know How?

The table shows data about the students in three classes.

Teacher	Boys	Girls
Ms. Green	15	14
Mr. Nesbit	12	12
Ms. Jackson	12	16

4. What is the mean number of boys in the three classes? What is the mean number of girls in the three classes?

5. What is the mode of the number of girls in the three classes?

6. What is the median number of students in the three classes?

Name: _____

Practice & Problem Solving

In 7–10, use the data shown in the table to find each mean.

7. Technical marks from judges

8. Presentation marks from judges

9. Find the combined marks, or total score, awarded by each of the 7 judges. Record your answers in the table.

10. What is the mean total score awarded by the judges?

A U.S. Figure Skater's Scores			
Judge	Technical Marks	Presentation Marks	Total Score
A	5.9	5.4	
B	5.8	5.7	
C	5.8	5.6	
D	5.6	5.3	
E	5.9	5.5	
F	5.6	5.3	
G	6.0	5.7	

In 11–14, use the data in the table.

States Traveled To or Lived In
1, 3, 5, 2, 5, 2, 10, 7, 1, 2, 4, 1, 2, 7, 12

11. Order the data from least to greatest.

12. What are the median, mode, and range of the data?

13. **Use Structure** The student who traveled to 3 states visited 3 new states during a vacation. Does increasing the 3 to 6 change the median? If so, how?

14. **Look for Relationships** Does increasing the 3 to 6 change the mode? If so, how?

In 15–17, use the data table.

15. What is the average low temperature forecasted for the five days?

16. What is the average high temperature forecasted for the five days?

17. The forecast for Wednesday is later changed to a high of 70°F. Without calculating the new mean, describe how this changes the mean high temperature for the 5 days.

Forecasted Temperatures

Day	Low (°F)	High (°F)
Monday	42	55
Tuesday	44	57
Wednesday	45	60
Thursday	34	45
Friday	40	50

18. **Vocabulary** What term is used to describe the difference between the greatest and the least values of a data set?

19. **Critique Reasoning** Lewis thinks that since the data 5, 0, 4, 0, 0 has a mode of 0, the data has no mode. Critique Lewis's reasoning.

20. Chester scored 84, 88, and 80 on his first 3 math tests. How can you find Chester's mean, or average, score on these tests?

21. **Reasoning** Use the information in Exercise 20. Suppose Chester scores a 90 on his next test. Without doing any calculations, will Chester's mean score increase, decrease, or stay the same? Explain.

22. On Monday, Jeremiah collects data on the number of cars that pass through an intersection each hour from 6 A.M. to 10 A.M. He records the following data: 15, 27, 37, 29, and 12. If Jeremiah removes the 12 from his data set, will the mean change? Explain.

23. On Tuesday, Jeremiah finds the mean number of cars that pass through the same intersection from 6 A.M. to 10 A.M. was 22. Using the data from Exercise 22, how many fewer cars passed through the intersection on Tuesday?

In 24–26, use the data table.

24. What are the median, mode, and range of these data?

25. What is the mean number of moons for the 8 planets, rounded to the nearest whole number?

26. If you include Pluto's moons in the data, the median is 5.

   a. How many moons does Pluto have? Explain.

   b. Would including Pluto affect the range of the data? Explain.

Known Number of Moons of the Planets	
Mercury	0
Venus	0
Earth	1
Mars	2
Jupiter	50
Saturn	53
Uranus	27
Neptune	13

Pluto is a dwarf planet.

27. **Higher Order Thinking** Is the median always, sometimes, or never one of the data values? Explain.

28. **Critique Reasoning** Maria says the mean of the scores 7, 8, 3, 0, 2 is 5, because she added the scores and divided by 4. Is she correct? Explain why or why not.

✓ Assessment Practice

29. The cost of 8 different sets of golf clubs is shown in the data table. A new brand of golf clubs for $533 is now being sold at the shop. Which of the following statements about the data is true?

   Ⓐ The mean cost will decrease.

   Ⓑ The range of the costs will increase.

   Ⓒ The mean cost will stay the same.

   Ⓓ The range of the costs will stay the same.

Price of Golf Clubs (dollars per set)
265
237
325
281
265
252
494
273

Solve & Discuss It! ACTIVITY

To track how many raisins are needed for packaging, a quality control inspector at a food processing plant collected data for the number of raisins in small boxes. Describe the data, including minimum value, maximum value, and median. Then describe what you notice about the values between the minimum and the median, and between the median and maximum.

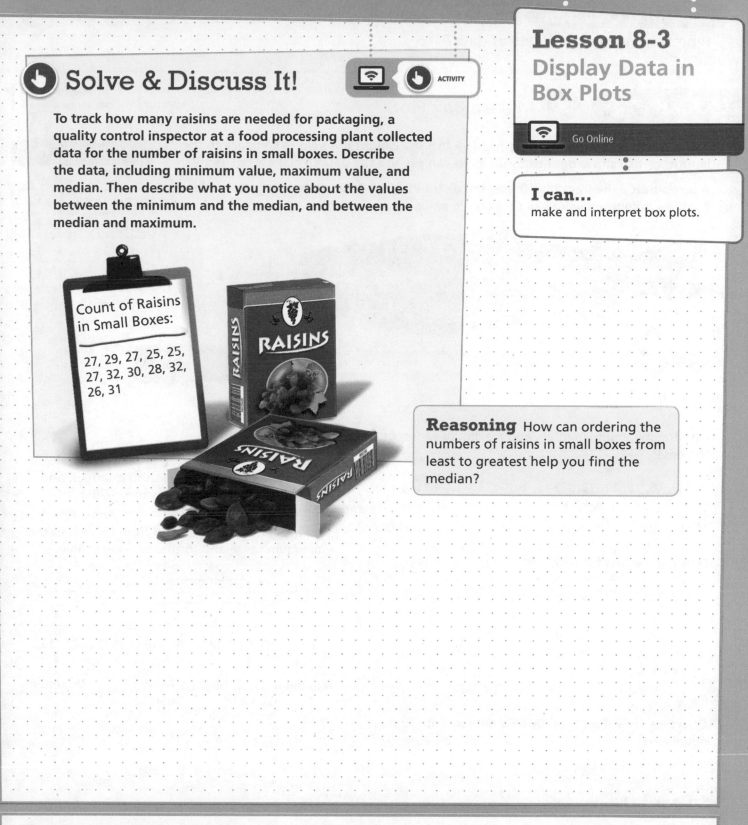

Count of Raisins in Small Boxes:

27, 29, 27, 25, 25, 27, 32, 30, 28, 32, 26, 31

I can...
make and interpret box plots.

Reasoning How can ordering the numbers of raisins in small boxes from least to greatest help you find the median?

Focus on math practices

Construct Arguments The median of the first half of the data is 26.5, and the median of the second half of the data is 30.5. Why would this information be helpful and what do those medians show? Explain.

VISUAL LEARNING   ASSESS

EXAMPLE 1 ◉ Make a Box Plot

Scan for Multimedia

Helen wants to display the lengths of 15 fish she caught this year to compare to the lengths of fish she caught last year. How can she use the data to make a box plot?

A box plot is a diagram that shows the distribution of data values using the median, quartiles, minimum value, and maximum value on a number line.

Length of Fish (in.)		
7	9	10
7	13	13
10	15	15
18	11	13
22	14	17

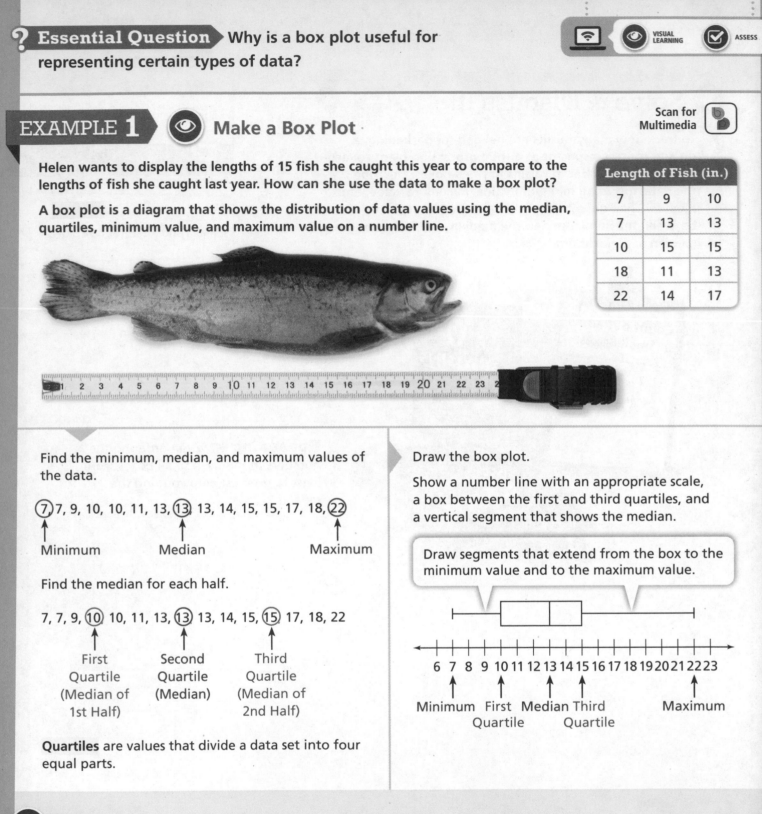

Find the minimum, median, and maximum values of the data.

⑦ 7, 9, 10, 10, 11, 13, ⑬ 13, 14, 15, 15, 17, 18, ㉒

↑ Minimum   ↑ Median   ↑ Maximum

Find the median for each half.

7, 7, 9, ⑩ 10, 11, 13, ⑬ 13, 14, 15, ⑮ 17, 18, 22

↑ First Quartile (Median of 1st Half)   ↑ Second Quartile (Median)   ↑ Third Quartile (Median of 2nd Half)

Quartiles are values that divide a data set into four equal parts.

Draw the box plot.

Show a number line with an appropriate scale, a box between the first and third quartiles, and a vertical segment that shows the median.

Draw segments that extend from the box to the minimum value and to the maximum value.

6 7 8 9 10 11 12 13 14 15 16 17 18 19 20 21 22 23

↑ Minimum   ↑ First Quartile   ↑ Median   ↑ Third Quartile   ↑ Maximum

☑ Try It!

The lengths in inches of 11 fish that Helen caught last year are listed below.

7, 8, 12, 12, 12, 13, 14, 15, 16, 17, 22

Circle the first quartile, median, and third quartile.

Convince Me! How is the distribution of Helen's data this year different from Helen's data last year? Draw a box plot of last year's data and use it to support your answer.

6 7 8 9 10 11 12 13 14 15 16 17 18 19 20 21 22 23

EXAMPLE 2 **Make a Box Plot When the Number of Values Is Even**

ACTIVITY ASSESS

The Earth Club collected enough donations online to build compost bins. How can the club record the donation information in a box plot?

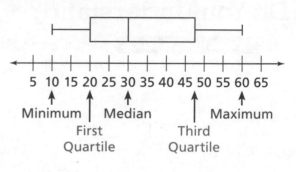

Earth Club Sign Up Log In

Fund-Raiser

Donations Received Thank you!			
$50	Ken M.	$25	Anon.
$35	Ann K.	$15	Jay T.
$45	J. W.	$15	Ben A.
$50	Anon.	$10	Anon.
$25	Anon.	$60	Nia M.
$25	Hal K.	$45	Anon.

COMPOST BIN

> **Model with Math** A box plot is helpful when analyzing a data set because it visually represents the data set by dividing it into four equal parts. A data table does not visually show the division of data.

STEP 1 Find the minimum, median, and maximum values as well as the first and third quartiles.

> There are 12 values. So, the median is the average of the two middle numbers.

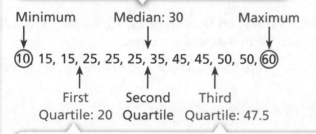

Minimum   Median: 30   Maximum

⑩ 15, 15, 25, 25, 25, 35, 45, 45, 50, 50, ⑥⓪

First Quartile: 20   Second Quartile   Third Quartile: 47.5

> There are 6 values in each half. The quartiles are the averages of the two middle numbers in each half.

STEP 2 Draw a box plot.

The donation values range from $10 to $60, in $5 increments. So, a good scale for the number line is $5 to $65, numbered by 5s.

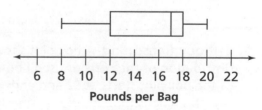

5 10 15 20 25 30 35 40 45 50 55 60 65

Minimum | Median   Maximum
First Quartile   Third Quartile

EXAMPLE 3 **Interpret a Box Plot**

The box plot shows the distribution of the weights, in pounds, of bags of donated clothing. What information do you know from the box plot?

The minimum is 8, so the lightest bag weighs 8 pounds.

The maximum is 20, so the heaviest bag weighs 20 pounds.

The median weight for the bags is about 17 pounds.

The first quartile weight is 12 pounds, and the third quartile weight is 18 pounds.

Bags of Donated Clothing

6   8   10   12   14   16   18   20   22

Pounds per Bag

✓ Try It!

The ages of 12 volunteers participating in a beach clean-up are shown:

15, 27, 9, 15, 21, 9, 21, 9, 15, 21, 21, 24

Record the ages in a box plot.

A box plot shows a distribution of data values on a number line. A box plot visually represents a data set divided into four equal parts.

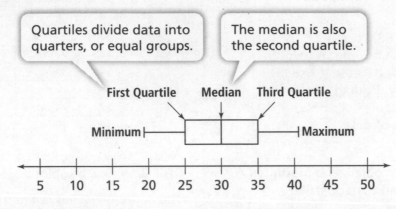

Quartiles divide data into quarters, or equal groups.

The median is also the second quartile.

Do You Understand?

1. **Essential Question** Why is a box plot useful for representing certain types of data?

2. What values are included inside the box of a box plot?

3. **Critique Reasoning** A box plot shows the distribution of the costs of used books. The box of the box plot starts at $2 and ends at $5. Alex says this means that about one-quarter of the books cost between $2 and $5. Is Alex correct? Explain.

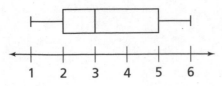

Do You Know How?

Sarah's scores on tests were 79, 75, 82, 90, 73, 82, 78, 85, and 78. In 4–8, use the data.

4. What are the minimum and maximum test scores?

5. Find the median.

6. Find the first and the third quartiles.

7. Draw a box plot that shows the distribution of Sarah's test scores.

8. Eric is in Sarah's class. This box plot shows his scores on the same nine tests. How do Eric's scores compare to Sarah's?

Eric's Tests

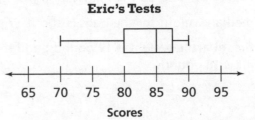

Scores

Practice & Problem Solving ✏️ ⏻

Scan for Multimedia 🅱️

Leveled Practice In **9** and **10**, use this data set, which shows how many minutes Enzo practiced violin each day for 10 days.

40, 25, 45, 55, 30, 25, 30, 50, 30, 40

9. Find the statistical measures that you need to make a box plot of Enzo's practice times.

[ ] 25, [ ] 30, 30, 40, 40, [ ] 50, [ ]

↑ Minimum ↑ First Quartile ↑ Median: [ ] ↑ Third Quartile ↑ Maximum

10. Complete the box plot to represent Enzo's practice times.

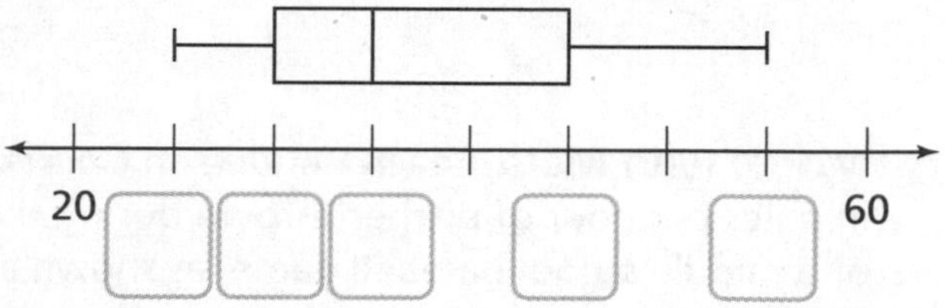

[box plot with labels 20 and 60, five empty boxes below]

In **11** and **12**, use this data set, which shows the prices, in dollars, of tickets to 10 plays at the community theater.

14, 22, 8, 14, 16, 8, 20, 14, 10, 18

11. Find the minimum, maximum, median, and quartile ticket prices.

Minimum: [ ]   First Quartile: [ ]

Median: [ ]   Third Quartile: [ ]

Maximum: [ ]

12. Make a box plot to display the ticket prices.

In **13** and **14**, draw box plots using the data provided.

13. The sprint times, in seconds, of students who tried out for the track team:

44, 40, 40, 42, 49, 43, 41, 47, 54, 48, 42, 52, 48

14. Scores earned on science tests:

73, 78, 66, 61, 85, 90, 99, 76, 64, 70, 72, 72, 93, 81

In **15** and **16**, use the box plot to answer the question.

15. How many words per minute does the fastest keyboarder type?

Keyboarding Speeds

[box plot]

20 30 40 50 60 70 80 90 100 110

Words per Minute

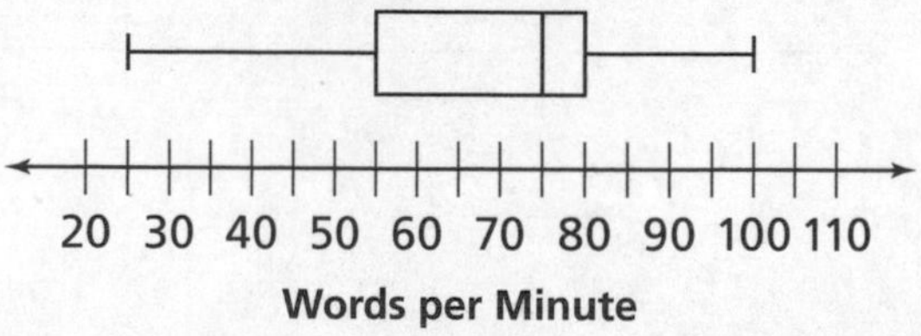

16. How many words per minute do the fastest 50% of keyboarders type?

Keyboarding Speeds

[box plot]

10 20 30 40 50 60 70 80 90 100

Words per Minute

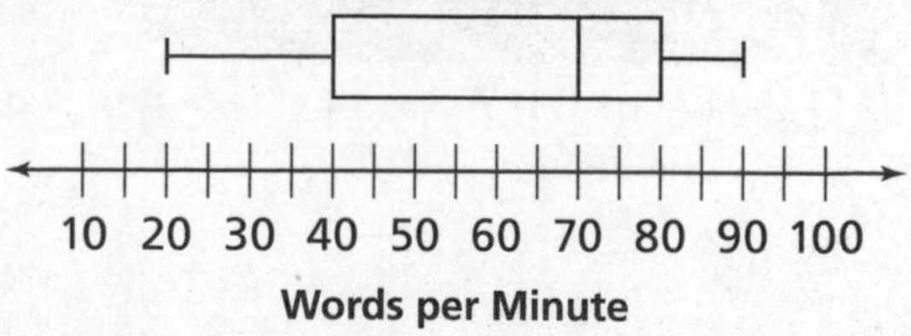

17. **Reasoning** The price per share of Electric Company's stock during 9 days, rounded to the nearest dollar, was as follows: $16, $17, $16, $16, $18, $18, $21, $22, $19.

Use a box plot to determine how much greater the third quartile's price per share was than the first quartile's price per share.

18. **Make Sense and Persevere** The temperature forecast for Topeka, Kansas, for the next 8 days is shown. Use a box plot to determine the range for the lower half of the temperatures.

19. **Model with Math** Coach Henderson clocked the speeds in miles per hour of pitches thrown during the first inning of a middle school baseball game, as shown at the right.

Draw a box plot to display the data and write two conclusions about the data shown in the box plot.

Speeds of Pitches Thrown (in miles per hour)
45.3 47 48.1 51.3 55.8 61.1 48.5 60.7 49

20. **Critique Reasoning** Tanya recorded the ages of 10 local babysitters: 20, 16, 18, 13, 14, 13, 12, 16, 22, 18. She says that the box plot below shows the distribution of ages. What error did she make?

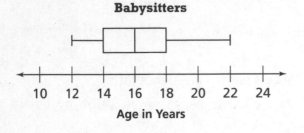

Babysitters

Age in Years

21. **Higher Order Thinking** Alana made this box plot to represent classroom attendance last month. Without seeing the values, what conclusions can you make about whether attendance was mostly high or low last month? Explain.

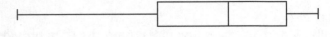

22. Use the data given to complete the box plot.

The ages in years of the students in Caryn's gymnastics class are shown in the table.

Ages of Students in Years
12 11 9 18 10 11 7 16 14 11 6

Complete the box plot to show the distribution of the students' ages.

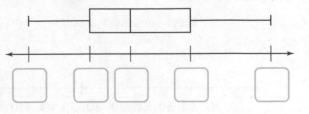

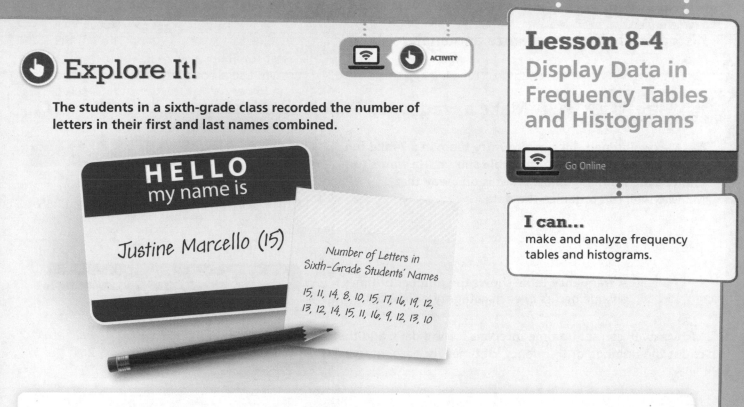
Explore It!

ACTIVITY

The students in a sixth-grade class recorded the number of letters in their first and last names combined.

HELLO
my name is

Justine Marcello (15)

Number of Letters in Sixth-Grade Students' Names

15, 11, 14, 8, 10, 15, 17, 16, 19, 12,
13, 12, 14, 15, 11, 16, 9, 12, 13, 10

I can...
make and analyze frequency tables and histograms.

A. How can the data be organized? Describe one way to organize the data.

B. Describe another way to organize the data.

C. Compare the two ways. What do you notice about the data in each way?

Focus on math practices
Generalize What generalization can you make about the data set?

EXAMPLE 1  **Make a Frequency Table and a Histogram**

Scan for
Multimedia

Mr. Maxwell timed the cross-country team in a 2-mile run and recorded the times in the table shown. He wants to analyze the runners' times. What is one way that Mr. Maxwell can organize the data?

Team Times					
16:45	14:25	18:40	16:03	15:12	19:15
17:14	14:02	16:52	15:18	17:49	17:55

A **frequency table** shows the number of times a value occurs in each category or interval.

Mr. Maxwell can set up time intervals for the data, and then count the number, or frequency, of times for each interval.

Running Times	Tally	Frequency
14:00–15:59	IIII	4
16:00–17:59	LHT I	6
18:00–19:59	II	2

Then he can use the frequency table to make a histogram.

Display the data by drawing a bar for each interval.

Look for Relationships How is a histogram similar to and different from a bar graph?

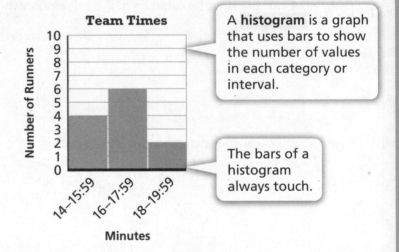

A **histogram** is a graph that uses bars to show the number of values in each category or interval.

The bars of a histogram always touch.

✓ **Try It!**

This histogram shows a different way to represent Mr. Maxwell's data. Fill in the boxes with appropriate times and shade the bars for the last three intervals. How have the intervals changed?

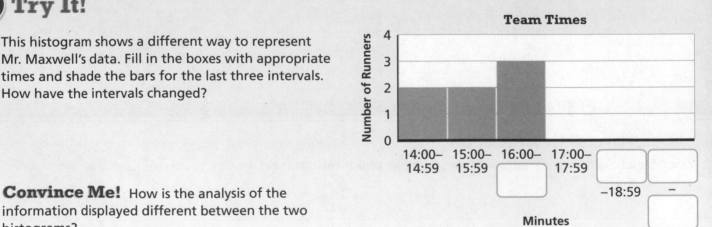

Convince Me! How is the analysis of the information displayed different between the two histograms?

EXAMPLE 2 ▶ Use a Frequency Table to Solve Problems

Zack surveys a group of middle school students and asks them how many texts they sent yesterday. The table shows the results.

a. **Is the greatest number of texts sent between 60 and 79?**

The greatest frequency is 11, which corresponds to students who sent 60–79 texts. However, the greatest number of texts sent is between 80 and 99.

b. **Is the lowest number of texts sent between 20 and 39?**

The lowest frequency is 4, which corresponds to students who sent 20–39 texts. However, the lowest number of texts sent is between 0 and 19.

Number of Texts	Tally	Frequency
0–19	卌	5
20–39	‖‖	4
40–59	卌 卌	10
60–79	卌 卌 ‖	11
80–99	卌 ‖‖	8

✅ Try It!

How many students sent between 20 and 59 texts?

EXAMPLE 3 ▶ Use a Histogram to Solve Problems

The histogram shows the number of points that Kendra scored during each basketball game she played last season.

a. **How many games did Kendra play last season?**

The total number of games can be found by adding the number of games shown by each bar.

$3 + 0 + 6 + 2 + 1 = 12$

Kendra played 12 games.

b. **In how many games did Kendra score from 5 to 9 points?**

There is no bar on the histogram for 5–9 points. Kendra did not score 5–9 points in any games last season.

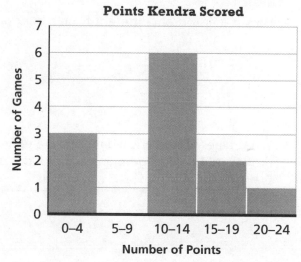

✅ Try It!

Does the histogram show the mode of the number of points Kendra scored in the games? Explain.

Data displays can be used to help make sense of data.

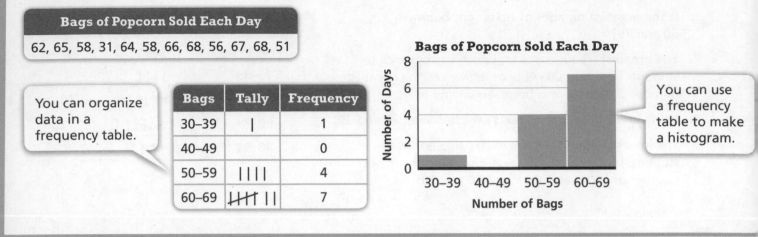

Bags of Popcorn Sold Each Day
62, 65, 58, 31, 64, 58, 66, 68, 56, 67, 68, 51

You can organize data in a frequency table.

Bags	Tally	Frequency
30–39	I	1
40–49		0
50–59	IIII	4
60–69	⫟⫟⫟ II	7

Bags of Popcorn Sold Each Day

You can use a frequency table to make a histogram.

Do You Understand?

1. **Essential Question** How can a frequency table or histogram help you organize and analyze data?

2. How is a histogram different from a bar graph?

3. What types of numerical data sets are easier to display using a histogram instead of a dot plot? Explain.

4. **Reasoning** How are frequency tables and histograms alike and how are they different?

Do You Know How?

5. A data set contains ages ranging from 6 to 27.

6, 11, 9, 13, 18, 15, 21, 15, 17, 24, 27, 12

Complete the frequency table and histogram.

Ages	Tally	Frequency
6–10		
11–15		
16–20		
21–25		
26–30		

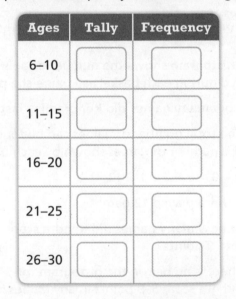

Ages in Data Set

Name: _____

Practice & Problem Solving

Leveled Practice In 6–11, use the data in the chart.

Number of Songs on Phones
125, 289, 115, 203, 192, 178, 256,
248, 165, 233, 147, 209, 225,
184, 156, 201, 143, 125, 263, 210

6. Complete the frequency table below for the number of songs stored on phones.

Song Range	Tally	Frequency
100–149	~~IIII~~	5
150–199	~~IIII~~	5
200–249	~~IIII~~ I	7
250–299	~~IIII~~	5

7. Use your frequency table to complete the histogram.

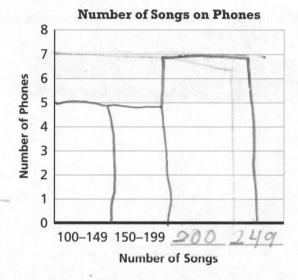

8. How many people have between 150 and 199 songs stored on their phones?

5

9. Do more than half of the phones have fewer than 149 songs stored on them?

NO

10. Is the greatest number of songs stored on phones between 200 and 249 songs?

Yes

11. Are there more phones that have between 200 and 249 songs stored on them than have between 150 and 199 songs?

Yes

In **12–14**, use the data in the histogram.

12. How many students in Ms. Gioia's class took the science test?

27

13. How many more students had scores that were 80 or lower than had scores that were higher than 90?

1

14. **Be Precise** Can you tell from the histogram how many students scored 83 on the test? Explain.

None because

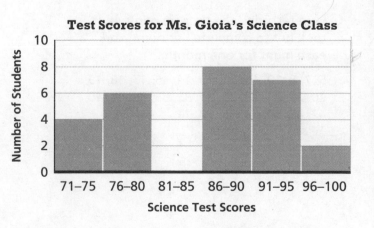

In **15–17**, use the data in the chart.

Bicycle Stopping Times (in seconds)
15, 25, 11, 8, 10, 21, 18, 23, 19, 9, 14, 16, 24, 18, 10, 16, 24, 18, 9, 14

15. **Reasoning** Todd wants to know how many people took 20 seconds or more to stop a bike safely. Would a frequency table or a histogram be the better way to show this? Explain.

16. **Higher Order Thinking** When organizing the data, what interval should Todd use? Explain.

17. **Model with Math** Make a frequency table and histogram for the data.

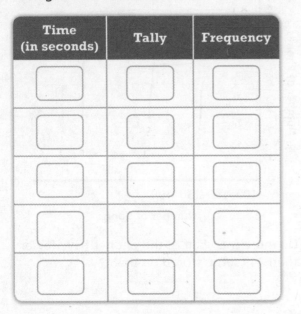

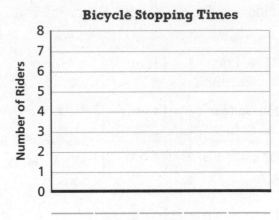

Bicycle Stopping Times

Number of Riders

Number of Seconds

✓ Assessment Practice

18. Use the data given to complete the histogram.

Lissa recorded the time, in minutes, it took her to complete her homework each night for one month.

5, 7, 8, 10, 10, 11, 13, 14, 15, 15, 18, 19, 20, 20, 25, 26, 29, 31, 33, 35, 38, 40, 40, 42, 48, 50, 51, 55, 58, 71

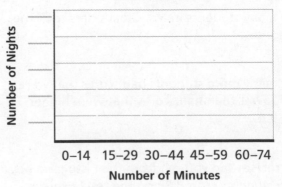

Time Lissa Takes to Complete Her Homework

Number of Nights

0–14   15–29   30–44   45–59   60–74

Number of Minutes

1. **Vocabulary** Which of the following describes the mean of a data set? *Lesson 8-2*

Ⓐ The data value that occurs most often

Ⓑ The middle data value

Ⓒ The sum of the data values divided by the total number of data values

Ⓓ The difference of the greatest and least data values

2. A P.E. teacher recorded how many sit-ups the students in her class did in one minute. Select all the statements that describe the data. *Lesson 8-4*

☐ Every student did at least 10 sit-ups in one minute.

☐ Two students did 50 or more sit-ups in one minute.

☐ Eight more students did 30 to 39 sit-ups than did 10 to 19 sit-ups.

☐ More than half of the students did 40 or more sit-ups in one minute.

☐ There are 30 students in the class.

P.E. Class Results

(bar graph: Number of Students vs. Sit-ups per Minute)

Sit-ups per Minute	Number of Students
10–19	2
20–29	6
30–39	10
40–49	11
50–59	1

In 3 and 4, determine whether each question is *statistical* or *not statistical*. Explain.

3. How many pages did Liz read yesterday? *Lesson 8-1*

4. How many books did each of the students in grade 6 read last year? *Lesson 8-1*

In 5 and 6, use the table of cousins' ages at a family reunion.

5. Make a box plot of the ages. *Lesson 8-3*

Cousins' Ages (years)

10, 9, 10, 14, 21, 11, 16, 10, 16

6. One 8-year-old cousin could not make it to the reunion. Select all the ways the measures of center of the data set change if she had attended the reunion. *Lesson 8-2*

☐ The median increases by 1   ☐ The mean decreases by 0.5

☐ The mode decreases by 1   ☐ The median decreases by 0.5

☐ The mean increases by 0.5

How well did you do on the mid-topic checkpoint? Fill in the stars.

MID-TOPIC PERFORMANCE TASK

Antonia surveys a group of students entered in a school science fair. Her results are shown.

Hours Spent on Project

8, 12, 10, 5, 2, 10, 17, 20, 14, 22

PART A

What statistical question could Antonia have asked to gather these data? Explain why the question is a statistical question.

PART B

Find the mean, median, mode, and range of Antonia's data. Draw lines to match each measure to its value.

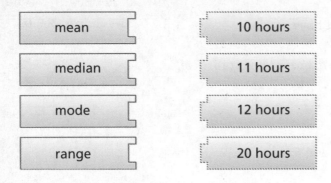

mean	10 hours
median	11 hours
mode	12 hours
range	20 hours

PART C

Choose reasonable intervals and then make a frequency table and a histogram to show Antonia's data.

Hours	Tally	Frequency

Hours Spent on Project

Number of Students

Total Number of Hours

👆 Solve & Discuss It!

📶 👆 ACTIVITY

Suppose you collected data from 11 people about the number of pieces of fruit they have eaten in the past week. The median number is 6 pieces of fruit.

Make two possible dot plots that could be used to display the data—one in which the data vary a little and one in which the data vary a lot. Explain how you created your dot plots.

Names

Reasoning How can you find values that have the same median?

I can...
use measures of variability to describe a data set.

Focus on math practices

Critique Reasoning Jackline says that only 3 people surveyed ate more than six pieces of fruit in the past week. Do you agree? Explain why or why not.

VISUAL LEARNING | ASSESS

EXAMPLE 1 | Find the Mean Absolute Deviation to Describe Variability

Scan for Multimedia

Ann is looking at her math quiz scores for one grading period. She wants to know how much her scores varied. She knows that her average (mean) score is 86%. How can Ann determine how much her scores varied during this grading period?

Ann's Math Quiz Scores (%)	
82	99
76	73
92	90
88	88

Model with Math
You can use a number line to show the spread and clustering of data in relation to the mean.

STEP 1 Find the differences between each of Ann's quiz scores and her mean (average) score. Show all differences as positive integers.

The **absolute deviation** is the absolute value of the difference between a value and the mean.

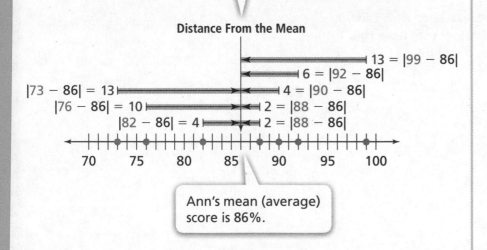

Distance From the Mean

$13 = |99 - 86|$
$6 = |92 - 86|$
$|73 - 86| = 13$ $4 = |90 - 86|$
$|76 - 86| = 10$ $2 = |88 - 86|$
$|82 - 86| = 4$ $2 = |88 - 86|$

Ann's mean (average) score is 86%.

STEP 2 Find the mean of all of the differences, or absolute deviations. This value is called the **mean absolute deviation (MAD)**.

Add all of the absolute deviations.

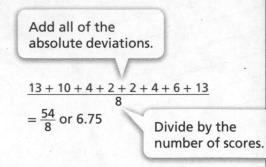

$$\frac{13 + 10 + 4 + 2 + 2 + 4 + 6 + 13}{8}$$
$$= \frac{54}{8} \text{ or } 6.75$$

Divide by the number of scores.

Ann can find the mean absolute deviation (MAD) to determine how much her math quiz scores varied during this grading period.

Her scores varied by an average of 6.75 points.

✓ Try It!

Ann's vocabulary quiz scores are 75, 81, and 90. The mean score is 82. What is the mean absolute deviation?

16

Score	Absolute Deviation
75	$|82 - 75| =$ 7
81	$|82 - 81| =$ 1
90	$|90 - 82| =$ 8

Convince Me! Can the mean absolute deviation ever have a negative value? Explain.

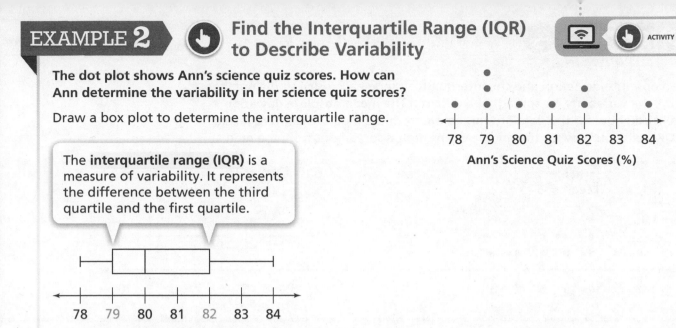

EXAMPLE 2 ► 👆 **Find the Interquartile Range (IQR) to Describe Variability**

The dot plot shows Ann's science quiz scores. How can Ann determine the variability in her science quiz scores?

Draw a box plot to determine the interquartile range.

> The **interquartile range (IQR)** is a measure of variability. It represents the difference between the third quartile and the first quartile.

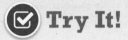

Ann's Science Quiz Scores (%)

The interquartile range is $82 - 79 = 3$.
So, at least half of Ann's science quiz scores were within 3 points.

 Try It!

The dot plot shows the distribution of Ann's health quiz scores. How can the IQR describe her scores?

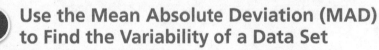

Ann's Health Quiz Scores (%)

EXAMPLE 3 ► 👆 **Use the Mean Absolute Deviation (MAD) to Find the Variability of a Data Set**

Jonah recorded the points his team scored during its last nine basketball games. The mean number of points scored was 42 and the MAD was 4.$\overline{4}$. How can Jonah use these measures to describe the variability of the points his team scored during the last nine games?

The MAD shows that the scores generally varied greatly from the mean. The scores were mostly less than 38 ($42 - 4.4 = 37.6$) or greater than 46 ($42 + 4.4 = 46.4$).

 Try It!

Jonah's team scored 36, 37, 38, 38, 41, 46, 47, 47, and 48 points in the last nine games. Find the IQR and range of the points Jonah's team scored in its last nine games. Are these good measures for describing the points scored?

The mean absolute deviation and the interquartile range each use a single number to describe the variability, or spread, of a data set. The **mean absolute deviation (MAD)** tells you how far the data are spread out from the mean. The **interquartile range (IQR)** tells you how far the middle of the data is spread out from the median.

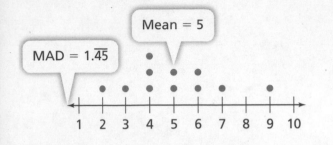

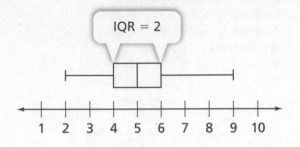

Do You Understand?

1. ❓ **Essential Question** How can the variability of data be described using a single number?

2. What does the IQR show that the range does not show?

3. **Reasoning** Two data sets have the same mean, 8. However, the MAD of Data Set A is 2 and the MAD of Data Set B is 4. What does this indicate about the variability of the data sets?

Do You Know How?

In 4–7, use these data.

Davita works at a shoe store. She measured the feet of nine customers and found that their shoe sizes were 4, 5, 5, 6, 7, 8, 8, 10, and 10.

4. Find the mean.

5. Find the sum of the absolute deviations from the mean.

6. Find the mean absolute deviation. Explain how you found the MAD.

7. Find the range and IQR. How is each calculated?

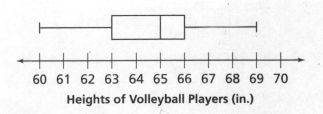
Name: _____

Practice & Problem Solving

8. **Leveled Practice** The mean of the data set is 3. Find the absolute deviation of each of the green values.

   a. The absolute deviation of 1 is ⬚.

   b. The absolute deviation of 2 is ⬚.

   c. The absolute deviation of 5 is ⬚.

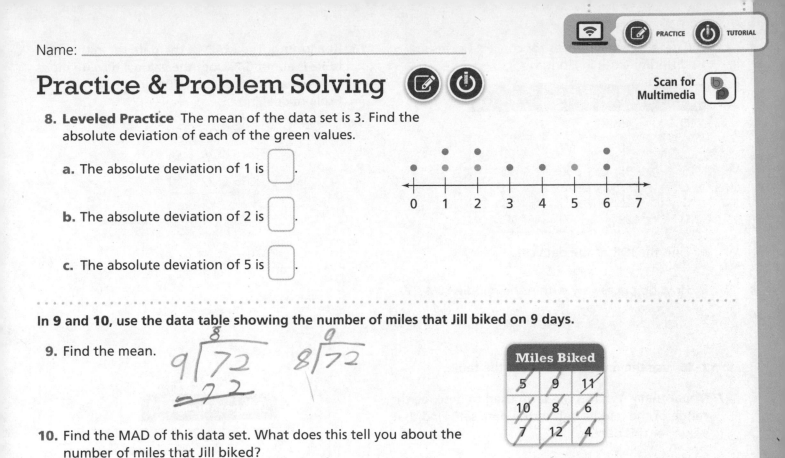

In 9 and 10, use the data table showing the number of miles that Jill biked on 9 days.

9. Find the mean.

$$9\overline{)72} \quad 8\overline{)72}$$
$$= 72$$

Miles Biked		
5	9	11
10	8	6
7	12	4

10. Find the MAD of this data set. What does this tell you about the number of miles that Jill biked?

   9

In 11 and 12, use the data shown in the dot plot.

11. What are the mean and the MAD?

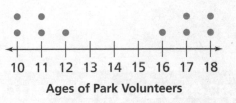

Ages of Park Volunteers

12. Describe the variability of the data.

In 13 and 14, use the data shown in the box plot.

13. What are the range and the IQR?

Heights of Volleyball Players (in.)

14. Describe the variability of the data.

15. The data set shows prices for concert tickets in 10 different cities in Florida.

City	Price ($)	City	Price ($)
Q	45	V	36
R	50	W	24
S	35	X	25
T	37	Y	27
U	29	Z	43

a. Find the IQR of the data set.

b. How do prices vary within the middle 50%?

16. **Reasoning** The MAD of the data set in the table is about 6.7. Does the value 4 deviate more or less than most of the values in the table? Explain.

4	28	25
19	7	13
16	22	10

In 17–19, use the data set shown in the table.

17. **Vocabulary** What is the term used to describe the range of the middle half of the data set? Find that value for this data.

Temperatures (°C)			
11	17	20	16
19	16	15	22

18. **Critique Reasoning** Dina said that the greatest absolute deviation will be found from the highest temperature because it has to be the farthest from the mean. Is she correct? Explain.

19. **Higher Order Thinking** What is the MAD for the data and what does it tell you about the temperatures?

✓ Assessment Practice

20. Harlo recorded the tide, in feet, every hour during an 8-hour period as shown in the table.

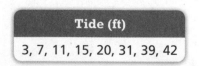

Tide (ft)
3, 7, 11, 15, 20, 31, 39, 42

PART A

What is the MAD for the data set?

PART B

Select all the statements that best describe the IQR, MAD, and variability of the data set.

☐ The middle 50% of the data is spread out more than the average variation.

☐ The IQR is greater than the MAD.

☐ The middle 25% of the data is spread out more than the average variation.

☐ The IQR is less than the MAD.

☐ The MAD shows that the tides generally varied greatly from the mean.

Solve & Discuss It! 📶 👆 ACTIVITY

The prices in dollars of athletic shoes in one store are shown below. Does the mean, median, or mode best describe the typical price for shoes at this store?

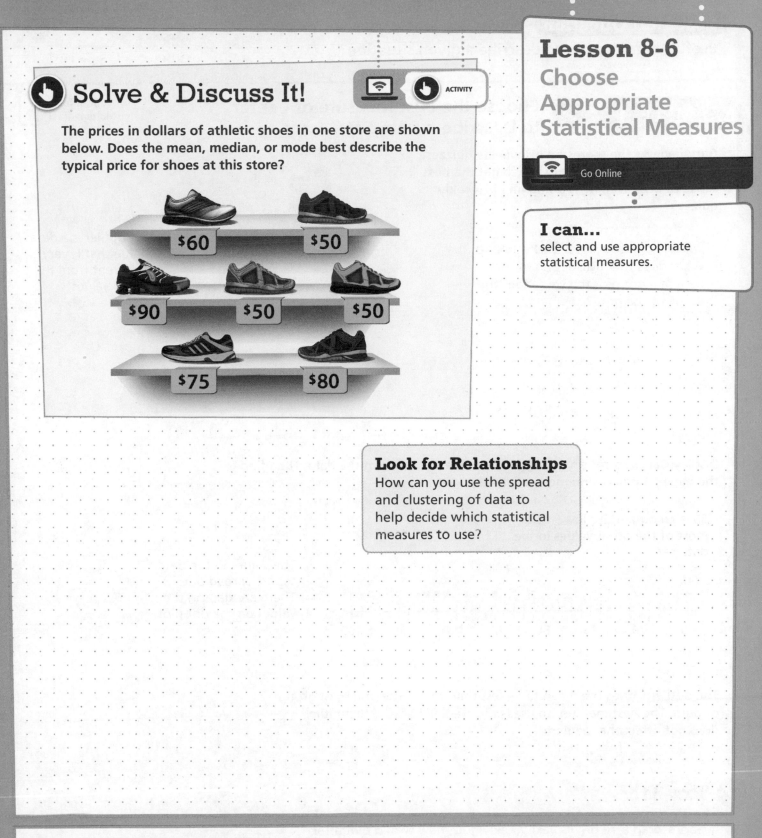

I can...
select and use appropriate statistical measures.

Look for Relationships
How can you use the spread and clustering of data to help decide which statistical measures to use?

Focus on math practices

Construct Arguments Which measure would the store most likely use in its advertising? Explain why this measure should be used.

? **Essential Question** Why is one statistical measure more useful than another to describe a given situation?

VISUAL LEARNING   ASSESS

EXAMPLE 1   👁 **Choose the Best Measure of Center to Describe a Data Set**   Scan for Multimedia

Gary reviews the scores on his weekly quizzes. What measure should Gary use to get the best sense of how well he is doing on his weekly quizzes?

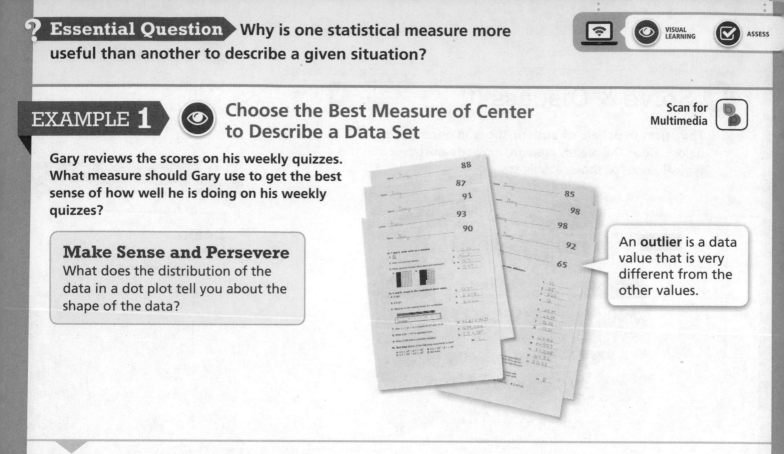

Make Sense and Persevere
What does the distribution of the data in a dot plot tell you about the shape of the data?

88
87
91
93
90

85
98
98
92
65

An **outlier** is a data value that is very different from the other values.

Display Gary's scores on a dot plot. Describe the shape of the data. Then find the mean, median, and mode of the data set.

65 is an outlier. It "lies outside" most of the other values in the data set.

The values in the data set are spread out. There are gaps in the values on the dot plot.

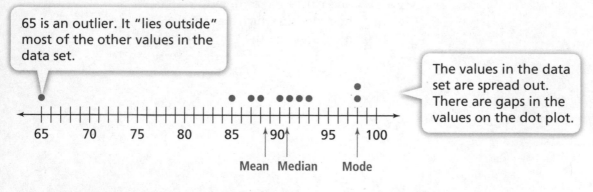

The outlier causes the mean to be less than the values of largest group of data. The best measure to use is the median because the outlier does not affect the median.

✅ Try It!

If Gary scored a 70 on his next weekly quiz, how would that affect his mean score?

Convince Me! Gary says that he usually scores 98 on his weekly quiz. What measure of center did Gary use? Explain.

EXAMPLE 2

Choose the Best Measure of Variability to Describe a Data Set

ACTIVITY   ASSESS

John and Yoshi are computer lab partners. During a spreadsheet project, they decide to enter their French quiz scores on their shared tablet.

A. Choose a measure of variability and use it to describe John's quiz scores.

John's scores contain an outlier, 65, so the median is a better measure of center for his data than the mean.

Use the IQR when the median is the appropriate measure of center.

First Quartile = 87   Third Quartile = 93

IQR = 93 − 87 = 6

At least half of John's quiz scores are between 87 and 93. This accurately describes how his scores are clustered.

B. Choose a measure of variability and use it to describe Yoshi's quiz scores.

Yoshi's scores range from 80 to 88, so there is no outlier. The mean, 84, is a good measure of center for her data.

Use the MAD when the mean is the appropriate measure of center.

$$MAD = \frac{4+4+2+2+0+0+2+2+4+4}{10} = \frac{24}{10} = 2.4$$

Yoshi's scores are typically within 2.4 points of her mean score of 84.

Quiz Scores

	A John	B Yoshi
1	65	80
2	87	80
3	87	82
4	88	82
5	90	84
6	91	84
7	92	86
8	93	86
9	93	88
10	93	88

10:15

✓ Try It!

Suppose the French teacher says that she will drop each student's lowest quiz score. Would the MAD now be a good measure of variability for John's quiz scores? Calculate the MAD without John's lowest score and use it to justify your answer.

John's lowest score is [ ].

Without the lowest score, John's mean score is [ ].

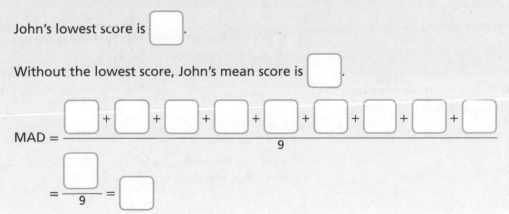

$$MAD = \frac{[\ ]+[\ ]+[\ ]+[\ ]+[\ ]+[\ ]+[\ ]+[\ ]+[\ ]}{9}$$

$$= \frac{[\ ]}{9} = [\ ]$$

The statistical measure that is most appropriate to describe the center and variability of a data set should be chosen based on an analysis of the spread, clustering, and outliers in the data set.

The **mean** is a good choice to describe the center of a data set when the data are clustered together.

When the mean is used, the **mean absolute deviation (MAD)** is a good choice to describe the variability.

The **median** is a good choice to describe the center of a data set when the data contain an outlier.

When the median is used, the **interquartile range (IQR)** is a good choice to describe the variability.

The **mode** is sometimes a good choice to describe the center of a data set if the data is not numeric or does not fall in intervals.

> The median and mode are the same, 30. Both describe the center of the data set.

> The outlier will increase the mean. The mean and MAD are *not* the best choices.

> The middle half of the data is clustered together. The IQR is a good measure of the variability of the data set because it uses the median.

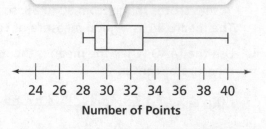

Do You Understand?

1. **Essential Question** Why is one statistical measure more useful than another to describe a given situation?

2. **Reasoning** You cannot find a good measure of center for a data set. What is probably true of the data set?

Do You Know How?

In 3–5, use the basketball team's scores for one season: 44, 43, 42, 40, 42, 45, 39, 38, 18.

3. Find the mean, median, and mode of the scores.

4. Is the median or mean the best measure of center for these data? Explain.

5. Find the measure of variability that best describes the data set.

Practice & Problem Solving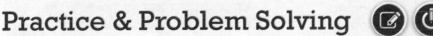

In 6–8, use the data to answer the questions.

Each of five different stores sell a quart of milk for one of the following prices: $1.50, $1.55, $1.80, $1.70, $1.50.

6. What are the mean, median, and mode of the data?

7. Which measure of center best describes these data? Which measure of variability?

8. Find the best measure of variability for these data. Describe the variability.

In 9–11, use the dot plot at the right.

The dot plot shows the hourly wages of cashiers at a supermarket.

9. a. Is the median, mean, or mode the best measure of center for these data? Explain.

10. Identify a good measure of variability for these data. Find the value.

11. Write a sentence describing the variability of the wages.

b. Find that measure of center.

12. Critique Reasoning Hayden looks at the dot plot. He believes that the data set contains outliers and argues that the best measure of variability is the IQR because the median is a good measure to describe a data set that contains outliers. Is Hayden correct? Explain.

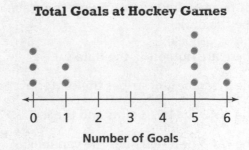

In **13–16**, use the table at the right.

The table shows measures of center based on 5 data points
for attendance at a national skateboarding competition.

Mean	Median	Mode
14,000	13,000	12,500

13. **Vocabulary** What is the term and the value of the middle
number of the data set?

14. **Make Sense and Persevere** Which value in the data set
occurs at least twice? Can it occur 3 times? Explain.

15. **Reasoning** Why must the other two
numbers in the data set be greater than
or equal to 13,000?

16. **Model with Math** What must be the sum of
the two remaining numbers, x and y? Write an
equation to show how to find this sum.

In **17 and 18**, use the table.

Game Scores for the Bravo Bowling Team								
Jessie	150	145	181	235	196	211	204	221	185
Sam	186	187	192	195	194	157	157	162	200

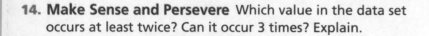

17. **Be Precise** The coach needs to choose the top
bowler for the next meet. If the coach bases her
decision on the player with the best average,
whom should she choose? Justify your answer
using measures of center.

18. **Higher Order Thinking** If the coach bases her
decision on the player who is most consistent,
whom should she choose? Justify your answer
using measures of variability.

☑ Assessment Practice

19. The table at the right shows the winning bowling scores during
the last five bowling events. Select the statements that best
describe the data.

Winning Scores				
121	159	146	132	149

☐ There are outliers in the data set.

☐ The mean best describes the center of the data.

☐ The MAD is 11.92 points and the IQR is 27.5 points.

☐ The MAD best describes the variability.

☐ The IQR best describes the spread.

Explain It!

ACTIVITY

George tosses two six-sided number cubes 20 times.
He records his results in a dot plot.

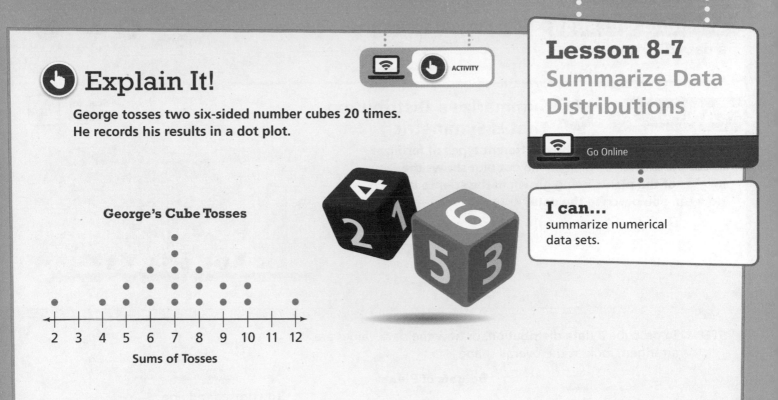

George's Cube Tosses

Sums of Tosses

I can...
summarize numerical
data sets.

A. Describe the shape of the data distribution.

B. Critique Reasoning George says that he expects to roll a sum of 11 on his
next roll. Do you agree? Justify your reasoning.

Focus on math practices

Construct Arguments Suppose George tossed the number cubes 20 more
times and added the data to his dot plot. Would you expect the shape of
the distribution to be different? Construct an argument that supports your
reasoning.

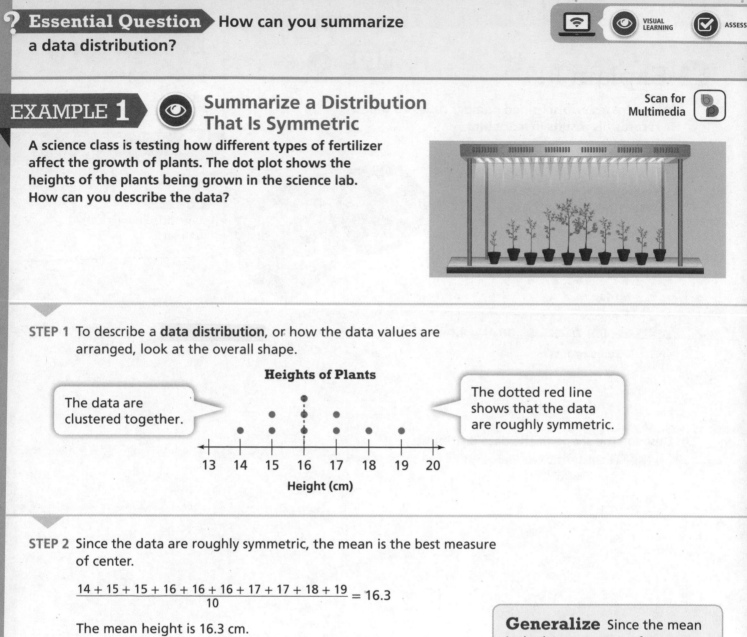

EXAMPLE 1 👁 **Summarize a Distribution That Is Symmetric**

Scan for Multimedia

A science class is testing how different types of fertilizer affect the growth of plants. The dot plot shows the heights of the plants being grown in the science lab. How can you describe the data?

STEP 1 To describe a **data distribution**, or how the data values are arranged, look at the overall shape.

Heights of Plants

The data are clustered together.

The dotted red line shows that the data are roughly symmetric.

13 14 15 16 17 18 19 20

Height (cm)

STEP 2 Since the data are roughly symmetric, the mean is the best measure of center.

$$\frac{14 + 15 + 15 + 16 + 16 + 16 + 17 + 17 + 18 + 19}{10} = 16.3$$

The mean height is 16.3 cm.

Find the mean absolute deviation (MAD).

$$\frac{2.3 + 1.3 + 1.3 + 0.3 + 0.3 + 0.3 + 0.7 + 0.7 + 1.7 + 2.7}{10} = 1.16$$

The mean absolute deviation is 1.16 cm, so a typical height is about 1.16 cm from the mean.

Generalize Since the mean is the best measure of center, the MAD is the best measure of variability.

☑ **Try It!**

Does the shape of the distribution match what you found when you used measures of center and variability? Explain.

Convince Me! What are some factors that might explain why some plants grew more or less than others in the science lab?

The fat content, in grams, was measured for one slice ($\frac{1}{8}$ pizza) of 24 different 12-inch pizzas. The data are displayed in the dot plot. How can the data be used to describe the fat content of a slice of pizza?

STEP 1 Look at the distribution of the data in the dot plot.

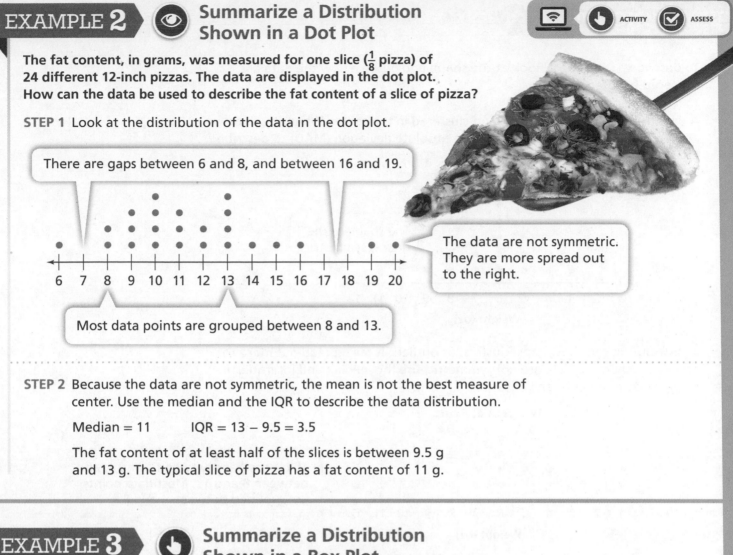

There are gaps between 6 and 8, and between 16 and 19.

The data are not symmetric. They are more spread out to the right.

Most data points are grouped between 8 and 13.

STEP 2 Because the data are not symmetric, the mean is not the best measure of center. Use the median and the IQR to describe the data distribution.

Median = 11   IQR = 13 − 9.5 = 3.5

The fat content of at least half of the slices is between 9.5 g and 13 g. The typical slice of pizza has a fat content of 11 g.

EXAMPLE 3 ▸ 👆 **Summarize a Distribution Shown in a Box Plot**

The box plot displays data for the number of days the temperature was above 80°F for the month of July. The data were collected over a ten-year period. How can you summarize these data?

First, look at the overall shape. Then find measures of center and variability.

Days above 80°F in July

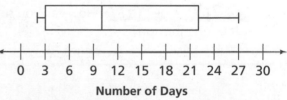

Number of Days

- The data are spread out to the right.

- The median is the center of the data.

- The first quartile is 3 and the third quartile is 22. At least half of the data fall between 3 days and 22 days. The interquartile range is 19 days.

- 25% of the years, the number of days with temperatures above 80°F in July was 3 days or less.

Model with Math You can select a box plot, dot plot, or other method to display data. You can use that display to help describe the data set.

☑ **Try It!**

Why does it make sense to look at the overall shape before deciding which measures to use?

To describe a set of data, look at the shape and observe how the data are clustered or spread out.

A distribution can be symmetric and clustered in the center. When the data are symmetric, use the mean and mean absolute deviation (MAD) to describe the data.

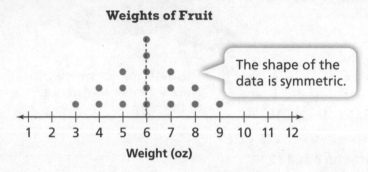

Weights of Fruit

The shape of the data is symmetric.

Weight (oz)

A distribution can show gaps, clusters, or outliers. It may spread out more to one side. When the data are not symmetric, use the median and interquartile range (IQR) to describe the data.

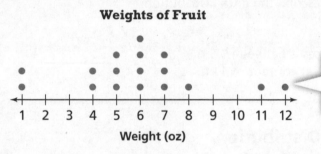

Weights of Fruit

There are gaps between 1 and 4, and between 8 and 11. Most data points are grouped between 4 and 8.

Weight (oz)

Do You Understand?

1. **? Essential Question** How can you summarize a data distribution?

2. **Reasoning** This data set has an outlier.

   0, 40, 50, 60, 60, 70, 80, 80

   How would the median and the mean be affected if the outlier was removed?

Do You Know How?

3. Five different students measured the length of a shadow in inches as follows: 38, $38\frac{1}{2}$, $37\frac{3}{4}$, 38, $38\frac{1}{4}$. Make a generalization about the data distribution of the shadow measurements.

4. What are the mean, the median, and the interquartile range of the data set in Exercise 3?

Practice & Problem Solving

In 5–8, use the data table.

Number of Home Runs Hit by Players on My Team									
Player Number	1	2	3	4	5	6	7	8	9
Home Runs	21	9	12	20	7	11	9	10	9

5. What are the mean and the median?

6. Draw a box plot of the data.

7. Describe the overall shape of the data.

8. Make a generalization about the data distribution.

9. Be Precise A doctor asked 15 people how many hours they spend exercising each week. The dot plot displays the data.

Hours Exercising per Week

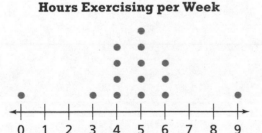

Number of Hours

What do any clusters and gaps in the dot plot tell you about the exercise habits of these people?

10. Look for Relationships Describe the pattern in the dot plot. Then write about a situation that this data could represent. Explain why your situation has this pattern.

Times Needed

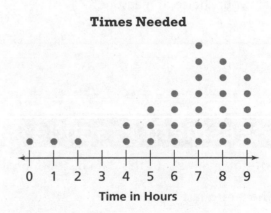

Time in Hours

In 11 and 12, use the data in the table.

Adult	1	2	3	4	5
Salary	$35,000	$46,000	$38,000	$34,000	$52,000
Adult	6	7	8	9	10
Salary	$99,000	$64,000	$435,000	$22,000	$88,000

11. **Model with Math** Make a box plot for the data. What are the median, first quartile, third quartile, and interquartile range?

12. **Higher Order Thinking** Which data value most affects your choice of a measure of center to describe the data? Explain.

In 13–15, use the data in the dot plot.

13. Describe the shape of the data.

Spanish Quiz Scores

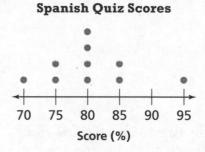

14. Describe the typical quiz scores of the students. Explain your choice of measure.

15. Describe the variability of the quiz scores.

Assessment Practice

16. Which statement about this data distribution is **NOT** true?

Ⓐ The interquartile range is 4.

Ⓑ The median is the preferable measure of center.

Ⓒ The data cluster from 2 to 7.

Ⓓ The distribution is symmetrical.

Number of Miles Students Ran in a Week

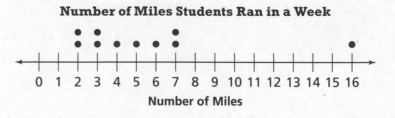

Number of Miles

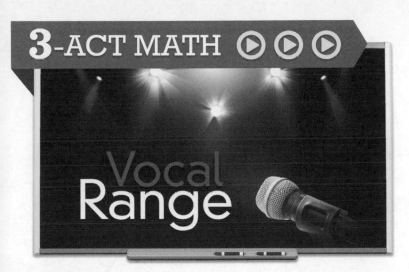

3-ACT MATH ▷ ▷ ▷

Vocal Range

ACT 1

1. After watching the video, what is the first question that comes to mind?

2. Write the Main Question you will answer.

3. Make a prediction to answer this Main Question.

The person who should win the competition is _____ .

4. Construct Arguments Explain how you arrived at your prediction.

5. What information in this situation would be helpful to know? How would you use that information?

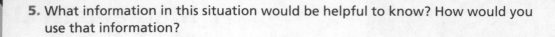

6. Use Appropriate Tools What tools can you use to solve the problem? Explain how you would use them strategically.

7. Model with Math Represent the situation using mathematics. Use your representation to answer the Main Question.

8. What is your answer to the Main Question? Does it differ from your initial prediction? Explain.

9. Write the answer you saw in the video.

10. Reasoning Does your answer match the answer in the video? If not, what are some reasons that would explain the difference?

11. Make Sense and Persevere Would you change your model now that you know the answer? Explain.

Reflect

12. Model with Math Explain how you used a mathematical model to represent the situation. How did the model help you answer the Main Question?

13. Use Appropriate Tools What tools or technology did you use to answer the Main Question? What other tools did your classmates use?

14. Be Precise Design your own singing competition. Explain how you would score each performance and how you would use those scores to choose a winner. Use a different method than you did to answer the Main Question.

❓ Topic Essential Question

How can data be described by a single number? How can tables and graphs be used to represent data and answer questions?

Vocabulary Review

Write *always*, *sometimes*, or *never* for each statement.

1. Intervals in a *frequency table* go beyond the values in a data set. _____

2. You can calculate the *IQR* from a *box plot*. _____

3. You can calculate the *mean* from a *histogram*. _____

4. The *MAD* is a negative value. _____

5. The *range* is a measure of variability. _____

6. The *mean*, *median*, and *mode* are the same value. _____

Use Vocabulary in Writing

Describe measures of variability and when you would use them to summarize a data set. Use vocabulary words in your explanation.

Concepts and Skills Review

LESSON 8-1 ▸ Recognize Statistical Questions

Quick Review

A **statistical question** anticipates that there will be a variety of answers.

Example

Ramon surveyed his classmates to determine the answer to the statistical question "How many hours do my classmates spend online each week?" The question yielded a variety of numerical answers. Ramon made this dot plot to display the data.

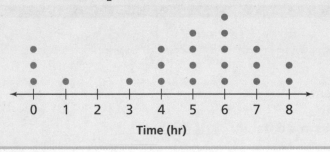

Time Spent Online Each Week

Time (hr)

Practice

In **1–4**, tell whether each question is statistical.

1. How many stations are there in a subway system?

2. How would passengers of a subway system rate the quality of service on a scale of 1 to 10?

3. How many passengers travel on each of the Green, Blue, Red, and Orange Lines of the subway system each day?

4. How much does it cost for a ticket to ride the subway from Station A to Station B?

LESSON 8-2 ▸ Summarize Data Using Mean, Median, Mode, and Range

Quick Review

The **mean** is the sum of all the values in a data set divided by the total number of values in the set. The **median** is the middle data value in a set arranged in numerical order. The **mode** is the value that occurs most often in a set. The **range** is the difference between the highest and lowest values in a set.

Example

Find the mean, median, mode, and range of the following set of data.

Total Game Points				
129	124	128	120	124

Mean: 125   Median: 124

Mode: 124   Range: 9

Practice

In **1–6**, find the mean, median, mode, and range of each data set.

1. 2, 5, 5

2. 11, 13, 13, 11, 13

3. 27, 26, 25, 20

4. 100, 200, 500, 300, 500

5. 1.4, 1.3, 1.1, 1.4, 1.9, 1.8, 1.7, 1.4

6. 450, 0, 500, 750, 0

LESSON 8-3 — Display Data in Box Plots

Quick Review

Quartiles divide a data set into four equal groups. A box plot uses the minimum, first quartile, median, third quartile, and maximum values in a data set to show how the data are distributed.

Example

Make a box plot of the distances, in feet, that seven paper airplanes flew: 60, 75, 45, 55, 70, 40, 65.

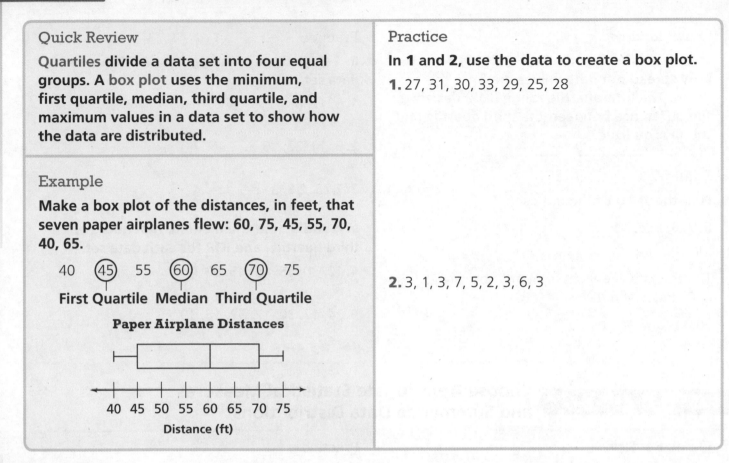

40 (45) 55 (60) 65 (70) 75

First Quartile Median Third Quartile

Paper Airplane Distances

40 45 50 55 60 65 70 75
Distance (ft)

Practice

In **1** and **2**, use the data to create a box plot.

1. 27, 31, 30, 33, 29, 25, 28

2. 3, 1, 3, 7, 5, 2, 3, 6, 3

LESSON 8-4 — Display Data in Frequency Tables and Histograms

Quick Review

A frequency table shows the number of times a data value or a range of data values occurs in a data set. A histogram is a graph that uses bars to show the frequency of equal ranges or groups of data.

Example

Organize the ages of the campers listed below in a frequency table.

12, 14, 12, 14, 10, 11, 15, 13, 13, 11, 12, 12, 7, 14, 12

Divide the data into equal intervals and mark the frequency of the data using tally marks. Then write the frequency.

Ages of Campers	6–8	9–11	12–14	15–17
Tally	I	III	JHT JHT	I
Frequency	1	3	10	1

Practice

1. Represent the data in the frequency table on the left in a histogram.

LESSON 8-5 ▸ Summarize Data Using Measures of Variability

Quick Review

The mean absolute deviation (MAD) describes how spread out data values are from the mean. The interquartile range (IQR) describes the difference between the third quartile and the first quartile.

Example

Find the MAD of the data set.

6, 7, 8, 8, 8, 11

Mean = 8

The absolute deviations from the mean are 2, 1, 0, 0, 0, and 3, and their sum is 6.

So, MAD $= \dfrac{6}{6} = 1$.

Practice

In 1–3, find the mean and the MAD for each data set.

1. 5, 12, 0, 7

2. 8, 14, 22, 16

3. 1.25, 2.5, 3

In 4 and 5, find the median, first quartile, third quartile, and IQR for each data set.

4. 10, 20, 35, 45, 45, 50

5. 24, 12, 30, 17, 32, 13, 19

LESSONS 8-6 AND 8-7 ▸ Choose Appropriate Statistical Measures and Summarize Data Distributions

Quick Review

You can summarize data by finding the measure of center and the measure of variability. Use the IQR when the median is an appropriate measure of center, and the MAD when the mean is an appropriate measure of center.

Example

Use statistical measures to summarize the data set shown.

Test Scores

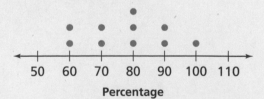

Percentage

The mean and MAD are good measures to describe this data set.

The mean test score is 78 points. The MAD is 10.4, so most test scores are within 10.4 points of the mean.

Practice

In 1–3, use the data below.

Game Sales

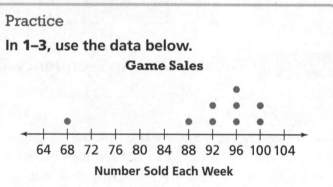

Number Sold Each Week

1. Describe the overall shape of the data. Include any outliers.

2. Which measure of center and measure of variability best describe the data set? Explain.

3. Summarize the data set.

Riddle Rearranging

Find each sum or difference. Then arrange the answers in order from least to greatest. The letters will spell out the answer to the riddle below.

I can...
add and subtract decimals.

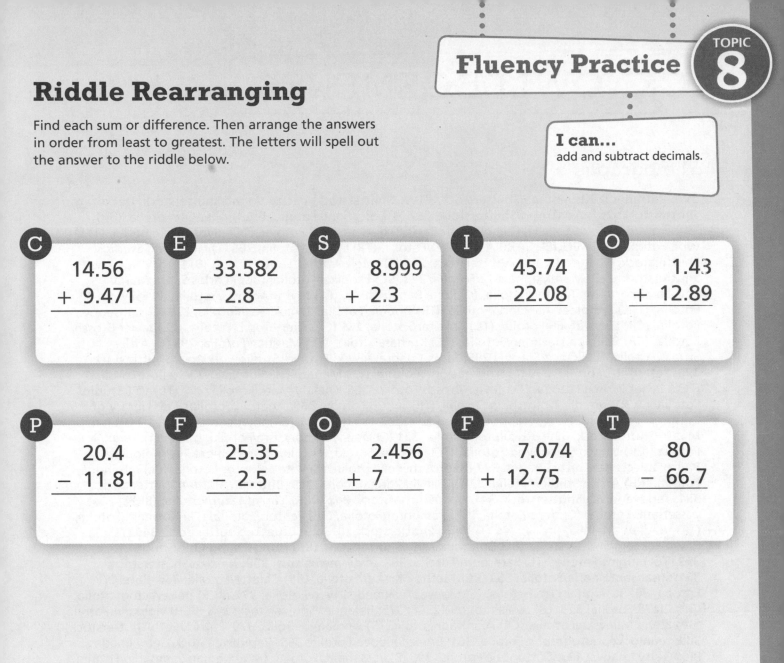

C
14.56
+ 9.471

E
33.582
− 2.8

S
8.999
+ 2.3

I
45.74
− 22.08

O
1.43
+ 12.89

P
20.4
− 11.81

F
25.35
− 2.5

O
2.456
+ 7

F
7.074
+ 12.75

T
80
− 66.7

What place's name is only two words long but has hundreds of letters in it?

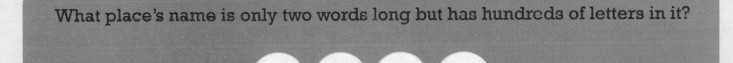

ACKNOWLEDGEMENTS

Photographs

CVR: Rattanasak Khuentana/Shutterstock, HTWE/Shutterstock, Vaclav Volrab/Shutterstock, Deckorator/Shutterstock; **261**: AsiaTravel/Shutterstock; **262** (B) yossarian6/Fotolia, (BCR) AlienCat/Fotolia, (BR) Monika Wisniewska/Fotolia, (CL) olly/Fotolia, (CR) donatas1205/Fotolia, (TC) glyphstock/Fotolia, (TCL) vvoe/Fotolia, (TL) MIGUEL GARCIA SAAVED/Fotolia, (TR) Svenni/Fotolia; **265** (T) LightField Studios/Shutterstock, (B) Beto Chagas/Shutterstock; **266** (T) Leigh Prather/Shutterstock, (B) Sergey Novikov/Shutterstock; **267**: Marekkulhavy12/Fotolia; **273** (BC) Exopixel/Fotolia, (BCL) Carlos Santa Maria/Fotolia, (Bkgrd) Mr Twister/Fotolia, (C) Ilona Baha/Fotolia, (CL) Jovica Antoski/Fotolia, (L) SSilver/Fotolia, (TCL) Ermolaev Alexandr/Fotolia, (TR) Doomu/Fotolia; **274**: Alekss/Fotolia; **279** (C) samsonovs/Fotolia, (CR) Elizaveta66/Fotolia, (TC) Raksitar/Fotolia; **285** (C) Javier Brosch/Fotolia, (CL) Javier Brosch/Fotolia, (CR) Philippe Devanne/Fotolia, (TC) Kurhan/Fotolia, (TL) Maridav/Fotolia; **293** (C) Africa Studio/Fotolia, (CL) Okea/Fotolia; **295**: Jacek Chabraszewski/Fotolia, Studioworkstock/Shutterstock; **298**: PeterBetts/Fotolia; **299** (C) Andreacionti/Fotolia, (CL) Manati8888/Fotolia, (TC) Steliost/Fotolia, (TCL) Javier Brosch/Fotolia, (TL) Javier Brosch/Fotolia; **305**: Oleksiy Mark/Fotolia; **307** (TC) VTT Studio/Fotolia, (TCR) Evgenia Tiplyashina/Fotolia, (TR) Jultud/Fotolia; **308**: Anatolii/Fotolia; **315**: Library of Congress Prints and Photographs Division[LC USZ62 113360]; **317** (CR) Injenerker/Fotolia, (TCR) Ian Maton/Shutterstock; **320**: 3dsculptor/Fotolia; **321** (C) Openyouraperture/Fotolia, (CL) Amridesign/Fotolia, (CR) Ljupco Smokovski/Fotolia, (TCL) Nikolai Sorokin/Fotolia; **326**: Hemera Technologies/PhotoObjects.net/Getty Images; **327** (Bkgrd) theyok/Fotolia, (C) Pete Saloutos/Fotolia, (CL) mbongo/Fotolia, (CR) Africa Studio/Fotolia; **328**: kirill_makarov/Fotolia; **329**: Butterfly Hunter/Shutterstock; **331**: TeddyandMia/Shutterstock; **341**: Vixit/Shutterstock; **342** (BCR) Yuriy Mazur/Fotolia, (BR) yossarian6/Fotolia, (C) tiero/Fotolia, (CR) kamonrat/Fotolia, (TC) Fenton/Fotolia, (TL) Kotomiti/Fotolia, (TR) Vladimir Melnik/Fotolia; **345** (T) Yatra/Shutterstock, (B) John Brueske/Shutterstock; **346** (T) Rawpixel.com/Shutterstock, (BL) Dangdumrong/Shutterstock, (BR) Hung Chung Chih/Shutterstock; **353** (TCL) jdoms/Fotolia, (TL) Sararoom/Fotolia; **358**: afxhome/Fotolia; **359**: Nattika/Shutterstock; **361**: susansantamaria/Fotolia; **363** (BCR) Jeffrey Kraker/Fotolia, (BR) Colette/Fotolia; **364**: PeterO/Fotolia; **367** (C) tigger11th/Fotolia, (CL) WavebreakmediaMicro/Fotolia; **372** (BCR) neuevector/Fotolia, (BR) Cla78/Fotolia; **373**: Lakov Filimonov/123RF; **375**: Belander/Shutterstock; **378** (BCR) vipman4/Fotolia, (BR) Elena Milevska/Fotolia, (CR) AlenKadr/Fotolia, (R) vipman4/Fotolia; **379**: Patrick Foto/Shutterstock; **380**: seanlockephotography/Fotolia; **381**: Bruce Shippee/Fotolia; **393**: RapidEye/iStock/Getty Images Plus/Getty Images; **433**: Cottonfioc/Fotolia; **396** (B) yossarian6/Fotolia, (BCL) Roman Samokhin/Fotolia, (BCR) fotonen/Fotolia, (BL) vlorzor/Fotolia, (BR) Coprid/Fotolia, (C) bravissimos/Fotolia, (CL) monticellllo/Fotolia, (CR) nito/Fotolia, (TCR) yvdavid/Fotolia, (TCR) Jaimie Duplass/Fotolia, (TL) viperagp/Fotolia, (TR) Carolyn Franks/Fotolia; **399** (T) Sigur/Shutterstock, (B) Tostphoto/Shutterstock; **400** (T) Kikovic/Shutterstock, (B) RedlineVector/Shutterstock; **406** (B): eboss6/Fotolia; **415** (TCR) Budimir Jevtic/Fotolia, (TR) Roman_23203/Fotolia; **427**: Andreas Metz/Fotolia; **432**: Zudy/Shutterstock; **443** (C) dadoodas/Fotolia, (CL) Photocreo Bednarek/Fotolia, (CR) littlestocker/Fotolia; (TC) Steve Byland/Shutterstock; **449** (TC) Bogdan Florea/Shutterstock, (TL) Lovely Bird/Shutterstock; **453**: Pixelrobot/Fotolia; **461**: Ryan Burke/DigitalVision Vectors/Getty Images; **463**: Yongcharoen_kittiyaporn/Shutterstock; **464** (BR) yossarian6/Fotolia, (CL) puckillustrations/Fotolia, (CR) andresgarciam/Fotolia, (TR) Ig0rZh/Fotolia; (BCR) Pisaphotography/Shutterstock; **467** (T) Diego Cervo/Shutterstock, (B) Agave Studio/Shutterstock; **468** (T) Kuznetcov_Konstantin/Shutterstock, (B) Monkey Business Images/Shutterstock; **475** (CL) mouse_md/Fotolia, (TC) Ljupco Smokovski/Fotolia; **477**: Csak Istvan/123RF; **482**: 3drenderings/Fotolia; **483**: ki33/Fotolia; **484** (C) aleciccotelli/Fotolia, (T) Racobovt/Shutterstock; **489**: bluecherrygfx/Fotolia; **497**: Gleb Semenjuk/Fotolia; **508** (CR) pixelrobot/Fotolia, (TR) Natsmith1/Shutterstock; (R) BillionPhotos.com/Fotolia; **511**: OmniArt/Shutterstock; Amnachphoto/Fotolia; Bonzami Emmanuelle/123RF; Chaivit/Fotolia; Coprid/Fotolia; Pavlo Vakhrushev/Fotolia; **F16** (BL) Natis/Fotolia, (TR) Natis/Fotolia; **F17** (BL) mike166146/Fotolia, (BR) macrovector/Fotolia; **F18**: Gelpi/Fotolia; **F19** (T) blueringmedia/Fotolia, (TC) lukeruk/Fotolia; **F20** (C) piai/Fotolia, (CR) Fotolia, (CR) Natis/Fotolia; **F21**: Taras Livyy/Fotolia; **F22** (T): duke215/Fotolia; **F23** Fotolia, mike166146/Fotolia; Geargodz/Fotolia; GraphicCompressor/Fotolia; Koya979/Fotolia; Kurhan/Fotolia; Lars Christensen/Shutterstock; Popova Olga/Fotolia; Stephen VanHorn/Fotolia; Taras Livyy/Fotolia.

A2